THEORY OF COOKERY
A TEXTBOOK

THEORY OF COOKERY
A TEXTBOOK

Prof. PRANSHU CHOMPLAY, *M.Phil.*
Head of the Department and Programme Leader
Amity School of Hospitality,
Amity University, Noida, India

Prof. SHAILENDRA KUMAR SINGH
Director, Amrapali Institute of Hotel Management,
Haldwani, Nainital, Uttrakhand, India

AMAN PUBLICATIONS
NEW DELHI

Published by
Rajiv Jain for Aman Publications
LG-4A, Ganpati Bhawan,
4675-B/21, Ansari Road,
Darya Ganj, Delhi - 110002
PH: 23255012, 23282127
E-mail: sshjbs@yahoo.com

First Published - 2010

Second Revised Edition - 2011

Third Revised Edition-2013

Reprint **2020**

ISBN–81–8204–068-X
ISBN–978-81–8204–068-7

SOLE DISTRIBUTOR
JINDAL BOOK SERVICES
LG-4A, Ganpati Bhawan,
4675-B/21, Ansari Road,
Darya Ganj, Delhi - 110002

Jacket Designed by :
S.M. Graphics

Printed by:
Balaji Offest, Delhi, India

Preface

The book has been written by keeping the interest of the students those are aspiring to become the food production professional in the hospitality industry. As there are very few books on this subject are available in the market serving dual purposes, the examination need and the industry requirement. Since a long time there was a wide gap could be felt between the industry and academia as the norms and technology of food industry is changing very rapidly. The Book also carries the required syllabi portion of most of the university food production paper requirement on all level like post graduate, bachelor degree, diploma and certificate level. For the practical session earlier most of the practical were based on European or continental cuisine but in the book apart from the continental cuisine, the different international cuisine title in all aspects have been added like middle east cuisine, American cuisine etc. this all is due to he change in the taste of consumer likeness and preferences.

There are certainly new topics related to latest changes in the hotel industry have been added in this book where students had faced the difficulty to understand the certain topics earlier as the detailed structure was not available easily. Especially the uses of pictures have been done extensively to explain the complete concept. A wide spectrum of Indian cuisine is also available in the book as the details of Indian food prospective are not easily available.

All possible efforts have been made to keep this book useful for the students of hotel management, culinary art and the practicing chef in the hospitality industry to widen their theoretical knowledge. Also the suggestion to make this book more effective is welcomed so that they can be effectively implemented in the next edition.

Pranshu Chomplay
Prof. Shailendra Kumar Singh

Contents

1

Fundamentals of Food Production

OBJECTIVES

In this lesson, students will be familiar with the basics of cooking. This will assist them for pursuing as a professional chef in their hospitality career

The chapter includes following topics:

1. Introduction and definition of cooking
2. History of cuisine.
3. Cooking as an art and science
4. Methods of cooking
5. Developing elementary skills

After studying this chapter students should know:

1. Definition of cooking - cooking as an art or science
2. History and development in food habits globally.
3. Benefits of cooking food
4. The process of food cooked
5. Various methods of cooking
6. Table of British measure conversion.

Additionally, the lesson explains how the method of heat transfer affects various food products. The basic principles of cooking are an important foundation in a food service operation. In order to cook food, heat must be transferred; this can be done in a variety of ways. The method of heat transfer affects the texture, appearance, aroma, and flavour of the finished food product. This lesson discusses the specific cooking methods used to transfer heat including dry heat, moist heat, and a combination of the two.

INTRODUCTION

The best way to get into the heart is through the routes of stomach.

Such kind of quotes clearly shows the importance of food in modern life. Food is not only consumed to fill the stomach but it is the professional phenomena now a days. From the simple form of domestic kitchen it has changed the shape into an art and science. It is no more a formality but an essential element to live the modern life and way to perform as a good host.

Along with a time it has changed various times and is still changing as per the requirement of human being. Learning the skill of food is not only learning the cooking part but to get into the deep and to start from the ingredient knowledge and learning the science behind the cooking.

DEFINITION

Cooking is an art of preparing food for human consumption by the application of heat. In layman language Cooking is the technique of converting raw material into finished one. But modern cuisine is more then mere cooking that why it is called culinary art.

Professional cooking is not only preparation but it involve different methods of cooking, using advance tools and technique, flavour like herbs, wine, spices etc., measuring specific ingredient, temperature, mixing technique and above all skill with knowledge of production.

Cooking chemically break down the plant cells; soften the fibers of meat 'thus making the food digestible and palatable.

HISTORY OF FOOD

Prehistoric event historic people used to eat abnormal food like animals, insects like lizards and birds. Food was raw and unseasoned. Food was mostly hunted and the storage was minimal.

Until fire was invented, humans did not cook. Although, they probably ate animals cooked in forest fires. Raw food is hard to digest and sometimes is not healthy. Early human life expectancy was about 30 to 40 years and food is probably one of the main reasons

With the invention of fire, people could now eat a lot of other different variety of food including meat and vegetables. Eating cooked food has allowed people to live longer

In 8000 - 7000 BC Mankind first learn the art of farming. He become social and start growing crops and raising animals for food instead of hunting and gathering for food. This allowed towns and villages to grow as people no longer had to travel around to get supplies of food. By 4000 BC people were moving into towns and villages more and more.

Preservation of food started in this time Salting and drying, as well as the use of snow and ice, were developed for storing food for long times.

3,000 B.C. was the time of agriculture and man started cultivation in bulk. There were very few tools made of iron and stone for agriculture.

Between 4000 and 1000 BC, was the time of growth of cities and empires helped with the development of different types of foods. At some time during this period the plough was developed. Mankind starts using animal power-like horses and oxen - for many farming jobs.

In India food like beef, chicken, dear, pork, rice and vegetables was popular but by around 300 BC lots of Hindus felt that killing animal is not in favour of their religion and especially cows are sacred so they should show respect by not killing her for food purpose. They understood the role of cow in developed society like milk, cheese, butter and *ghee*. Pork is assumed to live in unhygienic condition so it was also unhealthy to eat.

Around AD 1100 Islamic introduce conquest India and they brought theirs food habits with them. People could eat chicken, mutton and fish as daily food habits but still non-veg food was popular only in Muslim culture.

In 1295 famous Italian traveller Marco Polo brought Chinese noodles as pasta from China.

The German word for pasta '*nudel*' gave us the English word 'noodle'.

A.D. 1400

The first French cookbooks imitated Moorish cuisine. Sugar, still a luxury, made food sweet. Saffron gilded it, rose water perfumed it, and milk of almonds made it rich. Today's taste for tajines and couscous is an echo of the middle ages.

1492 Discovery of America and the New World

In 1493 Columbus "discovered" the West Indies island of Guadeloupe. New plants and vegetables such as pineapple, potato, and tomatoes were discovered in America that did not grow in Europe. These were brought back and successfully grown and eaten in Europe.

1600

In India most of the states were ruled by Muslims rulers and the influence of Muslims food could be felt. Specially Delhi, Lucknow, Hyderabad, and some part of central India. Food was rich and carrying a long procedure of cooking.

Royal patronage promoted French cooking. Henri IV (1553-1610), who aimed to put "a chicken in the pot" of each peasant, funded banquets as lubricants of policy. The table of Louis XIII (1601-1643) featured 22 kinds of fish and 28 of fruit. Coffee, introduced in 1644, revived a taste for the exotic

The secrets of Louis's kitchen were divulged in cookbooks: by 1691, when François Massialot (1760-1733) published a book whose title, Cuisinier Royal et Bourgeois, summed up the process of social diffusion, this was the beginning of haute cuisine.

17th century

The agricultural revolution during this time meant people could eat more grains like wheat and oats. People became loyal to their land.

Agriculture moved from animal power to mechanical power. The seed drill replaced the old way of planting by throwing seeds by hand. This led to more food being grown.

England resisted, patriotically loyal to roast beef and sceptical of superfluous sauces. The English even flirted with Portuguese wines in their trade wars against the French. Imperialism inaugurated the age of sugar, chocolate, global grocery

1800

The invention of the steam engine allowed grains like wheat to be milled for flour without the need for water. People also started to use steam power for transport. This led to the development of the railways.

The 19th century consolidated French supremacy. Antonin Carême (1784-1833), founder of grande cuisine, organised spectacular, Roman-style meals. In 1825, Jean-Anthèlme Brillat-Savarin wrote what is still the world's best food book, La Physiologie du Goût. Brillat-Savarin exalted cooking as art and science,

Industrialization intervened, but the French exploited the new techno-logies to serve the table.

1900

Yet French food relied for its reputation on the inventiveness not of its industrialists, but of its chefs and gastronomes. Auguste Escoffier (1846- 1935), "the chef of emperors and Emperor of chefs", founded the professional style, this made a trend in cuisine. His books were the most influential culinary texts since the writings of ancient Rome's top chef, Apicius. He created dishes for the celebrities of the new century: cuisses de nymphe Aurore (a dish of frogs' legs) and peach Melba. His showy, ingenious, liquor-lashed, cream-besotted dishes dominated haute cuisine until the Seventies, when light-handed, digestion-friendly nouvelle cuisine became the last French fashion to reshape the way we eat.

Some foods brought from America were used for decoration, instead of being eaten. Tomatoes used to grow wild in South America. Spanish explorers took them to Europe, but northern countries like England and Holland grew them for decoration and did not eat them. The transport revolution allowed farmers to sell their food in far away places so more people could live in the growing cities.

1939-1945

The World War forced people to source more and more crops from the land and new inventions were used to do this.

- Food preservation developed during these years. Canning and refrigeration and freezing of foods became very important to countries in the war so they could store food for a long time.
- The invention of other wartime machines for example technology of submarines was used to build microwave ovens later on after the war was over.

1945-1965 Fashions in Food

In India *tandoor* was revolutionary equipment of culinary art given to world which brought a new concept of *tandoori* food, is popular now all over the world. It is a mud base oven used for making of breads and variety of kebab.

Nouvelle cuisine was born in France, thanks to some innovative chefs.

Some of the key feature of modern cuisine-

1. Cooking is complex and long in duration.
2. It was the mix match of various herbs and flavour.
3. More focused was on big portioning and full plate food.
4. Less emphasis was given on presentation part.
5. Garnish was large in size.
6. Name of the dish was on the garnish.

Expert chefs got together and said that they needed to make French cooking simpler because people had more modern tastes and health concerns.

Space food

The race to space has led to the invention of new types of food. This invents a type of technology which has allowed the storing of food without refrigeration. Food compliment to the nutritional requirement of human body.

Fusion cuisine combines elements of various culinary traditions whilst not fitting specifically into any. The term generally refers to the innovations in many contemporary restaurant cuisines since the 1970s. East meet West Food! In simple term: cuisine western food and Asia food mix match together which give an exotic flavour

Fusion food tastes good when Cooking is taken as a living art which changes and develops with lots of innovation, experiments and thought.

2000

Modern French cooking is an answer to complex nouvelle cuisine. This trend, spearheaded by the famous chef Fernando Point in the early 20th century, is characterized by simpler, less time consuming dishes, lighter sauces, smaller portions, and a greater emphasis on local, high quality, in season ingredients. Nouvelle cuisine exploded onto the American culinary scene in the 1970s and remains a significant culinary influence. But now nouvelle cuisine is loosing shine and Europe is returning back to old one. Taste of Asian food is getting place like Tandoori chicken of India, Thai curry, Japanese *sushi*, Indonesian sate, Chinese noodles and many others dish.

COOKING AS AN ART/SCIENCE

Since beginning Cooking has always been considered as an art, where food is prepared in creating art that are pleasing to the palate .as every one couldn't afford to learn this skill.

Science is just starting to analyze these new creations of the cooking art, and can't even seem to see the end considering their gigantic number.

Terms of fats, protein, carbohydrates, minerals, and vitamins are associated with cooking.

Cooking & Science

Now days there are so many experiment and techniques with food are happening. Adding texture, changing flavour, taste and presentation to food caused change in the nature. Only by adding or subtracting a single ingredient will make a great difference in food. Use of technology makes the cooking as a science. Preservation or packed food are the new market in food areas. Professional cooking now required a deep understanding of subject thus making this is a great profession in modern era.

That's why there are so many culinary schools are coming up. Food can be different in much aspect like diabetic, invalids etc. which require a knowledge and nutritionally understanding of food.

Benefits of cooking:

1. Softening of tough fibers
2. Killing of harmful bacteria's and germs
3. Easily digestible food
4. Easily palatable food
5. Blending and mixing of different ingredients
6. Provide particular taste and flavour.
7. Convert the texture and shape of food.
8. Cooking bring varicty in food.

QUALITY IN FOOD PRODUCTION

1. Prepare all menu items using standardized recipes and including manufacturer's instructions for preparing convenience foods, that specify ingredients, preparation method and time, preparation equipment, serving pans and instructions, and portion sizes.
2. Always use quality top grade food items to produce the best food.
3. Selection of recipes and production methods must support the Healthy food.
4. Plan portion sizes based on their customers' nutritional needs and preferences, the menu planning option they use, and their food budget.
5. Have the food and supplies that are specified in the standardized recipe readily available for production.
6. Thoroughly check all food items for quality, including seasoning, texture, taste, and temperature, during preparation as well as 15 minutes before meal service and remove any unsatisfactory items.
7. Control quantities of food produced at all the time.
8. Follow prescribed procedures in the kitchen manual for monitoring food temperatures with thermometers that are calibrated periodically.
9. Discard stale or below standard food such as burned or overcooked, products.
10. Place food items on buffet no more than 10 minutes before serving them.
11. Garnish menu items attractively as indicated on the photographs of standardized recipe.
12. Use portioning equipment specified in the standardized recipe to ensure accurate and consistent serving sizes.
13. Keep the Accurate record of all the information.
14. Taste and test new recipes or products with customers and determine acceptability before adding to the menu cycle.
15. Provide quality food production training to all employees regularly to follow correct preparation procedures.
16. For the purpose of visual appeal, prepare, present on the line, and serve to customers foods prepared in accordance with established standards, including specifications reflected in. Cook all foods in a manner that best preserves nutrients, digestibility, colour, flavour, aroma, and texture.
17. Serve foods at the prescribed temperatures
18. Maintain or develop during preparation the texture that is regarded as desirable and characteristic of a given standard product.
19. Prepare food so that its form at service is uniform in size, thickness, and contour; is easy to serve; and is easy for customers to eat.
20. Cook food in the appropriate type and size containers called for by the standardized recipes.

21. Prepare food to promote quality and palatability through such factors as tenderness, flavour and aroma, juiciness, and colour.
22. Store foods that give off odors separately from foods susceptible to absorbing
23. Cook all foods as close to serving time as possible, observing standards for holding temperatures and maximum times indicated on the standardized recipe.
24. Store nonperishable foods according to the recommended shelf life and to achieve maximum quality.
25. Maintain a healthy and hygienic surroundings.

Professionalism in kitchen

A good attitude will not only help to acquire the skills are need to be successful but also allow you to overcome the many obstacles you may face in your career. There are some key qualities a professional should possess.

1. Positive look toward the job
2. Stamina for work pressure
3. Team work dedication
4. Learning attitude
5. Clarity of raw material understanding
6. Experiencing and creation
7. Commitment to quality product
8. Good understanding of the basics
9. Service and entertainment attitude
10. Hygiene consciousness.

COMPOSITION OF FOOD

Vitamins

Vitamin A is a fat-soluble (water insoluble) is essential in vision, bone growth, reproduction, cell making and strengthening of immune system. Eggs, milk, liver, cereals and vegetable like carrots, sweet potatoes, and spinach are the major source of vitamin A.

Vitamin B complex

Vitamin B6 is a water-soluble vitamin. It performs a wide variety of functions in body and is essential for red blood cell metabolism. The nervous and immune systems need vitamin B6 to function efficiently.

Body needs vitamin B6 to make hemoglobin. And helps in increasing the amount of oxygen carried by hemoglobin. A vitamin B6 deficiency can result in a form of anemia that is similar to iron deficiency anemia. Vitamin B6 is found in a wide variety of foods including fortified cereals, beans, meat, poultry, fish, and some fruits and vegetables.

Vitamin B12 helps maintaining DNA, healthy nerve cells and red blood cells and help in digestion of food. Vitamin B12 is naturally found in animal foods including fish, meat, poultry, eggs, milk, and milk products. Vitamin B complex -these are soluble in water. So can be destroyed on heating

Vitamin C soluble in water, antioxidant vitamin and can be destroyed when heated. Vitamin C is oxidized readily in light, and air when heated. Heating in water, causes the vitamin to leach out of the food into the water and also to be oxidized first to dehydroascorbic acid and then to diketogulonic acid. It is found mainly in citrus fruit, pepper, chillies and broccoli.

Vitamin D is a fat soluble vitamin (insoluble in water) that is found in food and by the rays from the sun. The major use of vitamin D is associated with calcium and phosphorus thus vitamin D helps to form and maintain strong bones.

There are only a few good sources of vitamin D like cod liver oil tuna fish, etc. but milk and some ready-to-eat breakfast cereals may be fortified with vitamin D

Protein a large molecule composed of one or more chains of amino acids, vital nutrients required for the structure, function, and regulation of the body's cells, tissues, and organs. Proteins are essential components of muscles, skin, bones and the body as a whole. Found in meats, poultry, eggs, milk, lentils, some vegetables and starches. **Soyabean** is a major source of protein for vegetarian. T V P (texture vegetable protein) is a food product made from soyabeans. It is produced from soya flour after the soyabean oil has been extracted, then cooked under pressure, extruded, and dried. TVP has a long shelf life and is an excellent source of protein.

On heating protein coagulate means protein become tough and expands. This is also called **coagulation of protein**. Therefore never over cook the protein base product like cheese, cream, egg, meat etc.

Followings are the few protein name of food ingredient:

i. Albumen - egg white

ii. Gluten(Glutenin+Gladinin) - wheat

iii. Myosin - meat

iv. Casein - milk

Carbohydrates / CHO is an organic compound, found in sugar, starch, cereal, fruits and vegetables that provide fuel for the body. Carbohydrates are a major source of metabolic energy. Aside from the sugars and starches that meet this vital nutritional role, carbohydrates also serve as a structural material (cellulose). Found in starch, sugar and lentils. When heated Starches gelatinize in presence of water, starch swallow and then burst like boiling of rice but in absence of water it become brown due to presence of carbon and then burned like cooking of sugar.

Sugars caramelize if cooked dry. This is due to the presence of carbon molecule sugar get brown colour and then caramelizes after certain degree of temperature. But in liquid it dissolves completely.

Types of sugar found in the food-

1. **Lactose** Naturally occurring in milk
2. **Fructose** Found in fruit
3. **Maltose** Crystallized from starch
4. **Dextrose** Crystallized from sugar cane, sugar beets and starches
5. **Corn Syrup** Produced from corn starch

Fat - fats are composed of fatty acids and are essentials as they provide energy. Although fats has the capacity to stay longer on heat but high Heat can destroy fats and oil if applied over a time. High temperature destroys the cells of fatty acids. This type of food is not good for human consumption. Two types of fats are:

1. **Saturated fats** are those which remain solid at room temperature like butter, margarine etc.
2. **Unsaturated fats** are those which remain liquid at room temperature like olive oil, mustard oil etc.

Zinc is an essential mineral to stimulate the activity of enzymes. Zinc is essential for normal growth and development during pregnancy, childhood, and adolescence, developing a healthy immune system maintaining sense of taste and smell. Zinc is found in a wide variety of foods like Oysters contain more zinc per serving than any other food, but red meat and poultry provide the majority of zinc in diet. Other good food sources include beans, nuts, certain seafood, whole grains, fortified breakfast cereals, and dairy products.

Iron is an integral part of many proteins and enzymes that maintain good health. It is also essential for the regulation of cell growth and differentiation. A deficiency of iron limits oxygen delivery to cells, resulting in fatigue, poor work performance, and decreased immunity. Iron is found in poultry, egg, apple, red meat plant such as spinach, lentils and beans

Magnesium: Magnesium helps in maintaining normal muscle and nerve function, keeps heart rhythm steady, supports a healthy immune system, and bones strong. Magnesium also helps regulate blood sugar levels, promotes normal blood pressure, and is known to be involved in energy metabolism and protein synthesis. Green vegetables such as spinach, legumes (beans and peas), nuts and seeds, and whole, unrefined grains are good sources of magnesium

Calcium, has several important functions. Like development of the bones and teeth, muscle contraction, blood vessel contraction and expansion, the secretion of hormones and enzymes, and sending messages through the nervous system. Sea food, Milk and Milk product like yogurt and cheese are the major contributors of calcium in the typical diet.

Ways of Heat Transfer for Cooking of Food

There are basically three ways of heat transfer for cooking of food:

- conduction
- convection
- radiation

Conduction is the transfer of heat by the interaction between molecules of a material. Heat transfer by conduction depends upon the contact with a solid object like metal. The resistance to heat transfer depends upon the nature and dimensions of the heat transfer medium. For example metal is always a solid way of heat transfer. Always brass or steel made utensils are better for cooking purpose.

Convection involves the transfer of heat in liquid and gases. As hot air becomes lighter, compare to cold air and on heating it rises and replaces the cold air. The same motion of molecules happen in liquids. These circulations are called convection.

Radiation heat transfer the heat involves either solid or fluid surfaces, separated by an air, or vapor, and fall on a object on the way. Example like salamander, Steamer.

Methods of cookingMethods of cooking

Cooking make the food digestible and available for use by the body. But it can damage the nutrient in food thus one must adopt the right method of cooking. Each method of cooking has its own role to play in taste development, nutrition preservation, healthy food etc.

Cooking techniques can generally be divided into three

1. Dry heat method
2. Moist heat methods
3. Combination

Dry methods - Dry-heat methods cook the foods with hot air or fat (sautéing, pan-frying, deep-frying, grilling, broiling, roasting, baking);

(a) Baking - Baking is cooking food in an oven with dry heat. Used for bakery products like. Breads, pastries, desserts etc.

The dry heat of baking causes the outside of the food to brown, giving it an attractive appearance and taste, as well as sealing in the food's moisture. Heat is transferred to the surface of the food through the convection of hot air, and then penetrates the food through conduction

To compensate for moisture loss, some items surface is applied with butter or oil or water is kept in oven for letting it steam up into or around the food.

(b) Broiling is the use of radiant heat for cooking. Typically this is done in an electric oven or griller. Broiling is used for developing flavour tender meat and poultry. The food should be exposed to intense heat and then browned sear all surfaces quickly and thus retain the juices. The food that is being broiled should be turned often. Once the outside is browned, the application of heat is controlled as per the requirement and texture of ingredient.

METHOD OF COOKING

Dry Heat Method	Wet/Moist Heat Method	Combination
❖ Baking	❖ Boiling	❖ Brainsing & Stewing
❖ Broiling	❖ Clay Pot Cooking	
❖ Frying	❖ Poaching	
❑ Deep frying	❖ Pressure Cooking	
❑ Pan frying	❖ Simmering	
❑ Stir frying	❖ Blauching	
❑ Sauteing	❖ Barbequing	
❖ Grilling	❖ Solar	
❖ Roasting	❖ Paper Bag Cooking	
❑ Pot Roasting		
❑ Tandoor		
❑ Microwave		

Also it is done without any medium like roasting of spice in Indian cuisine. This is best done in an electric oven, with the door partly open and only the top heating element in use.

(c) Frying is the cooking of food in oil. This takes several forms, from *deep-frying*, where the food is completely immersed in hot oil, to *sautéing* where food is cooked in a frying pan where there is only a thin coating of oil. Frying is the fastest way to cook, as it is the most efficient way to transfer heat into the food. Despite using liquid oil, frying is considered to be a dry cooking method as water is not used in the cooking process and ideally the cooking oil will not be absorbed by the food, thus no moisture is added by cooking.

From the method using the most oil to the least, the **types of frying** are:

Deep frying

Pan frying

Stir-frying

Sautéing

Deep frying involves fully immersing food in hot oil. It is an extremely fast cooking method.

Oil should be hot for frying purpose, the hot oil also boils the water within the food, and steams the food from the inside out. As long as the oil is hot enough and the food is not immersed in the oil for too long, no oil will enter the food itself. If the food stays in the oil too long, the water will steam out and the oil will penetrate the food. If the oil is too cool, the food won't be done before this happens.

Most fried recipes rely on either a coating of batter or breading, or on foods that have or produce a natural skin around the food such as potatoes or whole poultry with the skin on. The effect of this is that the outside of the food becomes crispy and browned while the inside is tender, moist, and steamed.

Rules for Frying

When starting with cold foods, generally frying temperatures are around 160-190 degrees Celsius. It may e higher for small foods. If the oil is too hot, the outside will burn before the inside is done.

- When starting with warm or hot foods, the oil can be much hotter.
- Change the oil after use as it is not good for health to reuse the oil.
- Don't add too much food at one time; it will lower the temperature of the oil.
- With breading with a moist batter, use a flour to make it stick to the food.
- Shake off excess batter or breading before frying; otherwise it will come off in the oil, requiring more frequent oil changes.
- Always store used oil with refrigeration. Used oil contains moisture and nutrients, which will allow for the growth of bacteria. This can cause food poisoning.

Pan-frying/Shallow frying - Pan frying is type of frying where the food is not fully sub-merged in oil. It is partially covered with oil.

Stir Frying involves frying food quickly over very high heat in an oiled pan. While stir-frying, you generally stir continually. A special slope-sided pan called a 'wok' is designed for stir-frying method normally used in Chinese cuisine.

Sauté is French word means "jumping", used to describe the action of the food in the pan as it tossed around to prevent burning. The term *pan-frying* is the English equivalent of *sautéing* (which is a French word). Some people consider it a different technique, which uses more fat and takes longer.

Sautéing is browning food first on one side and then on the other in a small quantity of fat .When sautéing, the fat is placed in a shallow pan, and when it is sufficiently hot, the food is put into it. When cooking, the fat should not come up the sides of the food being cooked.

(d) Grilling -This cooking method uses fire. It is usually done outdoors on barbecue grills over wood, charcoal, or propane fires. In some areas, the term **barbequing** is reserved for a slow low-heat cooking process that operates at about 220°F (104.4°C) and the term **grilling** is used for a fast high-heat cooking process. In most areas, all Barbequing is considered grilling and all grilling over a fire is considered Barbequing.

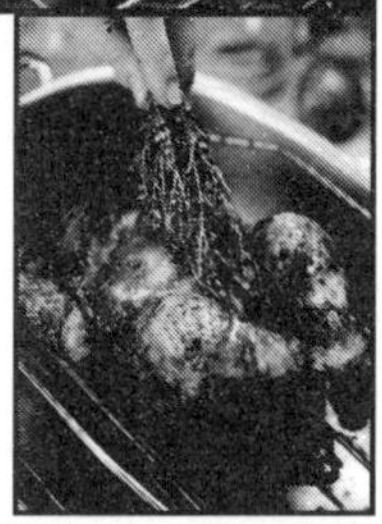

The meats may be prepared by marinating or by applying a combination of spices known as a dry rub. Marinated meats can also be 'mopped' with the marinade while cooking. A barbecue sauce added before, during, or after cooking.

Barbecue also can mean a device for cooking such food, a social event at which such food is served, or any food served with barbeque sauce.

(e) Roasting is a type of baking (in oven) with very little moisture and higher temperature. Roasted foods get drier and browned on the outside, which keeps most of the moisture from being cooked out of the food. Meats and vegetables are good roasted. Roasting can be done in and oven or over an open fire. It is like baking except in roasting it for meat and vegetables. Spit-roasting is a variation where the meat is impaled on a spit and rotated as it roasts

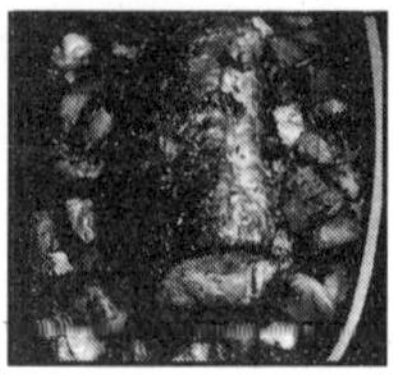

A. **Pot roasting** (poele): - pot-roasting is cooking on a bed of root vegetables in a covered pan. Known as poele, this method retains maximum flavour of all ingredients.

B. Tandoor is also a type of oven made of mud have been used in Indian tandoori cooking for centuries. Tradition-ally used for baking bread, vegetables, cheese, chicken and meat. Foods are cooked quite rapidly in these ovens due to very high interior temperatures of up to 900° F.

The heat source is generally very hot burning charcoal or wood but may also be gas. Three types of **heat transfer** [(a) radiant, (b) convective, and (c) conductive] occur depending on what food is being cooked and how it is placed in the oven. Breads are placed directly on the inside surface of the clay oven, while chicken and meats are skewered on long iron rods and placed through the top opening.

Tandoor clay ovens have typically been installed in retail food establishments in custom- built, permanent installations made of concrete blocks, bricks, and mortar, with sand insulation and tile exteriors. These ovens have been a source of many concerns, including;

- use of clay and other questionable materials in the manufacture of the ovens,
- extreme **heat** and smoke production,
- sparking,
- disposal of ashes that may contain embers,
- deterioration of exterior tile finishes,
- cracking of the clay oven itself,
- inferior workmanship

Microwave - this is a method of cooking and reheating food using electromagnetic waves in a microwave oven using electricity. The microwaves are similar to those which carry television signals from the transmitter to the receiver but are at a higher frequency. The microwaves activate the water molecules or particles of food and agitate them, causing heat by friction, which cooks or reheats the food.

Wet methods/Moist-heat cooking methods - Cook the food with a liquid, usually water, stock or steam (poaching, simmering, boiling, and steaming

(a) Boiling, as term applies to cooking, means cooking foods in boiling water. In most populated parts of the world, plain water boils at temperatures from about 100°C. Boiling has various effects on foods. It toughens the albumin in eggs, toughens the fiber and dissolves the connective tissues in meat, softens the cellulose in cereals, vegetables, and fruits, and dissolves other substances in many foods.

A cover placed on a saucepan or a kettle in which food is to be boiled retains the heat, and thus save the energy and causes the temperature to rise more quickly; besides, a cover so used prevents a loss of water by condensing the steam as it rises against the cover. As water boils, some of it constantly passes off in the form of steam, and for this reason sirups or sauces become thicker the longer they are cooked. Besides serving to cook foods, boiling also renders water safe, as it destroys any germs that may be present. This explains why water must sometimes be boiled to make it safe for drinking.

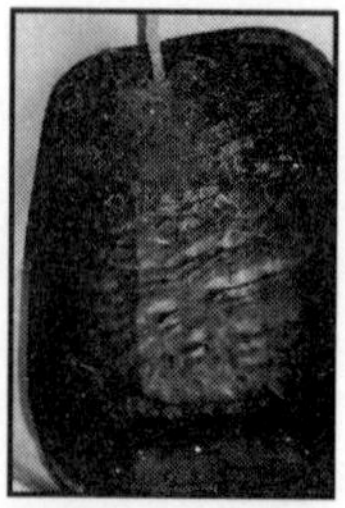

(b) Clay pot cooking is a technique of cooking food in an unglazed clay pot which has been soaked in water so as to release steam during the cooking process. This technique has a long history, streching back at least to ancient Roman times. Because of the heat lost to the evaporation of water, clay pot cooking requires higher oven temperature and longer cooking times than traditional roasting with dry heat. Clay pots may be cleaned by scrubbing them with salt; soaps or detergents should not be used, because the clay may absorb them.

(c) Poaching is a method of cooking that employs a liquid, usually a small amount, that is hot but not actually bubbling. The ideal temperature is between 70°C and 92°C. The cooking liquid is often water, but broth, stock or juice can also be used. Delicate foods such as fish, eggs out of the shell, or soft meat are commonly cooked by poaching. The cooking method is also used to partially cook certain foods such as sweetbread in order to eliminate undesirable flavors and to firm the product before final cooking.

Use a thermometer to gauge the temperature of the cooking liquid or watch for bubbling and adjust the heat as necessary. Do not allow the food being cooked to touch the bottom of them pan or it may cook too rapidly or burn. When poaching eggs, add a splash of vinegar to the water. This will help quickly firm the egg white so multiple eggs can be cooked at once without all sticking together.

(d) Pressure cooking is a method of cooking in a sealed vessel that does not permit air or liquids to escape below a preset pressure. A safety valve releases steam when the pressure exceeds the safety limit for the cooker. Because water's boiling point is affected by the atmospheric pressure, the pressure built up inside the cooker allows the liquid in the pot to rise to a temperature higher than 100°C (212°F) before boiling. The higher temperature causes the food to cook faster. A pressure cooker is often used by mountain climbers to compensate for the low atmospheric pressure at high altitude. Without it, water boils off before reaching 100°C, leaving the food improperly cooked.

(e) Simmering, or stewing, is a type of slow boiling done on a simmer fire. By this method, food is cooked in liquid at a temperature below the boiling point, or anywhere from 185 to 200° Fahrenheit (85-95 Celsius). Water at the simmering point always moves gently–never rapidly as it does in boiling. Less heat and consequently less fuel are required to cook foods in this way,

(f) Steaming is the cooking of food by the application of steam. In this cooking process, the food is put into a perforated tray over water. As the water boils, steam rises

and cooks the food in the upper, or perforated, vessel. Steamer can do the cooking of several foods at the same time without the need of additional fuel, because a different food may be placed in a row open above the other. Steaming is preferable to boiling because there is no loss of mineral salts nor food substances. The flavour is remain same as it does not break up as it might in boiling water. Vegetables prepared in this way prove very palatable, and very often variety is added to the diet by steaming bread, cake, and pudding mixtures and then, provided a crisp outside is desired, placing them in a hot oven to dry out the moist surface. It is one of the healthiest type of cooking.

(g) Blanching or parboiling is a cooking technique involving boiling food (usually vegetables and fruits) in water for a very short time. Blanching is often followed by plunging the food into cold water to stop the cooking process and to retain the colour. Blanching is similar to, which also involves boiling food briefly in water.

(h) Barbequing is cooking food in or above a fire. Traditionally this is done with hickory or mesquite wood, which gives a nice smoke flavour to the food. Propane is commonly used for convenience, but it does not produce a smoke flavour unless smoke chips (small bits of wood wrapped in foil) are added. Moulded chunks of charcoal are also often used; these can produce an awful taste especially when soaked in lighter fluid.

The following instructions assume that you wish to cook using a common cheap barbecue grill with a wood fire. Wood for this purpose is commonly available in bags, and may be used in any normal barbecue grill.

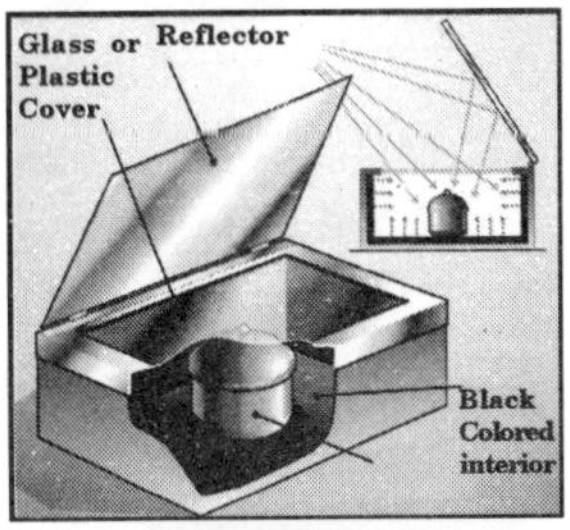

(i) Solar oven cooking - Acheap method of cooking and can be used for bulk cooking style. It involves A device, usually a parabolic dish, to concentrate and focus sunlight onto a cook pot or food item. (A parabolic dish is a concave, bowl shaped device with a reflective material lining the inside surface of the dish). The dish focuses sunlight onto a dark cooking pot, typically suspended or set on a stand in front of the cooker. These devices provide immediate, intense heat when exposed to direct sunlight.

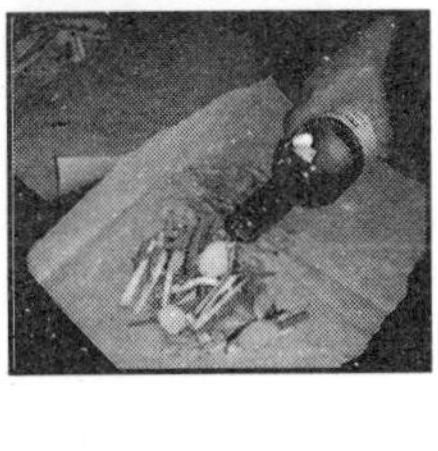

(j) Paper bag cooking (en papillotte) - this is a method of cookery in which the food is tightly sealed in oiled greaseproof paper or foil so that no steam escapes during cooking and maximum natural flavour and nutritive value is retained.

Combination method **–** uses both dry heat and moist heat procedures. Foods are first browned in hot fat, then covered and slowly cooked in a liquid over low heat. These include:

Braising and Stewing

Braising

- **The Similarities and Differences between Braising and Stewing.**
- Stewing are first sautéing the item, then adding liquid and simmering. While in braising meat joints are first roasted and then simmered in liquid. This is done to seal the juices of meat.
- Generally foods that are cut into dices are stewed, whereas larger items (poultry legs, lamb shanks, etc.) are braised.

Mise en place

Mise en place is a French term for having all ingredients measured, cut, and peeled, sliced, grated, and keeping on a place before start cooking. Pans are prepared. Mixing bowls, tools and equipment set out .it is basically to organize the work station and to prepare meals so quickly and effortlessly.

Mise en place has several benefits

1. Any missing ingredients can be spotted before it's too late for a quick trip to the store
2. Small preparation for ingredients — such as cutting, letting certain ingredients come to room temperature, etc. — can be handled before cooking rather than in the midst of another preparation step when time delays may affect food quality.
3. There is time to clean the mixing area as you go along rather than face a counter full of mixing equipment when you're done.
4. You can group ingredients or place them in the order used to assure all recipe steps are included.
5. It makes complicated recipes more fun to prepare when you're no longer doing a juggling act, trying to complete several tasks simultaneously.

Mise en Place involves several steps which will insure the necessary ingredients and tools are at your fingertips. The actual cooking process will be much quicker, smoother and more enjoyable!

1. As per the recipe, determine which ingredients and equipment one will need and have them arranged.
2. Prepare the work-space.
   - Start with a clean area in kitchen.
   - arrange the area as per requirement .keep necessary items like pans and pot, knife, vegetables, meat spices etc. in working area. Remove unnecessary items off the counter tops.
3. Do the starting.
   - Preheat the oven, prepare pans, etc.

- Chop, dice, grate, and sift; pre-measure ingredients and put into small bowls or tray in the cooking area

4. Keep the area neat and clean. This is the most important step

Following are the some terms associated with mise en place:

1. **Peeling** - means cleaning and removing surface dirt by taking off the skin of vegetables. This is done by using peeler and few of the vegetables like carrots, cucumber, celery etc. required thorough peeling.
2. **Chopping** - it is cutting into very small coarse or fine regular/irregular pieces. They are used for mirepoix and garnish.
3. **Mincing** - this is a very fine cut, stage after the chopping . When chopped vegetables are cut very-very finely.
4. **Turning** - vegetables can be turned by cutting into various series which simultaneously trim and shape the vegetable. Like barrel shapes of potatoes.
5. **Paring** is removing of skin in circular motion by pressing the edge of knife.
6. **Grating** - It is done by rubbing fruit, vegetable etc. against the grater for smaller pieces.
7. **Slitting-to** divides the vegetable by inserting knife in between .like for green chilies and carrot.
8. **Grinding** - It is done through a friction into very very smaller pieces. Done on a grinder.
9. **Mashing** - rubbing of the soft food by using pressure on it.
10. **Puree** - minute tiny pieces by straining through strainer or processing through blender.
11. **Sieving** - specially use for flour straining through a fine wire siever.
12. **Skimming** - removing the floating fat or impurities from the top of the boiling liquid.
13. **Folding** - Term is associated with blending of the different ingredient. In such a way that retain the enclosed air like mixing flour in whipped egg white.
14. **Beating** - lifting the liquid with the help of the beater which help in expanding and blending of different ingredient.
15. **Whipping** - it is a continuous and vigorously beating of egg by using whisker to incorporate air in it.
16. **Rolling**-flattening of dough by using rolling pin.
17. **Reducing** - evaporation of liquid by heating continuing.
18. **Emulsification** - The process of dispersing one liquid into another liquid with which it is immiscible; the action of breaking up fats, oils, and other lipids into small particles that remain suspended within a cleaning solution until extraction may be accomplished.

19. **Creaming** - lightening of fat by friction. As in case of cake making fat is mixed sugar.
20. **Scoring** is a term associated with fish, meat or vegetables by inserting knife deeply to penetrating the heat.
21. **Sealing-** to keep the meat or fish on high heat for very short period to close the pores of surface which helps in retaining the juice.
22. **Kneading** - mixing flour with liquid and then apply pressure to make a mass.

Traditional British measures distinguish between weight and volume.

Weight is measured in pounds and ounces (16 oz = 1 lb = 0.4545 kg)

Volume is measured in pints and fluid ounces (20 fl. oz = 1 pt = 568 ml)

U.S. recipes are almost always in terms of volume.

Dry Measures

pinch = approx. 1/8 teaspoon

1 dry ounce (oz.) = 16 drams = 1/16 pound = 28.35 g

1 peck = 8 quarts = 2 gallons = ¼ bushel = 9 lt. approx.

1 pound (lb.) = 16 ounces = 453.6 g

Fluid Measures

1 drop = 1/76 teaspoon

1 dash = 6 drops

1 teaspoon (t. or tsp.) = 76 drops = 1/3 tablespoon = 4.93 ml

1 tablespoon (T. or tbsp.) = 1/16 cup or ½ fluid ounce = 3 teaspoons = 14.79 ml

1 fluid ounce (oz.) = 1/16 pint = 29.57 ml

1 jigger = 1½ fluid ounces = 44.36 ml

1 gill = 4 fluid ounces = 118 ml

1 cup (c.) = 8 fluid ounces = 16 tablespoons = 237 ml

1 pint (pt.) = 16 fluid ounces = 2 cups = 473 ml

1 fifth = 25.6 fluid ounces = 757 ml

1 quart (qt.) = 32 fluid ounces = 2 pints = 946 ml

1 gallon = 128 fluid ounces = 4 quarts = 4.5 lt.

Formula to convert Fahrenheit to centigrade

C=5/9*(F-32)

Formula to convert centigrade to Fahrenheit

F = 32 + (C*9/5)

Oven Temperatures conversion chart

Electric		Gas mark	Description
Fahrenheit	Celsius		
225° F	110° C	1/4	Very cool/very slow
250° F	130° C	½	
275° F	140° C	1	cool
300° F	150° C	2	
325° F	170° C	3	very moderate
350° F	180° C	4	moderate
375° F	190° C	5	
400° F	200° C	6	moderately hot
425° F	220° C	7	hot
450° F	230° C	8	
475° F	240° C	9	very hot

BTU = British Thermal Unit

BTU × 1054 = Joules

Watts × Seconds = Joules

BTU = Watts × (Seconds/1054) = Watts × 3.415

Electric Cooktops typically range from 35 watts to 2900 watts.

To help you compare gas burners to electric elements:

BTU	**Watts**	
100	35	
200	70	<- gas burners lowest setting
3400	1000	
6500	1900	
8000	2300	<- most electric tops stop here
10000	2900	
12000	3500	

QUESTIONS

1. Define cooking and what are the benefits of cooking?
2. Explain in detail the development of various cuisines in past internationally?

3. What are the different methods of cooking?
4. If we cook the sugar the what changes will occurs?
5. What are the various essentials nutrients found in food? How they are useful for human body?
6. Differentiate the following:
   (a) Boiling and Broiling
   (b) Conduction and Convection
   (c) Braising and Stewing
   (d) Effect of heat on protein and carbohydrates
7. Define following-
   1. Microwave cooking
   2. Solar cooking
   3. B T U
   4. Stir frying
   5. Sautéing
   6. Fusion cuisine
   7. Conduction
   8. Radiation
   9. *Tandoor*
   10. Barbeque
   11. T V P.

Baking

Deep frying

Pan-frying

Stir Frying

Sauté

Broiling

Grilling

Roasting

Pot roasting

Tandoor

Clay pot cooking

Poaching

Simmering

Steaming

Blanching or parboiling

Barbequing

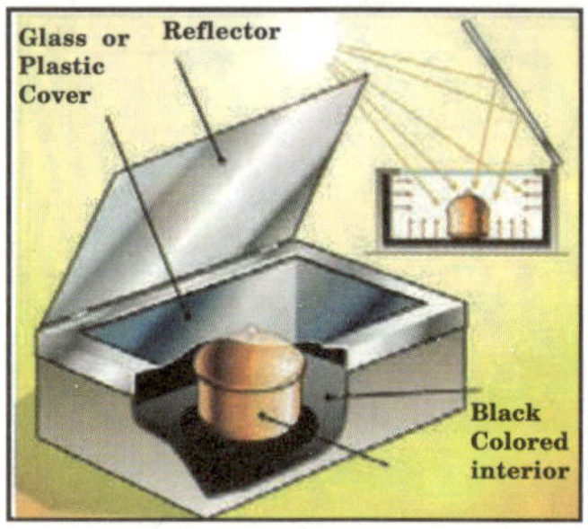

Solar oven cooking

Braising

Paper bag cooking

2

Organization of Food Production

OBJECTIVE

1. Organizational hierarchy of food production department
2. Duties and responsibilities of chef
3. Layout of kitchen

ORGANIZATION OF FOOD PRODUCTION

Objective - after studying this chapter student should know:

1. organizational hierarchy of food production department
2. layout of kitchen
3. planning production in kitchen
4. duties and responsibilities of chef

Brigade de cuisine is the term used to describe the hierarchy of the apprentice system in a professional kitchen. The concept was created by Auguste Escoffier.

There are many types of kitchen organization, but a general outline is as follows:

1. corporate chef
2. Executive Chef / Chef de Cuisine
3. Sous Chef /premiur chef
4. chef tournant
5. Chef de partie
6. Sauce chef or saucier
7. Fish cook or poissonier

8. Vegetable cook or entremetier
9. Roast cook or rotisseur
10. Larder Chef or Chef Gardemanger
11. Pastry chef or pâtissier
12. The butcher ,meat chef
13. Cooks and Assistants
14. aboyeur

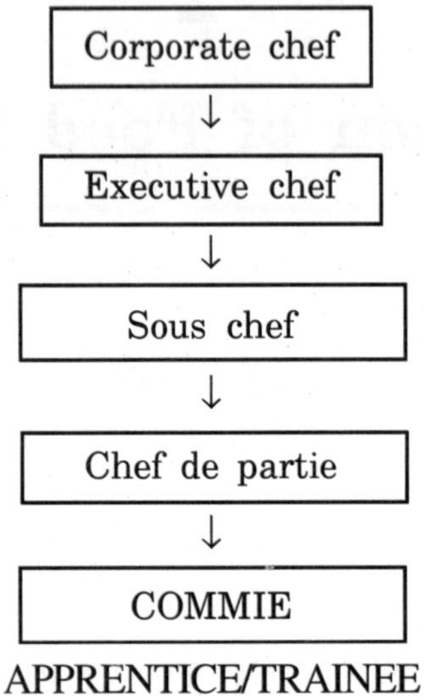

Corporate chef –usually corporate chef is chief chef in a chain hotel or cruise liner. He is above the Executive Chef, usually responsible for making policy in the kitchen.

Executive Chef / Chef de Cuisine

The Executive Chef is in charge of everything related to the kitchen, including menu planning, making, and quality and set up. He is responsible for the recruitment and selection of employee.

He is responsible for—

- Kitchen lay out and planning
- Food quality and standards
- Staff recruitment and training
- Maintaining hygiene and cleanliness.
- Costing and budgeting
- Answerable to top management like general manager, director.
- Allotment of different sections and administration.

- Making standard recipe, garnish, accompaniments and service style.
- Menu planning and designing.
- Represent the hotel management

Executive Sous Chef

The Executive Sous chef is the direct assistant of the Executive Chef. The executive Sous Chef often as a liaison between the top management and middle management. He also shares some duties with the executive chef, such as menu planning, costing and ordering. Each section in-charge is equal to Sous chef such as the banquet Sous chef, in charge of all banquets, Indian chef for Indian kitchen Larger kitchens often have more than one Sous chef, with each having his or her own area of responsibility, or the executive Sous chef, in charge of all other Sous chefs.

Sous chef

Generally known by the section chef like Pastry Chef, Coffee Shop kitchen chef etc. Sous chef, the expediter serves as the liaison between the customers in the dining room and the line cooks. With the help of proper coordination and timing, they make sure that the food gets to the wait staff in a timely fashion, so that everyone sitting at a particular table is served simultaneously.

Chef de partie

A *chef de partie*, also known as a "station chef" or "line cook", is in charge of a particular area of production. In large kitchens, each station chef might have several cooks and/or assistants. In most kitchens however, the station chef is the only worker in that department. Line cooks are often divided into a hierarchy of their own, starting with "First Cook", then "Second Cook", and so on as needed. Station chef titles can include:

Saucier - prepares sauces, stews, and hot *hors d'oeuvres*, and sautés foods to order. This is usually the highest position of all the stations.

Poissonier - Prepares fish dishes (this station may be handled by the saucier in some kitchens).

Vegetable cook or Entremetier - Prepares vegetables, soups, starches, and eggs. Large kitchens may divide these duties among the vegetable cook, the fry cook, and the soup cook.

Roast cook or Rotisseur - Prepares roasted and braised meats and their gravies, and broils meats and other items to order. A large kitchen may have a separate broiler cook or grillardin (gree-ar-dan) to handle the broiled items. The broiler cook may also prepare deep-fried meats and fish.

Indian chef - responsible for the preparation of Indian food included curry cook, tandoor cook and *halwai.*

The pantry chef or garde manger - is responsible for cold foods, including salads and dressings, pâtés, cold *hors d'oeuvres*, and buffet items.

Pastry chef or patisserie - prepares pastries and desserts.

The relief cook, swing cook, or Tournant - replaces other chef when they are on leave.

Aboyeur is the person on hot-plate who announces the order in kitchen.

COOKS AND ASSISTANTS

In larger kitchens, each station chef would have cooks and assistants (commis) that help with the particular duties that are assigned to that area. With experience, assistants may be promoted to station cooks and then to station chefs.

Factors which affect the layout of kitchen:

1. *Type of kitchen* - like small or large. Banquet kitchen would be large.
2. *Type of cuisine* - like Chinese kitchen will be smaller then Indian kitchen
3. *Number of customer* - it is catering to - for large number kitchen would be big.
4. Types of equipments and size
5. Menu and dish content
6. Size of hotel
7. Location of kitchen
8. Availability of water, store and fuel.

LAYOUT OF KITCHEN

Although the layout of kitchen varies as per the requirement but there are certain basic rules.

Following points should be taken care while making the layout of kitchen:

1. The area should be in proportionate to the restaurant capacity.
2. Store should be close the kitchen.
3. There must be enough space for movement of staff.
4. All required equipment and machinery installation first should be considered.
5. Enough provision should be kept for chef office, store, and pot cleaning and service area.
6. There should not be any obstacles in the movement.
7. One style of cooking should be arranged in one row.
8. Proper arrangement of water and drainage should be made.

SAMPLE KITCHEN LAYOUT

(Note: This is only a example and the layout and equipment may vary depending on the facility)

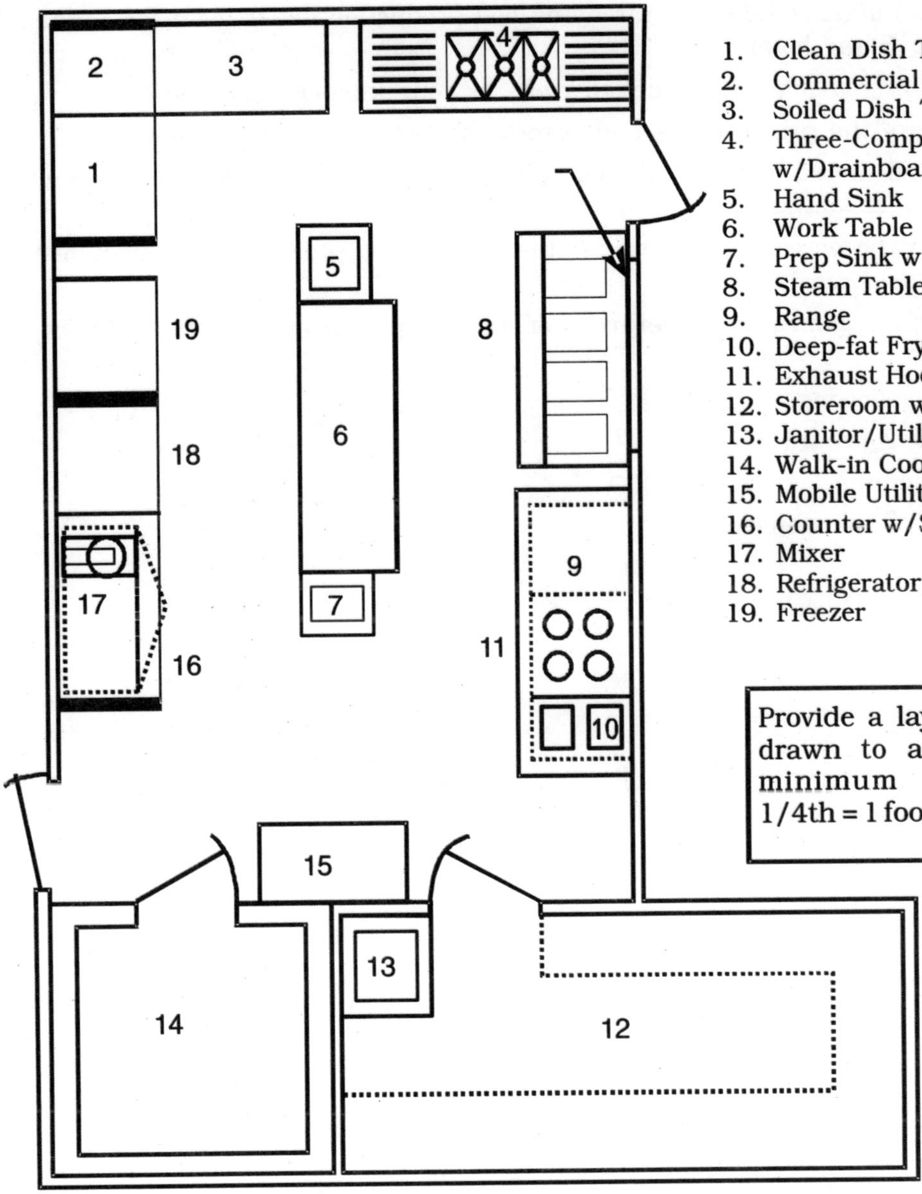

1. Clean Dish Table
2. Commercial Dishwasher
3. Soiled Dish Table
4. Three-Compartment Sink w/Drainboards
5. Hand Sink
6. Work Table
7. Prep Sink w/Air Break
8. Steam Table
9. Range
10. Deep-fat Fryer
11. Exhaust Hood
12. Storeroom w/Shelving
13. Janitor/Utility Sink
14. Walk-in Cooler
15. Mobile Utility Cart
16. Counter w/Storage
17. Mixer
18. Refrigerator
19. Freezer

Provide a layout plan drawn to at least a minimum scale of 1/4th = 1 foot.

9. A provision for gas bank, pipeline and exhaust should be made.
10. There should be synchronization of activity.

QUESTIONS

1. Draw a layout of coffee shop kitchen.
2. Draw an organizational hierarchy of food production department for 3-star and one for 5-star hotel.
3. How will you plan a production cycle in your kitchen as a chef?
4. What are the prime duties and responsibilities of chef de cuisine?
5. If a hotel should have one kitchen or two and more kitchen for food production. Give yours views.
6. Explain the necessity for close relationship of food production department with others department.
7. Draw an organizational hierarchy of kitchen preparing all three food for 100 pax.
8. Define followings:
   a. Chef Tournard
   b. Aboyeur.
   c. Chef Gardemanger.
   d. Pantry.
   e. Chef de Cuisine
   f. Satellite Kitchen.

3

Professionalism and Hygiene

OBJECTIVES

The purpose of this course is to provide the student with a base understanding of the need for cleanliness, sanitation, personal hygiene, general consciousness about safety, and an overall understanding of the workplace, and foods used in the work-place, as potentially harmful and hazardous. The need for students to learn the requirements in dealing with foods, and situations, which may be potentially hazardous to fellow human beings can never, be overstated

1. role of hygiene and sanitation in kitchen
2. different types of bacteria's and germs found related with food
3. effect and remedies of these bacteria's
4. food poisoning and its cause
5. danger zone – meaning and use.

CREATIVITY AS QUALITY

Creativity is most essential quality for chef in food preparation and presentation. This creativity rests on the constantly changing nature of the environment. While not as pervasive, the interest for many in novelty and complexity also drives the importance in developing our creative skills.

Because of the vast availability of basic ingredients, cooking techniques, cultural approaches attitudes, and existing recipes, as well as the quick and daily nature of food preparation, cooking offers many opportunities to develop innovative ideas and to test their usefulness simply by tasting.

Another aspect of creativity is that it should be useful to the individual, and society Cooking affords ample opportunities to understand this difference as beginners create—in most cases re-create—new recipes or techniques on the individual level and, as their learning progresses, move on to create new recipes or techniques that are innovative and that others can appreciate as well.

INTRODUCTION

Hygiene

The spread of certain infectious diseases may cause serious unhygienic practices or conditions in food service areas. The remedies are started with a proper layout that is properly designed and constructed to be free of conditions that are hazardous to food and service.

There should be an adequate supply of potable hot and cold water shall be provided. Steam supplies, whether used directly on food or food-contact surfaces, must be clean and non-toxic. Floor drains shall be trapped, vented and sealed into the floor surface and should be provided with grilles which can be easily removed. Ventilation systems must conform to fire regulations and be designed so as to prevent a back flow of contaminating material on to food or food preparation surfaces from vents or hoods. Air intakes should be designed to prevent the entrance of dirt, dust and insects. Filters shall be removable and cleaned at regular intervals, and systems must be kept free of grease and dust accumulation.

Washrooms and personnel locker or changing rooms should be structurally separated from food storage, handling, preparation and serving areas. Staff washrooms shall have an adequate supply of hot and cold water, soap, nail brushes, and single service disposable towels or an approved hand drying device. Food wastes and garbage wastes must be handled, stored or removed in such a way as to prevent food contamination or nuisances, the following measures shall be taken:

Cleanliness in all areas, including corners and behind the equipment, is mandatory. All food shall be properly covered and stored. Tight fitting window screens and self-closing screen doors shall Be provided for all food service areas proper and regular pest control should be done.

EQUIPMENT AND UTENSILS

All equipment and utensils must be designed in such a way that they can be easily cleaned and should be constructed of an approved material that is durable and resistant to corrosion.

The following measures shall be observed in the installation and maintenance of equipment:

- Non-mobile equipment shall be either sealed into the floor or mounted on legs with a minimum six-inch clearance between the floor and the base of the equipment.

- The sides and back of this equipment shall also be either sealed into adjacent walls or installed with an eight-inch clearance to enable cleaning.
- Wooden-topped preparation tables, meat blocks and cutting boards shall be kept clean and in good repair.
- Items with splits or open cracks shall be repaired or replaced.
- Locally made plywood cutting boards shall not be used.
- All chipped or cracked plastic ware or crockery, and other utensils or heavy equipment items which have surface damage rendering them difficult to sanitize shall be replaced. Plastic ware which has lost the glaze finish shall be replaced.
- Always use three sink method for cleaning utensils.

FOOD HANDLERS

As food services personnel can be carriers of disease organisms which contaminate food the following precautions shall be taken:

- Food services personnel who incur a common cold, sore throat, gastro-intestinal upset, skin rash or an infected cut or sore shall A high standard of personal hygiene is essential to prevent the transmission of infectious diseases through food. In order to maintain this standard, food services personnel shall adhere to the following:
- Smoking, combing hair, applying cosmetics, and changing clothing in food service areas are prohibited.
- Female personnel shall wear a hair net. Male personnel shall wear a cap. Beards worn by food handlers shall be kept short, neatly trimmed and clean.
- Personnel shall thoroughly wash their hands prior to starting work, and also after using the toilet facilities, handling raw foods, using a handkerchief, coughing or sneezing.

STORAGE AND REFRIGERATION

Food that does not require refrigeration or frozen storage shall be stored:

a. in clean, well-ventilated, rodent-proof areas;

b. on racks or pallets with a minimum of six inches clearance from the floor to facilitate cleaning and pest control; and

c. in unbroken packages or in closed containers to prevent insect contamination.

d. Proper temperatures shall be maintained

e. Perishable foods, both cooked and uncooked, when not actually being used in the preparation of meals or being served, shall be stored according to the following temperatures (degrees):

	Fahrenheit	Celsius
a. vegetables and fruits	39° to 50°	4° to 10°
b. meats	33° to 39°	0.5° to 4°
c. dairy products	35° to 38°	1.5° to 3.5°
d. frozen foods	0° or lower	-18° or lower

During meal preparation and service, cold foods shall be kept below 45°F (7°C) while hot foods must be maintained at a minimum of 140°F (60°C). Left over foods shall be cooled rapidly to 45°F (7°C), otherwise it will lead to contamination, and stored in the refrigerator. Maximum storage periods for leftover foods shall conform to recommended food service industry standards.

FOOD INTOXICATION

This type of illness is caused by toxins. Under favorable conditions certain bacteria produce chemical compounds called toxins, which, if ingested, cause food intoxication. Staphylococcus is the most commonly reported food intoxication.

Staphylococcus is the most prevalent carrier of food intoxication in food service personnel. Commonly involved are pork products, fowl foods, meats, fish, cheese, milk products (including cream- and custard-filled pastries), and potato and macaroni salads associated with outbreaks of staphylococcus. Thus the food should be cooked properly to avoid this kind of intoxication .

Botulism is a second type of food intoxication. This disease, usually fatal, is caused by the toxin produced by the rod-shaped bacterium called clostridium botulinum. Botulinum organisms are found in the soil and gain access to foods through contact with soil, dust, and possibly

FOOD INFECTION

This type of food illness is caused by micro-organisms such as the salmonella, shigella, clostridium species and the streptococcus, bacillus, and typhoid fever bacteria. A large percentage of food infections are transmitted by foods that have been allowed to remain at room temperature for a prolonged period of time.

Salmonellosis salmonella bacteria are transmitted by foods, usually from under-cooked or semi-cooked raw foods, or from foods that have become infected after cooking by persons who are harboring the bacteria. Since salmonella bacilli leave the body through the intestinal tract, the main source of salmonella infection is people who do not wash their hands after leaving the head.

Ones most likely to harbor the salmonella bacilli are:

(1) those that are usually eaten raw such as salads and greens;

(2) cooked leftover foods that are not reheated thoroughly;

(3) foods that are under-cooked, especially poultry and uninspected meats; and

(4) infected eggs that are eaten raw or under-cooked.

Streptococcus - Infections such as septic sore throat and scarlet fever are transmitted by contaminated milk and by certain other foods, including meat, meat products, and dressings.

ANIMAL PARASITES

Animal parasites sometimes enter the body in food and produce infections. Some of these forms of animal life are one-celled. All are so tiny that they are not visible when the food is being prepared.

Amoebic Dysentery, by flies, or by having been grown in fields where animal excreta was used as fertilizer.

Trichinosis - Eating infected pork that has not been thoroughly cooked is the most common cause of trichinosis. All fresh pork products must be cooked to an internal temperature of 75°C or above to kill the trichinella worm.

Beef Tapeworm Infection - Beef tapeworms are transmitted by infected beef that has not been cooked long enough to kill the encysted larvae.

Fish Tapeworm Infection - Fish tapeworm is transmitted by infected fish that has not been thoroughly cooked.

MOLDS AND YEASTS

Other types of cell life that may not be harmful are molds and yeasts.

Molds - Molds are composed of many cells and maybe very small or large enough to cover an entire wall. They grow best in dark, damp places where temperatures are favorable. Some molds are valuable in the production of medicines such as penicillin; other molds may cause certain infections in human beings. Molds spoil the taste of food and eventually destroy it. Molds may be removed from certain foods and the remainder of the food used. Consult your medical department on the precautions to be taken.

Yeasts like bacteria, yeasts are single-celled. They reproduce by budding. When a bud becomes sufficiently large, it separates from the original cell and becomes an independent cell. Certain yeasts are used in bread-making, vinegar fermentation, and the manufacture of beverages.

FOOD PREPARATION

It is evident that the food service worker is the most important link in the transmission of disease through food. The workers' health, personal habits, understanding of bacteria, and the methods of preparing and serving of food are of concern not only to themselves but also to their shipmates as well.

BACTERIA

An understanding of bacteria is valuable to all personnel and essential to those who work with food in any way. Bacteria are one-celled microorganisms; so small they are visible only under a microscope. They are widely distributed in the air, water, soil, and in animal and plant tissues

DANGER ZONE

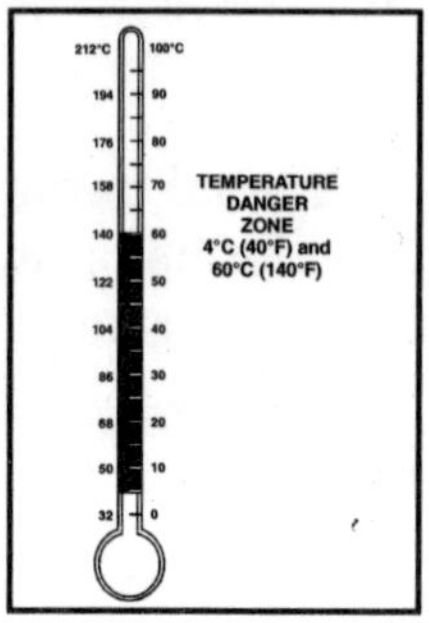

Danger Zone is the area of rapid growth of bacteria and production of toxins. Food should move through this temperature range within 2 to 3 hours to avoid spoilage. This occurs fast on room temperature i.e. 20°-40°C.

PROCEDURE OF FOOD HANDLING

Some types of foods are more likely than other foods to grow germs that may cause food poisoning if kept at room temperature. Such types of Foods are moist and contain protein are the most potentially hazardous. This includes meat, fish, poultry, dairy, eggs, cooked food like rice, dry beans, tofu, potatoes, and cut fruits.

Here are some important things to be done before cooking food in kitchen.

Wash Hands Properly

Wash hands with warm water at least for 20 seconds by using soap/sanitizing solution which helps in getting rid of the germs. One must wash hands regularly before touching food(raw & cooked)including raw meats, fish & poultry. One should wash hands even after coughing or sneezing or re-entering the kitchen from outer environment. If using gloves they should be changed frequently.

Avoid Cross-contamination

Cross contamination happens when germs from raw or unclean foods transfer to cooked food through knife, chopping board, storing using bare hand or even by handling in wrong way therefore always.

- Put store raw meat, fish, and poultry separate from the cooked one.
- After cooking place them in a clean container.
- Use a separate and clean chopping board for cutting meat and vegetables depending on the color codes eg. red-red meats, blue- seafood, green- vegetables & fruits, white-dairy products, yellow- poultry.

- Wash, rinse and sanitize the utensils, chopping board, tools and equipments.

Avoid danger zone

- Potentially hazardous food items should never be kept outside for long periods, they can attract germs and bacteria.
- Reheating the food needs to be done as quickly as possible (within 1 hour) to maintain the temp at 60°C and above.
- Reheat foods to 60°C or store food up to 6°C as fast as possible to avoid "danger zone."
- Thaw food in proper temperature. Usually in thawing room.

QUESTIONS

1. Why the Hygienic Conditions are essentials for food preparation areas?
2. Why it is necessary to cook raw meat for long period.
3. Define professionalism and its effect.
4. What are different mold and bacteria's can be grown on improper storage of food?
5. What is danger zone? How to quickly cross the stage of danger zone?
6. Define following:
   A. Food Intoxication
   B. Salmonella
   C. Danger Zone
   D. Potentially Hazardous Food
   E. Cross Contamination
   F. Thawing.

4

Tools and Equipment

It is important to understand the importance of using the proper tools and equipment when preparing, cooking, storing, and presenting food. Many times the quality of the finished product is determined by the tools and equipment used. In addition, the efficiency of the kitchen is impacted by the ability to select the correct tool and use it correctly. This chapter discusses most of the tools and pieces of equipment used in a professional kitchen and how the kitchen should be designed for optimal performance

OBJECTIVES

- Role and use of tools and equipment
- Various types of tools and equipment found in kitchen
- Knife and its parts
- Types of fuel

ROLE OF TOOLS AND EQUIPMENT

Without tools and equipment it is impossible to prepare a good food. On professional level it is difficult to prepare the food which serves a large quantity. Specially when different types of preparation method has to be used one need latest equipment.

1. small tools and equipment
2. heavy and bulky equipment
3. knife and parts
4. Indian culinary equipment

Small Equipment

- Cutting board
- Rubber spatula
- Set of measuring cups
- Set of measuring spoons
- Wire whip
- 2 lb. capacity portion scale
- Colander or strainer
- Vegetable peeler
- Flour sifter
- Wooden mixing spoons
- Ladle
- Stainless steel serving spoon (solid)
- Stainless steel slotted serving spoon
- Fine mesh china cap
- Double broiler
- Sauté pan
- Sauce pans with lids
- Mixing bowls
- Food storage containers
- Rack popover/muffin pan
- Baking sheet
- Custard cups
- Shallow roasting pan
- Round cookie cutter
- Hammer and many more.

Heavy and Bulky Equipments

- Cooking range with burners-available with gas or electricity operated. Comes in various sizes like low pressure, high pressure, plate etc. make sure that they are durable, easy to clean, easy to use and cover less space.
- Refrigerator like two or four door, table top, walk in freezer, chillers. They should be easy to manipulate, maintain temperature, as per the requirement and suitability.

- Baking oven is used for baking and cooking. Usually available with proving chamber and steam line:
  1. *Combination ovens*: Combination microwave convection ovens combine the speed of micro waving with the even cooking of convection baking.
  2. *Convection oven*: in this oven A fan circulates hot air to cook faster and more evenly. Such even browning means superior results, especially when baking. Also, because the air circulates, more of the oven space can be used.
  3. *Halogen/microwave combination oven*: These combine light waves with microwaves to cook food four times faster than a conventional oven would - with the same oven-quality browning and crisping.
  4. *Microwave oven*: These appliances use electro-magnetic waves to cook and warm food in much less time than conventional ovens. It has a great convenience for professional chef. It works on the base of friction as the waves agitate the food molecules. Resultant friction of molecules produces heat. Specially made utensils are used.
- *Work-table* - available in various sizes.
- *Salamander* - usually mountain top is available as it save the space and easy in handling.
- *Tilting pan* - a large pan used for bulk cooking can be tilted as per the requirement.
- *Mincing machine* - used for mincing the meat for force meat, pate and kebab.
- *Boilers* - used for heating stock, water, soup etc.
- *Bain Marie* - hot /cold water well
- *Steamer* - large equipment used for steaming the food. Available manual and electric base.
- *Tandoor* - for Tandoori items. Can be coal or gas base.
- *Griller* - for grilling meat, poultry, steak, patties etc.
- *Hot-plate* - for cooking flat dishes like pan cake, etc.
- *Ice-cream machine* - for making of ice cream.
- *Dish-washing machine* - for cleaning and washing of utensils. It can be hood or chain type. Available in 1, 2, 3 tanks.
- *Mixer blender Juicer* - available in various size and shapes. Should be stable, durable and high power resistance.
- *Band saw machine* - is used for cutting strong joints and bones of animals. Be very careful while using.
- *Buffalo chopper* - is used for blending and fine chopping of different ingredients. It carries very sharp and strong blades.
- *Bread slicer machine* - for slicing of bread.
- *Potatoes peeler* - for peeling potatoes and hard skin vegetables.

SMALL EQUIPMENT

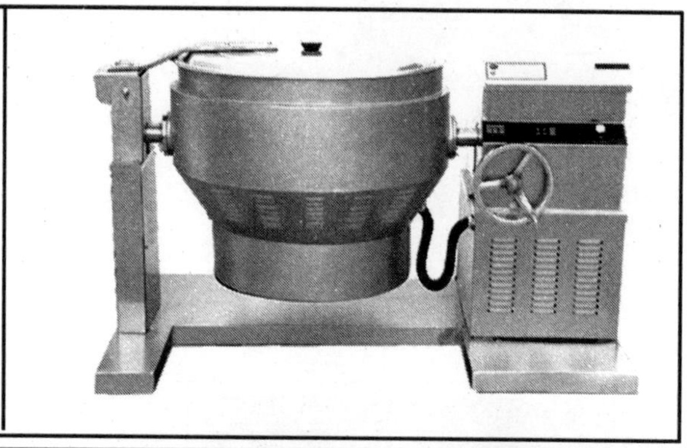

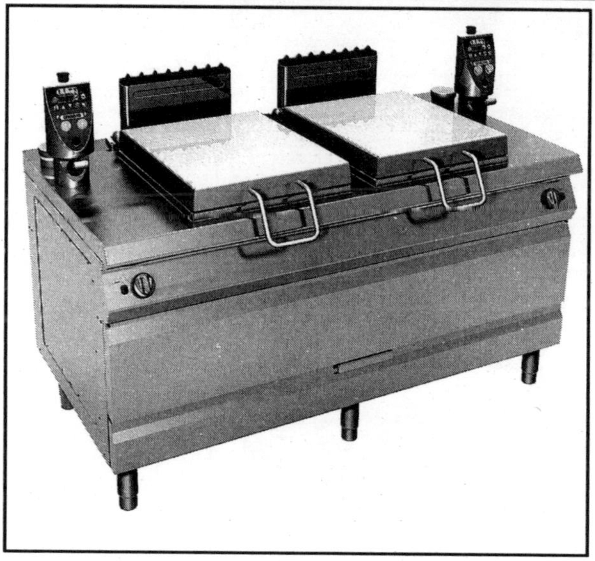

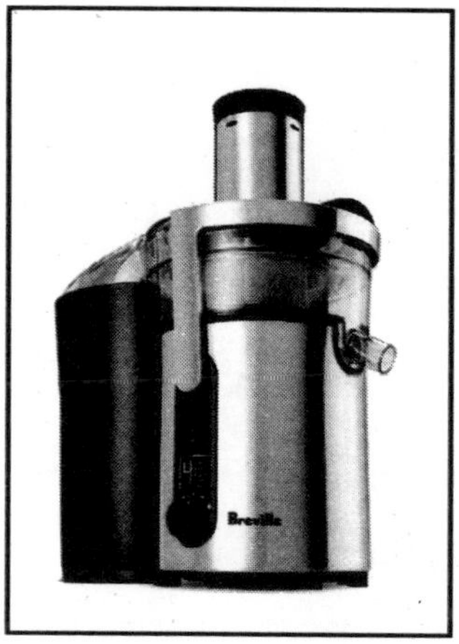

SMALL EQUIPMENT

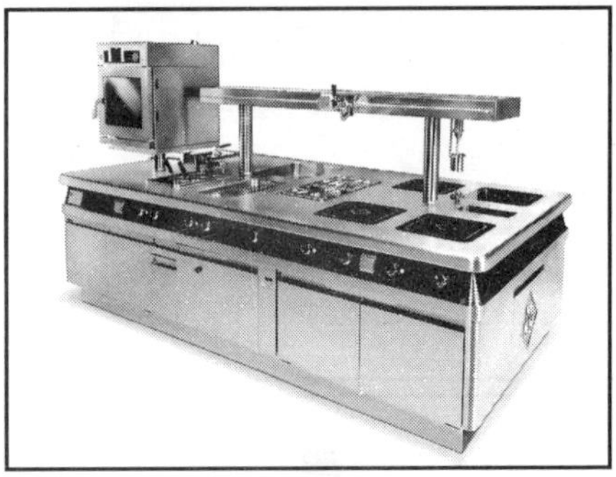

- *Steam cooker* - for bulk cooking.
- *Blast freezer* - for fast chilling.
- *Toaster.*
- *Walk in* - large deep freezers.
- *Deep fat fryer* - used for bulk frying.
- *Cookies making machine* - for quick cookies making
- *Bun divider* - dividing the dough.
- *Vegetable cutting/slicer machine* - for various type of vegetable cuts.
- *Dough making machine* - is used for various things with its various attachment like dough kneading, egg whipping, creaming etc.

KITCHEN EQUIPMENT

Kitchen equipment can be conveniently grouped into six categories:

1. Storage equipment,
2. Preparation equipment,
3. Cooking equipment,
4. Accessory equipment,
5. Steam fuelled equipment and
5. Service equipment.

Storage Equipment

Storage equipment consists of industrial food-grade shelving. It may be wire or solid. There are upright, chest, and walk-in freezers. Chest freezers preserve cold air but utilize more floor space, whereas upright freezes use less floor space but allow cold air to escape rapidly each time the door is opened.

Walk-in freezers are recommended for operations using considerable amounts of frozen foods. In every walk-in installation, care should be taken to position the freezer to open into a refrigerator in order to preserve at least part of the cold air, which inevitably escapes each time the door is opened. There are standard- or blast freezers for quick freezing of vegetables or plated food. Cryogenic freezers use liquid nitrogen or carbon dioxide and freeze fast.

They are recommended for hospitals and institutions feeding large numbers of people at set times

Preparation Equipment

Preparation equipment constitute all equipment employed in food preparation (chopping, dicing, cubing, peeling, slicing, mixing, processing). They speed up all these functions, reduce labour, facilitate quality control and promote consistency.

Specify sturdy brands, backed up by a good supply of spare parts, warranties, guarantees and service. Foreign suppliers should be specified only if local manufacturers are inadequate or do not exist.

Cooking Equipment

All equipment used in cooking fall under this category, and may be fuelled by electricity, propane, natural gas, oil, wood, or steam. The fuel must be selected with due care according to availability and style of cooking being envisaged. Steam generators are available, so are cooking equipment with self steam generating installations. Always specify cooking equipment with the least number of moving parts. The following are the cooking equipment

Ranges : hot top
open burners

Deep fryers : electric or gas

Broilers : ceramic brickets
radiant
infra red
open

Salamanders : (top heat)
electric
infrared
gas

Steam Fuelled Equipment

Steam jacketed kettles

Pressure steamers are suitable for quantity batch cooking. Combi-ovens combine steaming and roasting, and are popular due to their space saving features.

Ovens

A wide range of ovens is available. They can be under ranges, freestanding, electric or gas, steam injected or not. **Convection ovens** are practical for roasting and rotate hot air speeding up cooking time. **Conveyor type ovens** are appropriate in high volume pizza operations or in very busy bakeries. **Micro wave ovens** are used mostly for re-thermalizing. **Rotatory ovens** are used for bread making.

Griddles

Griddles consist of a stainless steel non-stick surface fuelled either by gas or electricity, equipped with appropriate grooves and grease collectors. They are versatile and very much in demand in short order kitchens and cafeterias.

Tilting Frying Pans

Tilting Frying Pans may be gas or electric fuelled. They are practical in large banquet halls or hotel banquet kitchens catering to huge banquets. Cooking equipment is rated either in units per hour or BTU's (British Thermal Unit) One British Thermal Unit is the amount of energy required to raise the temperature of one pound of water by one degree Fahrenheit. The rating is important to calculate power requirements.

Accessories Equipment

Electronic thermostats, energy load levelers (reduce peak electricity demand) and automatic shut off switches fall under this category.

Service Equipment

Service equipment help to keep prepared foods hot. Steam tables, flambé carts, gueridons, coffee machines, small wares (pots, pans, whips, scoops) self levelling plate dispensers, dishwashers, compactors, filtering devices fall into this category.

REFRIGERATORS

Refrigerators prevent bacterial growth and prolong the shelf life of perishable foods. There are electricity or gas fuelled, reach-in, roll-in, drawer and walk-in refrigerators. Electricity powered refrigerators are the most common.

Reach-in and walk-in refrigerators are readily available in a variety of sizes and configurations. Walk-in refrigerators can be specified modular or custom made. Drawer and roll-in refrigerators are practical and save labour but must be custom manufactured and expensive.

All commercial refrigerators must be equipped with thermostats both inside and out. Interiors of all must be easy to reach, clean, and well lit.. Walk-in refrigerators must have non-slip floors and equipped to open from inside and outside. All doors must be airtight and equipped with self-closing mechanisms to minimize cold air loss.

A well-designed compressor maintenance programme will help prolong usable life. Wooden storage shelving is not recommended. Tempering refrigerators to re-thermalize plated frozen food is practical in hospital and correctional institutions.

KNIFE AND PARTS

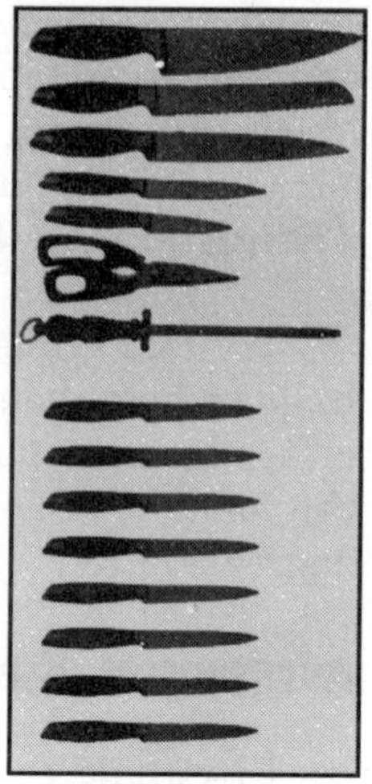

- French knife,
- Serrated slicing knife,
- Paring knife,
- Fish knife
- Meat knife
- Peeler
- Vegetable knife
- Steak knife and fork
- Cheese knife
- Carving knife
- Bread knife
- Pallet knife
- clavet

Identify Basic Knife Parts

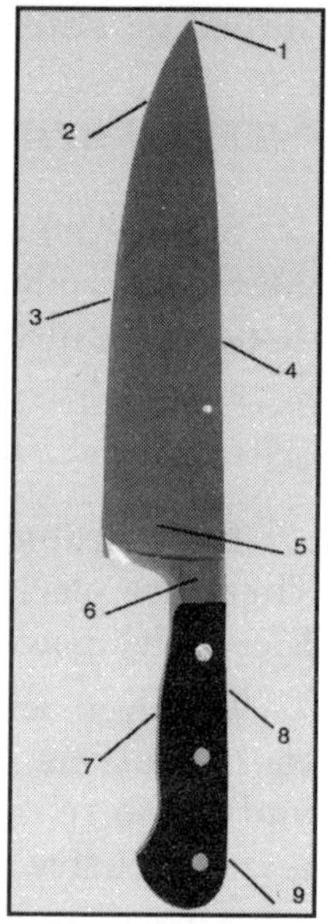

1. Point
2. Tip
3. Edge
4. Spine
5. Heel
6. Bolster
7. Tang
8. Scales
9. Butt

INDIAN TOOLS AND EQUIPMENTS

1. *Kadhai* - like a Chinese wok
2. *Belan* - rolling pin
3. *Chakla* - stone made platform for rolling
4. *chimta* - type of tongue
5. *Parat* - hollow container
6. *Degchi* - large deep bowl
7. *Sil pathar* - stone grinder

8. pestle and mortar
9. *Poni* - perforated spoon
10. *Dosa plate* - flat hot plate
11. *Chapatti* maker - for rolling Indian bred
12. *Idli* steamer - for steaming rice cakes
13. *Dhokla* steamer - for gram flour dumplings
14. potato masher
15. *Chilmachi* - large bowl
16. *Bhigona* - cooking cotainer
17. *Chhalani* - a siever

Meat slicer

Buffalo chopper

Microwave oven

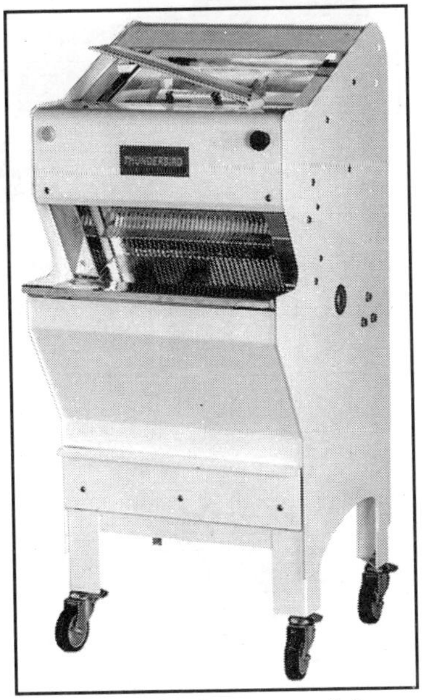

Bread slicing machine

Steam cooker

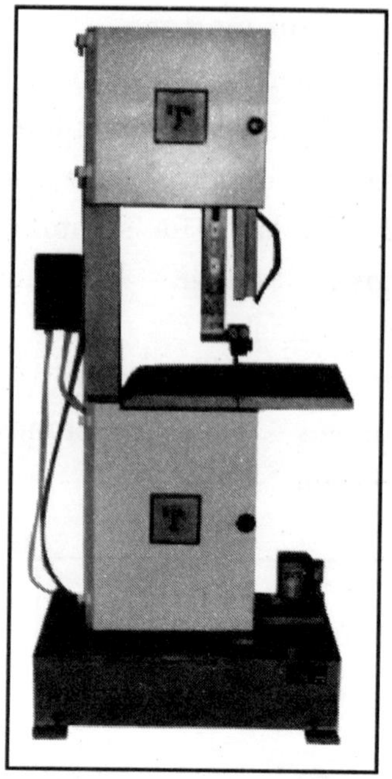

Band saw machine

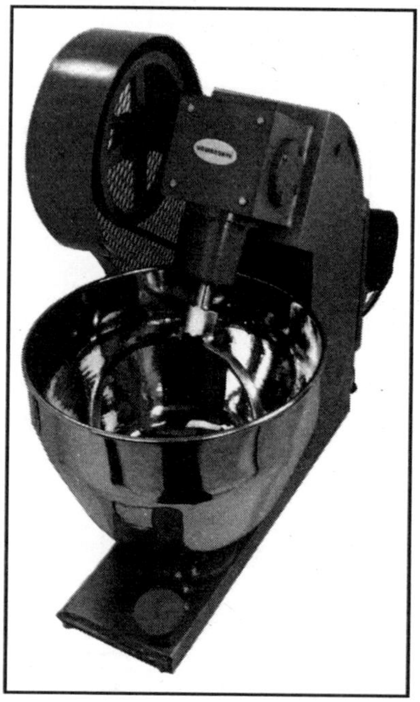

Dough kneader

Mincing machine

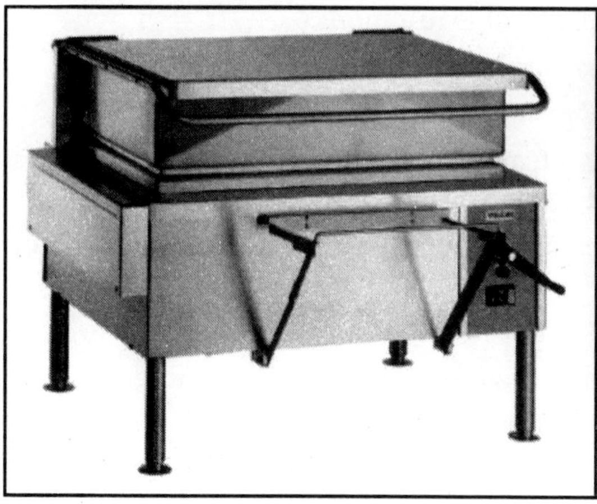

Tilting pan **Convection oven**

There are five types of fuels can be used:

1. *Electric* as it is a fast, reliable, easily available, eco friendly but expensive type of fuel
2. *Gas* is also a easily controlled, reliable, cheap, co friendly kind of fuels.
3. *Charcoal* is expensive, eco unfriendly but used for smoky flavour in Indian foods and barbeque.
4. *Solar* is cheap but slow and unpractical source of energy.
5. *Wood* is rarely used as fuel. Reason is of its smoky burning.

Bun divider

Safety precautions to be taken before using equipments. Follow these guideline while using heavy equipment:

- Staff should be trained in their use as per the manufacturer instruction.
- Wear personal protective cloth as prescribed for using equipment
- Use machine guarding specially for blender, dough kneading machine and buffalo chopper
- Always ask for help if not sure how to use.
- Be aware that age restrictions exist for workers under the age of 18 from using or cleaning certain equipment.
- Follow the manufacturer's instructions for machine use, cleaning and maintenance.
- Be alert and in proper consciousness while using heavy equipment.
- Always use a sign board while using heavy equipment. This helps in informing others to about machine use.

- Always report for the faulty or week parts of equipment.
- Always unplug the machine before cleaning and after use.

While using mincers, choppers, dicers, slicers one should follow the rules like:

- Do not use hands to feed smaller pieces of meat or to stir contents but always use push sticks to feed or remove food from these types of machines.
- Make sure to use machine guarding that is provided to prevent access to cutter blades. Do not ignore safety guards.
- Wear suitable protective clothing.
- Turn off and unplug the machine before disassembling and cleaning.

While using food processors, mixers follow the rules like:

- Do not attempt to remove items during operation (for example, a spoon that falls into the mixture) from dough while the machine is mixing.
- Do not open up the lids of processors to stir contents while food is processing.
- Make sure the processor is switched off before opening the lid or adding items.
- unplug machinery before cleaning or removing a blockage.
- Use any machine guards provided.
- Do not wear loose clothing or jewelry that could become caught in machinery.

While using steamers/oven follow the rules like:

- Do not open the door while the steamer is on, shut off the steam, and then wait a couple of minutes before releasing the pressure and opening.
- Clear the area around the steamer/oven before opening.
- Open the steamer door by standing to the side, keeping the door between you and the open steamer.
- Use oven mitts to remove hot trays from the steamer/oven.
- Place hot, dripping trays on a cart to transport. If trays are carried by hand, they will drip on floors and create a slip hazard.

QUESTIONS

1. Why tools and equipments are necessary for professional chef?
2. Classify different type of tools and equipments.
3. What are different fuels available for heating equipment? Explain each of them.
4. Explain different types of knife and their parts.
5. What are the safety precautions you will take while using the equipments?
6. Explain following:
   a) Conical strainer
   b) Deep fat fryer

SMALL EQUIPMENT

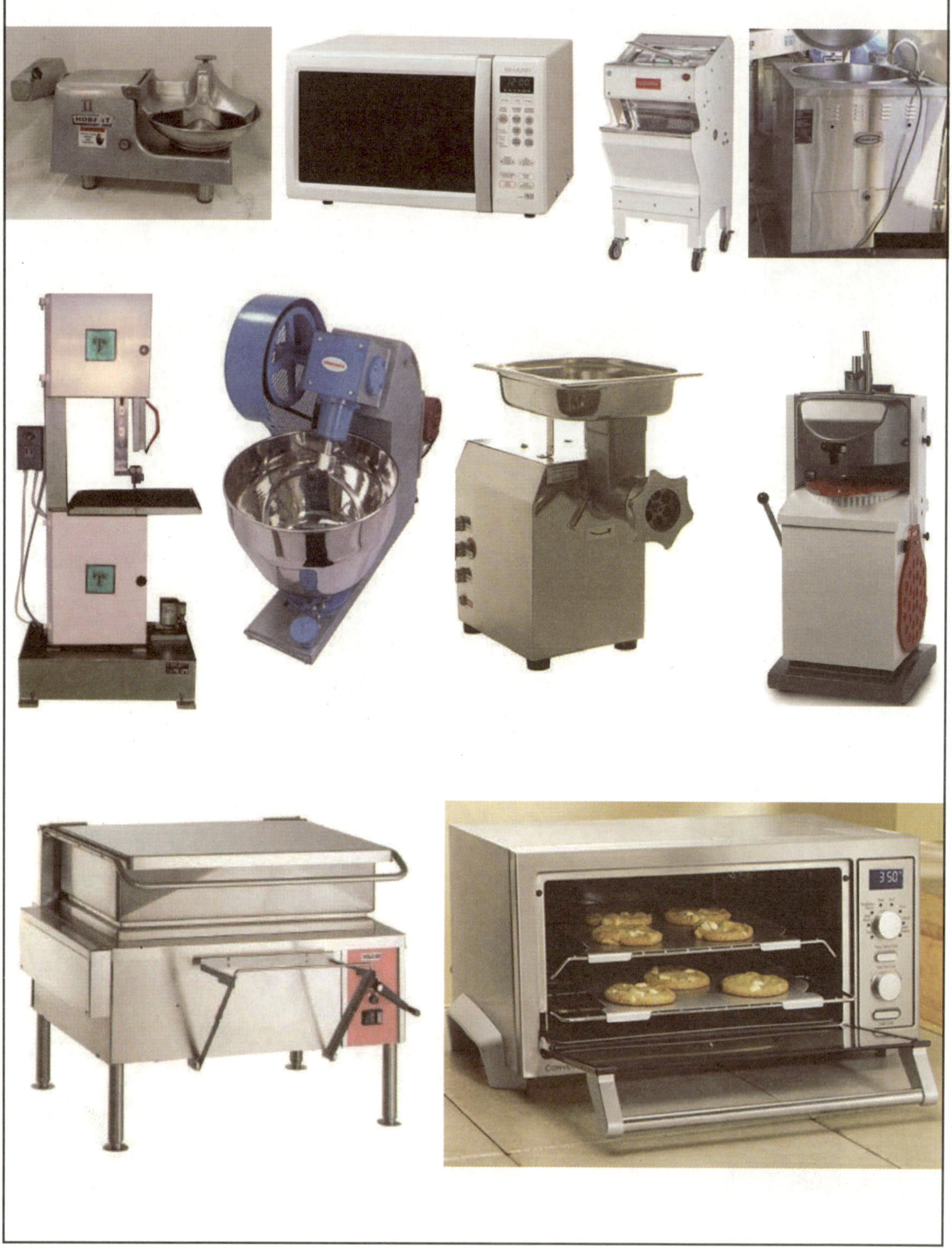
350°

c) Spine
d) Butt
e) Bain-marie
f) Buffalo chopper
g) Band saw machine.

5

Menu and Culinary Terms

OBJECTIVES

After studying this chapter student should know—

1. culinary and French terms
2. menu planning and menu compilation
3. kinds of menu
4. difference between various types of menu
5. points to be consider while planning a menu

Menu planning or menu compilation

A menu or a bill of fare is a list of prepared dishes of food which are available to a customer.

The compiling of a menu is one of the most important jobs of a chef and there are a number of factors that must be taken into consideration before any menu is written. Aim is to give the customer what he wants. In general it is better to offer fewer dishes of a good standard rather than having a wide choice of dishes of mediocre quality.

It is necessary to make certain that menu terms are expressed accurately so that the customer receives exactly what is stated on the menu.

The description on the menu should be clear and practically followed as per the quality, size, preparation and composition of the dish.

KINDS OF MENU

It must be clearly understood what kind of menu is required, whether a special party menu, table d'hôte or a la carte.

Table d'hôte

It literally means 'table of the host'. This is a set menu forming a complete meal at a fixed price. A limited choice of dishes may be offered at all courses; no separate prices are charges for individual dish.

Advantage

1. easy to organize
2. In case of large numbers of guest this is a best type.
3. Low cost because of less wastages.
4. easy to serve
5. Economy for the guest.

Disadvantages

1. less numbers of choice of dishes
2. no personnel service
3. useless if the guest numbers are very less

A la carte

In French 'a la carte' means 'according to the card'. This is a menu with all the dishes individually priced. The customer can therefore compile his own menu. It lists all the dishes available, arranged in courses & priced separately. A true a la carte dish should be cooked to order and the customer should be prepared to wait for this service.

Advantages

(i) Large number of choices
(ii) Personalise services
(iii) Ideal for less number of guests
(iv) Can be used for specialised service style.

Disadvantages

(i) Require Control
(ii) High cost
(iii) Expertise services

Apart from this others type of menus are:

(a) *Special party menu* - these are menus for banquets and parties of all kinds.

(b) *Function menu* - This menu is for special occasion such as wedding or parties, & has a fixed price. It is similar to table d'hôte menu but offers little to no choice. There can be 4 to 8 courses depending on time & cost

(c) *Cyclic menu* - This is a series of fixed meals that are rotated overtime. It is used mainly in hospitals, institutions and camps. A cycle can be from 7 days to 5 or more weeks. It offers limited choice for three meals in the day. A cyclic menu can be planned to give a balanced diet. Used in hospital and schools.

(d) *Ethnic or specialty menu* - This menu is for special occasion such as wedding or parties, and has a fixed price. It is similar to table d'hôte menu but menu is offered as per the occasions.

(e) *Hospital menu* - This menu types of food served in hospital is called "invalid food". Specialty of such type of food is:

1. Food carries no spices.
2. Nutritional aspect is major criteria for selected menus.
3. Food is prepared in extreme hygienic condition.
4. Always fresh and useful ingredients are used.
5. Menu and preparation of dish may differ from one patient to another patient as per advice given by doctor.

(f) *Menu for children* - In schools, colleges there are an emphasis on healthy eating and a balanced diet particularly in boarding schools.

(g) Dietic Menu - for dietic specific requirement like low in fat or gluten free diet.

Requirements of a Menu

The menu should:

1. Carry a wide range of nutritional aspects and better common preferences.
2. Accommodate the eating habits in dining. For example, there is an increasing trend towards healthy eating, while rich gravies or high calories food is less in demand
3. Be little innovate and different in taste, presentation and unique style of cooking.
4. Provide a variety as per the choice of occasion.
5. Explain through the description about dishes which help the guest to decide about the particular dish.

Factors that influence a menu

A style of an operation may influence menu items in the following ways:

- type of an establishment to an area:
- Using local ingredients and availability of them

- The spending power of the target market is also an important consideration
- Customer choice and likes: It is the customer not the chef who selects menu items, so analysis of dish popularity is necessary. Unpopular dishes must be removed from the menu.
- Competition in the local area in terms of style of food, price and quality
- The type of people catered like young old, kids etc.

Range of resources to consider in planning a menu:

1. Number of staff
2. Staff Knowledge & Skills
3. local Supplies of ingredients
4. availability of Equipment
5. preparation Time

CULINARY TERMS

- *Au Gratin*—A French phrase meaning foods that are browned on top, or cooked with a coating such as bread-crumbs or cheese until it is brown and crunchy like on pizza/ baked vegetable.
- *Au Jus*—*(oh szhoo)* A French phrase meaning "with juice," most often referring to a sauce made with pan drippings or liquid from roasted meats.
- *Au Jus Lié*—*(oh szhoo lee-ay)* A slightly thickened *Au Juice*. French translating literally to "with thickened juice," loosely referring to juices that have been thickened with a flour or others thickening agents
- *Au Sec*—The French phrase meaning to cook things until dry.
- *Bake*—To cook food in oven by surrounding it with hot air. Most often refers to breads, rolls, pastries and other sweet confections.
- *Baste*—To pour a fat or liquid over food before and/or while it is cooking to add moistness and to keep it from drying out and burning.
- *Blanch*—To cook food briefly in hot fat or boiling liquid. Most often, foods that are cooked in this manner are finished cooking using another method at a later time.
- *Blend*—To combine two or more liquids thoroughly together until they are indistinguishable from one another and have become one.
- *Boil*—To cook food in a liquid that is 212°F or 100°C (at sea level).
- *Bouquet Garni*—*(bookay garnee)* A French term for a small bundle of fresh herbs (bouquet) which are tied together and added to simmering foods as a flavoring agent.
- *Braise*—The method of cooking food first browning it in hot fat, and then cooing the food in a small amount of liquid. Braising includes both dry and moist cooking methods.

- *Breaded*—Food that is coated with bread-crumbs, or other appropriate coating (cornmeal, cracker crumbs, etc.). Food that is breaded is most often fried or sautéed.
- *Break*—When a liquid looses its emulsification and separates. When referring to dairy products, this may also be referred to as curdling.
- *Broil*—The cooking food by using no medium a radiant heat source that is above the food.
- Caramelization—The browning of sugars on a food's surface that occurs when exposed to heat
- *Carry-Over Cooking*—The continued cooking of a product after it is removed from an oven. Heat is transferred from the outside of an item inward, which continues to cook the food for sometime after removed from the oven.
- *Celsius*—The measure of temperature where 0°C is freezing and 100°C is boiling.
- *Cross Contamination*—The transfer of bacteria from one food or work surface to another.
- *Danger Zone*—45°F to 140°F. The temperature in which bacteria are most likely to multiply, the ideal temperature for bacteria multiplication.
- *Deep-Fry*—The process of cooking food buy totally immersing or submerging it in hot fat.
- *Deglaze*—(Fr. Déglacé) The process of removing caramelized sugars and proteins from the bottom of a pan by adding a liquid and gently scraping and swirling the Caramelization.
- *Degrease*—To skim or remove the fat off the surface of a stock, sauce or other liquid.
- *Dredge*—the process of coating a food in (usually) flour, prior to sautéing, or as part of the process of breading.
- *Emulsification*—two or more liquids that normally do not blend together (such as oil & water) that are held in a temporary or permanent suspension. Two examples: vinaigrette (temporary), and mayonnaise (permanent).
- *En Papillote*—The French term meaning "in paper." Also refèrring to the healthy method of cooking foods wrapped in parchment paper or aluminum foil.
- *E. P. Weight*—Edible portion. The edible portion of meat, fish or vegetables after the skin, fat and other inedible portions have been trimmed away.
- *Fold*—The process of gently mixing and turning two ingredients together, such as whipped egg whites and flour. The ingredients are very gently turned (folded) over and over; to avoid breaking the bubbles formed in the whipped egg, or other whipped ingredient.
- *Garnish*—The small decoration or artistic compliment that is added to a finished dish or platter to make the food more appealing to the eye. A garnish should

be edible and compliment, rather than clash or overpower the food that is to be garnished.

- *Gluten*—the protein which is prevalent in various amounts of all wheat flours, and builds structure to most baked goods, particularly breads.
- *Gram*—A basic unit of measure in the Metric system. 1 gram equals 1/30th of an ounce. Or, more specifically, 1 ounce equals 28.35 grams.
- *Grill*—the method of cooking foods on a metal grid, or grill, where the heat source is located under the food.
- *Herb*—A wide variety of aromatic plants used for seasoning and garnishing foods. An herb is generally the leafy portion of the plant.
- *Infusion*—Liquid derived from steeping herbs, spices, etc.
- *Julienne*—A vegetable cut into thin slice, a match-stick size.
- *Kosher Style*—Foods that have been cooked in accordance to Jewish dietary laws.
- *Marinate*—The process of soaking foods in a flavorful acidic liquid to add flavour and moistness.
- *Mise en Place*—The French phrase meaning "everything in its place." In professional kitchens this term is used often, referring the gathering of ingredients for specific recipes, and also referring to the general state of readiness of the kitchen. *"Is your mise en place complete?"*
- *Mirepoix*—*(meer-pwa)* A combination of vegetables used in flavoring dishes. Traditional mirepoix consists of onion-celery and carrots; a white mirepoix (used in light colored dishes) consists of onions and celery.
- *Navarin*—French-Style Lamb stew.
- *Nouilles*—The French word for Noodles
- *Pan-Fry*—The process of cooking food in a moderate amount of fat. The fat should 1/2 to 1/3 the depth of the food to be cooked.
- *Purée*—The process of mashing a food to a fine pulp in a blender or food processor
- *Quenelle*—An oval dumpling, usually poached and made of veal, chicken or fish
- *Reduce*—term is used for simmering liquid until it decreases in volume through evaporation. Used to increase to flavour of a liquid. Or to thicken the gravy/ sauce
- *Roast*—The process of cooking food by surrounding it with dry heat.
- *Roux*—A combination of 50% fat and 50% flour cooked together to form a smooth paste. Most often made with butter and flour. Roux is used as a thickening agent in cooking liquids such as soups and sauces.
- *Sachet*—Herbs and/or spices tied together in a piece of cheesecloth to form a small bag or satchel (the sachet) and used to flavour a soup sauce or stew. Once the food is flavored the sachet may be removed from the dish.

- *Sauté*—The French word meaning "to jump." The process of cooking food very quickly in a small amount of fat.
- *Sear*—The process of caramelizing the surface of foods by cooking it briefly in a small amount of extremely hot fat. Seared foods are often finished cooking with other cooking methods, such as roasting.
- *Spice*—Any number of vegetable-based aromatic seasonings other than the leafy portion (which is the herb). A spice is generally a root, seed, bark or stem.
- *Stir fry*—Very similar to sautéing. The main difference is that stir-fried items are usually cut small and are used in Asian preparations.
- *Sweat*—The process of cooking food in a small amount of fat or liquid over low heat, when sweating, the pot or pan is most often covered while cooking.
- *Truss*— To bind meat or poultry with twine in order to "hold its shape during cooking.
- *Véloutá*—The French word meaning "velvety." A sauce made of chicken, veal or fish stock that has been thickened with roux.
- *Whip*—The process of beating liquids or semi-liquids vigorously in order to incorporate air, and ultimately volume, into the product
- *Zest*—The thin, colored portion of citrus fruit skin. The white part, located below the surface of the skin (zest) is bitter, therefore undesirable in cooking.

QUESTIONS

1. Define following culinary terms:
   (a) bouquet garni,
   (b) mire poix,
   (c) a al carte,
   (d) au gratin,
   (e) lard,
   (f) marbling,
   (g) score,
   (h) zest.
2. What are the different types of menu? State the benefit and limitation of each?
3. What are the basic points you will consider while planning a menu for a restaurant?
4. Differentiate between
   1. Cyclic menu and Hospital menu.
   2. Table de hote and A la carte.
5. Explain following:
   - Invalid food

- Menu planning
- Table d hote
- A la carte
- Cyclic menu
- Menu for school

6

Agents in Production

OBJECTIVES

After reading this chapter student should know:

A. Different types of agents

B. Use of herbs and spices

C. Use of wine and herbs in cooking

D. Role of spices in Indian cuisine

There are various agents are used for food preparations these are:

1. Thickening
2. Raising
3. Binding
4. Coloring
5. Sweetening
6. Salting
7. Flavoring

Thickening Agents

Thickening agents are the products and food commodities which gives body, consistency and palatability to the food to be cooked.

- Flavoured liquids are thickened and converted into soups, sauces, curries, mousses and puddings etc.

- They improve the nutritive value.
- They provide thick and smooth consistency to the soups which have pouring consistency.
- They give creaminess and richness to the liquid.
- They also give the shine and glow to the liquid.

TYPES OF THICKENING AGENTS

- *Roux*: A mixture of flour and fat cooked together, cooked to various degrees namely white, blond and brown.

  According to how much cooking you give the flour,

  1. the roux is white, for only a 3-4 minutes or till the colour doesn't change, (Roux Blanc),
  2. blonde roux (Roux Blonde) just until the colour begins to change,
  3. brown roux (Roux Brun) until the starch is toasted a fine light brown colour
- *Starch*: Arrowroot, corn flour, potato starch, tapioca are use to thicken the sauce. It gelatinizes at 93 deg centigrade. It gives clear sauce and thickens more as it cools.
- *Pork Blood*: it is usually used for game cooking. It thickens the sauce and gives the particular flavour.
- *Yolks of Egg and Cream*: It is a liaison which acts as a finishing agent at the end of cooking. It is added to thicken delicate cream and cream soups.
- *Refined flour*: It is used as a thickener for gravies and is mixed in a batter giving the smooth consistency.
- *Manie Butter (Beurre Manie)*: It is uncooked roux chiefly used for fish sauces i.e. Butter and flower needed together and desolve in stock / sauce.
- Puree of vegetable and flour-can be used in sauce, soup, curry, cullies
- *Rice Flour*: It is widely used in pudding, , oriental and south Indian cuisine for making Kolambu and Gotsu etc. it is also used for making indian sweets like phirni giving a thick consistency.
- *Coconut*: Paste of coconut is used for curries giving then a whitish colour and enhancing the taste.
- *Tamarind*: It is used in a pulpy form and giving a thick consistency to the gravies and a brownish appearance and an acidic taste.
- *Curd*: It is used for thickening gravies and also giving a whitish appearance and a good flavour.
- Poppy seeds, onion paste, coriander powder give body to the curries and slightly thickens the gravy and blend with the flavour of the curry
- *Gelatin*: It is protein base unflavored product available in crystal form. Commercially it is prepared from three materials:

- Pork Skin
- Cattle Skin
- Bones of Animals

Raising Agents

Raising agents are those which help in raising and expansion of the dough, batter or liquid through the escaping of the gas.

Following are categories as raising agents.

Biological Agent

Yeast

Yeast is a living, microscopic, single-cell organism, They multiply rapidly and converts its food (through a process known as fermentation) into alcohol and carbon dioxide. They grow the presence of:

1. Temperature (room)
2. Food (sugar)
3. moisture
4. air

Proceedure of Using Yeast

When yeast is placed in a lukewarm liquid at 40 to 50 °C, then the cell starts grow. They keep on multiply very rapidly. Buds on cell wall keeps growing until daughter cells acquire the same size as mother cell. Then the buds separate from mother and start producing other buds. Thus they grow and raise the volume of dough. It's categorized into three basic types-

- Active dry yeast
- Compressed fresh yeast
- Instant yeast

Composition of Yeast

- Proteins 14%
- Carbohydrates 10%
- Fat 0.5%
- Mineral Matter 2.3%
- Moisture 68-73%
- Enzymes and Vitamins are also present.

Chemical

1. Soda bicarbonate - pinch is added for 100 g flour while sieving.
2. Baking powder - (2 part of soda bicarbonate + tartaric acid).

Mechanical Aeration

It is done through incorporated Air into the batter by

- Rubbing-rubbing fat into sugar
- Whisking /Beating- Like beating egg white for meringue
- Sieving-sieving flour before making dough

Folding

Like folding the sheet for making of puff cause the steam to be raised.

Colouring Agents

Food can be colored apart from using synthetic colours in many ways-

1. Tomato puree for red orange colour
2. Turmeric and egg yolk for yellow colour.
3. Beetroot for bright red colour.
4. Squid ink for black colour.
5. Spinach and green leafy vegetables like parsley, coriander, mint for green colour.
6. Carrot or orange juice for orange colour.
7. Berries can be used for blue and black colour in dessert.
8. Milk and cream provide bright white colour.

Sweetening Agents

Followings are the sweetening agents:

Sugar this is the main sweetening agents used massively in the cookery, bakery and others sweet products. Sugar is a carbohydrate. It's found naturally in most plants, but especially in sugarcane and sugar beets—hence their names:

a. Low concentration of sugar speeds the effectiveness of baker's yeast by providing an immediate, fast cooking course of nourishment for its growth - thus hastening the leavening process.
b. A small amount of sugar is added to aid in the baking process. Sugar helps in fomentation process by feeding the yeast.
c. The ability of sugar to crystallize gives a delightful variety in cookery.

d. Sugar gives puddings, breads, buns and bread rolls a unique flavour (caramel), the characteristic golden brown colour, tender and even texture.
e. It is an energy food and can be stored for a long time without getting spoilt.

Types of Sugar

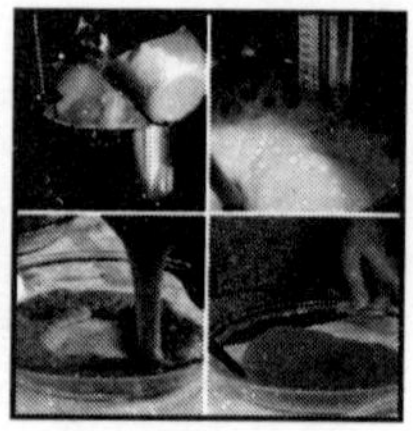

1. Granular sugar - regular sugar made from sugar cane. evenly size crystal.
2. Confectioner sugar - finely powdered can be used for breakfast also.
3. Icing sugar - very very fine powdered and mix with little corn flour for smoothness.
4. Brown sugar - sugar with some molasses.
5. Castor sugar - very fine dissolve easily.
6. Liquid sugar - cooked in water and lemon. Have a longer shelf life.

Stages of Sugar Boiling

• 110°C	Thread	Fruit paste and sweet
• 116°C	Soft Ball	Fondant and butter cream
• 119°C	Ball	Meringue, almond paste
• 121°C	Hard Ball	Meringue, almond paste
• 126°C	Small Crack	Nouget, Caramels, taffy
• 145°C	Crack	Pulled sugar, spun sugar, glaze fruit.

- final stage is caramelization.

1. *Corn syrup* - liquid extracted from corn, light in taste and colour
2. *Honey* - thick light brown in colour rich flavour and can be used as a medicine.
3. *Jaggery* - made from sugar cane juice used in rural areas of India.
4. *Maple*- syrup prepared from the maple fruit.
5. *Molasses* - is a byproduct of sugar refining and is base of making rum. Rich and less sweet in taste.

Salting Agents

Salt is an ingredient without which no food is complete. salt plays various role in cooking-notes

Sodium chloride or common salt is the chemical compound NaCl. Salt occurs naturally in many parts of the world as the mineral halite and as mixed evaporites in salt lakes. Sodium chloride crystals are cubic in form. Table salt consists of tiny cubes tightly bound together through ionic bonding of the sodium and chloride ions. awater has lots of salt; it contains an average of 2.6% (by weight) NaCl.

Types of Salting Agents

Black Salt

Other Names: *Kala Namak, Sanchal*

Black salt is an unrefined mineral salt. It is actually a pearly pinkish gray rather than black, and has a strong, sulfuric flavour.

Uses: Use in authentic Indian cooking for particular taste specially in salads. Available in very fine or coarse grain.

Coarse Salt

Other Names: *Gos Sel, Salė Grosso*

Coarse salt is a larger grained sea salt crystal. Most recipes calling for salt intend using finely ground salt, however, many professional chefs prefer cooking with coarse salt because they can easily measure it with their fingers. It is less moisture sensitive so it resists caking and is easily stored.

Uses: Salt crusts on meat or fish, and flavoring for soups, stews and pasta.

Flake Salt

Other Names: Flaky Salt

Flake sea salt is a light crystal reminiscent of snowflakes. Seawaters are evaporated using the natural processes of sun and wind producing salt brine that is fed into an open evaporating pan. This type of salt is light, flaky sea salt.

Sea Salt

Other Names: *Sal Del Mar, Sel De Mer*, Sale Marino

Sea salt is a broad term that generally refers to unrefined salt derived directly from a living ocean or sea. It is harvested through channeling ocean water into large clay trays and allowing the sun and wind to evaporate it naturally. it contains minerals, including iron, magnesium, calcium, potassium, manganese, zinc and iodine.. Sea salt is thought to be healthier and more flavorful that traditional table salt. Available in coarse, fine and extra fine grain size.

Table Salt

Table salt is the most common kind of salt found in the average kitchen. It usually comes from salt mines and once it's mined, it is refined and most minerals are removed from it until it is pure sodium chloride. Most table salt is available either plain or iodized.

Salt in Food

Salt serves many purposes. Humans and other animals have an inherent taste for this essential nutrient. Salt is the world's oldest known food additive. People use many types of sodium chloride in food processing, cooking or at the table—at home or in restaurants. Each makes its unique contribution.

Besides contributing its own basic "salty" taste, salt brings out natural flavours and makes foods acceptable, protects food safety by retarding the growth of spoilage microorganisms, gives proper texture to processed foods, serves as a control the rate of fermentation in food processing strengthens gluten in bread, provides the colour, aroma and appearance consumers expect and is used to create the gel necessary to process meats and sausages.

Salt preserves foods by creating a hostile environment for certain microorganisms. Within foods, salt brine dehydrates bacterial cells, inhibits bacterial growth and subsequent spoilage. Salting fish made long-range explorations possible in the age of sailing ships.

It also gives a smooth, firm texture to processed meats. Salt develops the characteristic rind hardness in cheese and helps produce the desirable, even consistency in cheese and other foods such as sauerkraut.

Salt helps extract the proteins in processed and formed meats, providing binding strength between adjacent pieces of meat. Water binding properties are increased and, as a result, cooking losses are reduced.

Salt promotes the development of colour in vegetables ham, bacon, hotdogs and sauerkraut. Used with sugar and nitrate or nitrite, salt produces a colour in processed meats which consumers find appealing.

FLAVORING AGENTS

Spices, herbs and seasoning

Spices, aromatic flavorings made from parts of plants. The term *spice* is usually applied to pungent plant products.

Herbs

Herbs can be used dry (tied in a cheese cloth and immersed in liquid, removed after use) or fresh and provide aroma to food.

Types of Herbs

Basil is available in fresh leaves and in dried leaves; Fresh leaves may be stored in a cool place or in the refrigerator for a very short time.

Add dried herbs at the beginning and during cooking and Add fresh herbs only at the end of cooking or upon serving. Many species of the basil herb exist, but the most popular is sweet basil. Basil is considered one of the most important and highly used herbs in the culinary world specially Italian cuisine.

The strong, clove like flavour is essential to many Italian recipes and it is paired most often with tomatoes. Basil is primarily used in sauces, pizzas, salads and pasta dishes. It is also the main ingredient used in pesto.

Chervil is a delicate herb with subtle taste and the flavour can be lost in cooking. Garnish salads with it, but serve it at the last moment. It is an important ingredient in the traditional French herb blend; Fines Herbs.Chervil is extremely delicate although it has very strong oil. Chervil is better used as a fresh herb used in the last of cooking.

Chives are a mild member herb of the onion family. Chives has many uses and best go with potatoes dishes like potato salad, baked potatoes, soups, salads, omelets, dips ,spreads, pastas and sauces.

Best used as fresh. The flavour is lost in drying. Add fresh or dried chives at the end of cooking to preserve the flavour and as garnish.

Dill is available in weed and seed both fresh and dried. Fresh leaves can be kept in a plastic bag in the refrigerator. Dill or dill weed is an herb that produces clusters of small flowers from which dill seed is gathered and dill weed is obtained from the thin, feathery leaves. Dill weed is good in soups, omelets, seafood dishes, herring, salmon, potato salads, and steamed vegetables. Dill seed is used in breads, pickling, cabbage dishes, stews, rice and cooked root vegetables.

Fennel also known as *finocchio*, common fennel, sweet fennel, wild fennel and sweet cumin. Fennel yields an herb and a spice. The stems and leaves are all edible. The spice comes from the dried seeds, the herb comes from the leaves and the stalk and root are the vegetable. It goes well with fish, sauce, meats and sausages. The leaves and stems can be finely chopped and used in salads and cooked vegetables. Also add to soups and stuffing.

Lemon Balm is a lemon scented herb of the mint family. When using whole leaves be sure to handle with care, as they tend to bruise and turn black. Mix lemon balm with other fresh herbs. Lemon For a tasty general seasoning, use it in tandem with tarragon. The taste of the leaves adds the perfect tangy note to fruit salads. Freshly steamed vegetables come alive when tossed with a chiffonade of Lemon Balm and a touch of cracked pepper.

Lavender is a member of the mint family and is close to rosemary, sage, and thyme .It has the green-gray needle like leaves and spikes of fragrant purple-mauve flowers .Lavender is an incredibly versatile herb for cooking. Flowers and leaves can be used fresh, and both buds and stems can be used dried. It is best used with fennel, oregano, rosemary, thyme, sage, and savory. English Lavender is the one most commonly used in cooking due to sweetest fragrance. Lavender has a sweet, floral flavour, with lemon and citrus notes. The potency of the lavender flowers increases with drying.

Marjoram has a mild, sweet flavour similar to oregano, also known as Sweet Marjoram, Knotted, Pot or Winter Marjoram. It is said to be "the meat herb". While fresh marjoram is excellent with salads and mild flavored foods, it has the best taste and greatest pungency when they are dried. Marjoram because it is more delicate should be added toward the end of cooking so its flavour is not lost. Marjoram goes well with pork and veal and complements stuffing for poultry, dumplings and herb scones or breads.

is available in fresh or dried leaves. Mint is an herb that comes in many varieties such as peppermint, spearmint, apple mint, lemon mint and even chocolate mint. Mint came to the New World with colonists, who used it in tea for medicinal purposes. it is widely used in Indian cuisine. Used for raita. Mutton chicken, rice, curry and breads. In other cuisine Mint is good in soups, salads, sauces, plain meat, fish and poultry, stews, sweet or savory recipes, extremely good with chocolate or lemon based desserts. Add in the end of cooking for a better flavour.

Oregano is also known as wild marjoram. Oregano means "the joy of the mountain" in Greek. Oregano goes well with vegetables, roast beef, lamb, chicken and pork. Marjoram goes well with all pork and veal and complements stuffing for poultry, dumplings and herb scones or breads. Generally used to season Mexican, Italian, Greek and Spanish dishes. Oregano has a warm, aromatic scent and robust taste. Its uses include seasoning soups, stews, meat pies, pasta sauces and shellfish.

Parsley is a great all around herb. It is use for colour and texture to any recipe. The aroma and taste of parsley is very mild and non obtrusive. Use fresh leaves as garnish.

Parsley is combined with other herbs like basil, bay leaves, chives, dill weed, garlic, marjoram, mint, oregano and thyme. Flat leaf or Italian is used primarily in cooking and curly parsley for garnish. Add at the end of cooking for better flavour.

Rosemary is a small evergreen shrub that is native to the Mediterranean and likes warm climates. It is produced all over the world. Rosemary's aromatic flavour blends well with garlic and thyme to season lamb roasts, meat stews, and marinades. Rosemary also enlivens lighter fish and poultry dishes, tomato sauces, and vegetables. Crush leaves by hand or with a mortar and pestle before using.

Sage is an herb from an evergreen shrub in the mint family. Fresh sage sprigs have long, narrow grayish green leaves and has a musty yet smoky aroma. Sage as standard goes well with pork but also enhances lamb, meats, and sausages. Chopped leaves flavour salads, pickles, and cheese. Crumble leaves for full fragrance. Use ground Sage sparingly as foods absorb its flavour more quickly. too much use will spoil the taste of food. Sage is a wonderful flavour enhancement for seafood, vegetables, stuffing, and other savory breads.

Tarragon is a Siberian herb with a subtle and sophisticated flavour and is an essential herb in French cuisine. Its flavour is delicate and almost licorice or anise-like. Tarragon, together with parsley, chervil, and chives make a traditional French blend, Fines Herbes. Tarragon is widely used in egg dishes, fish, mushrooms and other vegetables base dishes. Tarragon is good with chicken and in salad dressings. It is used in famous sauce béarnaise. Tarragon is also often used to infuse vinegar and olive oils.

Thyme is an herb that has thin grayish green leaves and a subtle lemon, yet different aroma and taste. Thyme is used in a wide variety of cuisine, but is most closely associated with French cuisine. It is often used in soups and sauces, with meat, poultry or fish. It is also a very important component of mixed herbs and bouquet garni. Fresh thyme has the most flavours used whole, with the stem. Thyme is commonly included in blends for marinating and seasoning for poultry and stuffing and also commonly used in fish sauces, chowders, and soups. It goes well with lamb and veal as well as in eggs and croquettes. Thyme if often paired with tomatoes.

Bouquet garni—Bouquet Garni is a French term means "a bundle of herbs". It can be made from fresh or dried ingredients. For a fresh, use 3 sprigs of parsley, 1 small sprig of thyme leaves and 1 small bay leaf. Tightly tie the bundle together using string or wrap securely in cheese cloth and tie. Use in soups, stews and sauces. Remove before serving.

USE OF WINE, HERB IN COOKING

A fundamental principle about the use of wine for cooking is about its quality. Wine's aromas and flavours, as well as its structure, are added to all the other ingredients of the recipe and this is the fundamental concept about using wine for cooking wine can be added to sauces, marinades, risottos, braises, ragus, broths, the stuck-on browned bits in a sauté pan, and many other foods enhances flavour.

As a cooking agent, wine and other alcoholic beverages have amazing ability to extract flavours that would otherwise remain trapped in food.

The alcohol in wine plays an important role. Some flavour components in foods dissolve in water, and some dissolve in fat. It dissolves not only water and fat-soluble flavours but also flavour components that neither water nor fat can dissolve. This ability of alcohol to extract and carry flavours makes it a great asset for cooks.

Alcohol boils at a lower temperature than water, but the alcohol doesn't completely evaporate before the water this happen. Flambéing removes about 25% of the original alcohol.

Wine can be used in marination, dressings and flambé. Preserving the meat, as well as for flavoring it,

The choice of wine to be used for cooking also depends by the type of food to the cooked. In general terms white wines are used for the preparation of soups, white meat, poultry, fish, vegetables and desserts, whereas red wines are more frequently used for red meat, stewed and braised meat and sometimes for desserts as well. Both white wines and red wines are widely used for the preparation of pasta and risotto. Even champagne or sparkling wines are used for cooking: Sweet sparkling wines are usually used for the preparation of desserts, fruit salads and dessert creams.

Sweet wines used in pastry cooking always add class, elegance and finesse both to creams and to baked cakes.

The use of herbs and spices Many early records reveal a mixture of medicinal and magical uses for herbs. But herbs were also used to mask unpleasant household odors and to enhance the taste of dull foods. When using herbs and spices to season foods, it is important to use them sparingly. Herbs should be used to enhance the food's natural flavours, rather than to dominate them. Only very heavily spiced, exotic dishes require a large amounts of flavoring in their preparation. Different parts of herbs are added to food recipes; leaves, flowers, and stems of plants. Each herb has its own distinctive taste, each with specific relationship to individual foods. They can enhance the foods natural flavour and create a livelier, tastier meal.

For centuries they have been an integral part of many of the world's great cuisines. At one time only kings and other wealthy people could afford such a delicacy as pepper and cinnamon. Today due to globalization and easy transportation they are available to common person.

The term "spices" is often used broadly to include all seasonings. Spices come from the bark, roots, leaves, stems, buds, seeds, or fruit of aromatic plants and trees with usually grow only in tropical countries. Pepper, allspice, cloves, nutmeg, mace, cinnamon, ginger, saffron, and turmeric are spices. Herbs are soft, succulent plants which usually grow in the temperate zone. Until recently cooks have had to make do with very few fresh herbs, such as sage, parsley, and thyme. Nowadays one can also find fresh basil, coriander, chervil, tarragon, rosemary, and dill. Since herbs are at their best when they are young and freshly picked.

HINTS FOR USING HERBS AND SPICES

Dried herbs are stronger in flavour than fresh leaf herbs. As a rule of thumb 1/3 of dry herb is equal to fresh ones in the recipe. When using dried herbs, crush and rub in the palm. This will releases the flavour quicker. There should be one domination of herb in a food. A strong-flavored seasoning may be combined with several mild-flavored ones. Whole herb leaves are a better choice than ground or powdered herbs because they hold their flavour longer in storage; pulverize just before using.

Don't season more than one dish in a meal with the same herb. Also, every dish on the menu does not need to be herbed - two or three at the most is enough.

Cooking with Dried Herbs

Most herbal flavours and aromas are released by heat. Although fresh herbs are usually preferred, dried versions can be used. When possible, grind whole spices in a grinder or use a stone/mortar and pestle just prior to using for enhanced flavour. Toasting or dry roasting whole spices in a dry skillet over medium heat before grinding will bring out even more flavour. A good rule of thumb is to substitute 1 teaspoon of crumbled, or 1/3 teaspoon powdered, dried herbs for each tablespoon of fresh herbs called for.

Cooking with Fresh Herbs

When using fresh herbs in cold dishes, they should be at room temperature. When preparing a dish that requires a lengthy cooking period, you can use a small, tied bunch of fresh herb sprigs. This bundle is generally known as a bouquet garni and customarily contains parsley, bay leaf, and thyme. Herbal combinations can also be minced and added to a meal immediately upon completion of cooking, and as a garnish before serving. This French practice is referred to as fines herbs. It contains chopped fresh chervil, parsley, tarragon, and chives. This blend is good on mild flavored cuisine like salads, scrambled eggs, and dishes containing poultry and fish.

There are no hard and fast rules when cooking with fresh herbs. Start to experiment using small amounts to see what you like. Here are a few ideas that will help you get started:

- Try not to mix two very strong herbs together. Try mixing one strong and one or more with milder flavours to complement both the stronger herb and the food.
- Usually, the weaker the flavour of the food (like eggs), the less added herbs are required to get a nice balance of flavour.
- Dried herbs are more concentrated than fresh, and powdered herbs are more concentrated than crumbled. Each herb is slightly different but a starting formula is: 1/4 teaspoon powdered herbs is equaled to 3/4 to 1 teaspoon crumbled or the equivalent of 2 to 4 teaspoons fresh.
- If chopping fresh herbs, chop the leaves very fine because the more of the oils and flavour will be released.
- Start sparingly with the amount of an herb used until you become familiar with it. The aromatic oils can be less than appetizing if too much is used.
- Usually extended cooking times reduces the flavoring of herbs, so add fresh herbs to soups or stews about 45 minutes before completing the cooking time. For refrigerated foods such as dips, cheese, vegetables and dressings, fresh herbs should be added several hours or overnight before using. Note: Fresh Basil is an exception. If you add it to salad dressing overnight or longer, it becomes bitter.
- For salsa, hot sauces and picante, add finely chopped fresh or dried herbs directly to the mixture.
- Make herbal butters and cream cheeses by mixing 1 tablespoon of finely chopped fresh herbs to 1/2 cup margarine, butter, cottage cheese, low fat yogurt or cream cheese. Let it set for at least an hour to blend the flavour; then taste test on a plain cracker or a melba round. You will gain a great feel for the dimensions of what the flavour will be good with by taste testing in this manner.
- Flavor vinegar for use in cooking and in vinaigrettes. Bruise one cup of leaves for every 2 cups of white wine or delicate vinegar. Allow to steep for two weeks.

Handling and Storage of Herbs and Spices:

Whole spices should be kept in tightly closed containers away from heat and light. Herbs in leaf form will keep longer than herbs in ground form. Ground spices and herbs will keep their flavour for up to a year after purchase (whether opened or unopened), as long as they were fresh when purchased and kept in tightly closed containers in a cool place. If kept at room temperature, in a pantry for example, herbs and spices will keep for only 6 months.

Never store herbs and spices in attack of moisture or above the hot range as this will shorten their life.

The Role of Spices in Indian Cuisine

Without Spices Indian food will not remain like an Indian food .Indian dishes are delicately spiced to enhance the flavour of the main cooking ingredient. Fresh ground spices are the order of the day in an Indian home and will be chosen according to the nature of the dish, season, individual and family.

The role of spices and herbs goes beyond just cooking. Ancient ayurvedic texts prescribe the herbs and spices for curative and therapeutic functions. Ayurvedic scripts dating back to 3000 years, list the preventive and curative properties of various spices.

Properties - Medicinal

An Indian cook has learnt to use this knowledge and weave them into everyday dishes. Ginger prevents dyspepsia, garlic reduces cholesterol and hypertension and fenugreek is a good resistance builder and with pepper often serves as antihistamines, turmeric is used for stomach ulcers and for glow of the skin.

Preserving Foods

Spices have been used to make the food last longer in the days when refrigeration was absent.

Aiding Digestion

India substitutes for the western after dinner mint are fragrant spices such as fennel, cardamom or cloves. Effective mouth fresheners, they aid digestion, prevent heartburn and curb nausea. Others such as asafetida and ginger root, have been known to counteract flatulence and colic, and are added to lentils, a must with every Indian meal.

Balancing Tastes and Properties of Food

Each spice has a property not just a taste property but warm or cooling property to it. It also has many other properties. The cook generally understands these properties and cooking is elevated to yet another level by using this knowledge of spices into the cooking

QUESTIONS

1. What is the role of different agents in cookery? Explain each in details.
2. What are the three types of leaveners? Give an example of each.
3. Explain following terms in details:
   A. Roux
   B. Beurre manie
   C. Beating
   D. Folding

E. Yeast
F. Fermentation
G. Herbs and Spices
H. Caramelisation
I. Icing sugar
J. Rock salt
K. Molasses

4. What is the use of wine and herbs in cooking?
5. What precaution one should take while using herbs?
6. What changes will occurs if spices are removed from Indian cooking?
7. Differentiate the followings
   a) roux and beurre manie
   b) white roux and brown roux
   c) herbs and spices
   d) thickening agent and raising agents
   e) caramel and sugar syrup
8. Fill in the blanks:
   a) For red meat ———— wine is used.
   b) White roux is cooked for ————.
   c) Salt is added in yeast base dough to ————the growth of yeast.
   d) Baking powder = ———— +2 ————
   e) ———— is used to obtain black colour
   f) To make soft balls ————temperature is required.
   g) Saffron is obtained from————.
   h) Icing sugar contain powdered sugar with————
   i) Salt is used to————the gluten in flour.

Thickening Agents

Types of Sugar

Basil

Chervil

Chives

Dill

Fennel

Lemon Balm

Lavender

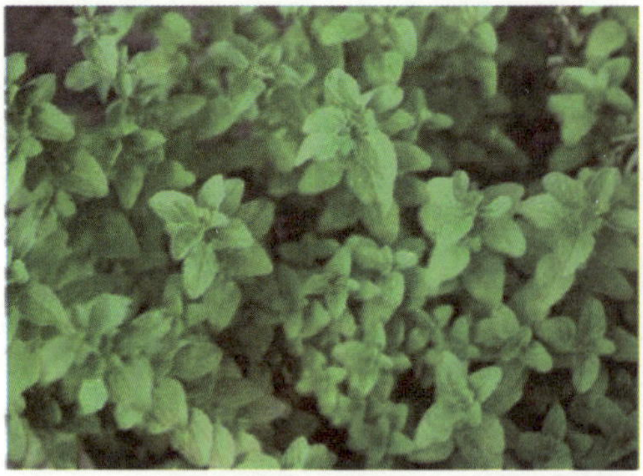

Marjoram

Mint

Oregano

Parsley

Rosemary

Sage

Tarragon

Thyme

Bouquct garni

7

Stock, Soup and Sauces

OBJECTIVES

After reading this chapter student should know-

1. Types of stock
2. Making of stock
3. Basic mother sauces
4. Derivatives of sauces
5. Classification of soup
6. Examples of soups.

This chapter covers three general topics: stocks, sauces, and soups.

This chapter explains the difference between stocks and sauces and offers the technique of how to produce a quality product. The chapter further discusses the versatility of stocks and sauces as they can be used to enhance numerous food dishes. Soups are also versatile menu items of their own on food service menus. Chapter 11 describes techniques to use when preparing quality soups and offers tips on what types of ingredients blend well in a variety of ways.

Stocks are flavorful liquids produced by simmering bones, meat trimmings, vegetables and other aromatic ingredients in water. Stocks are further categorized as white stock or brown stock, both of which are discussed below. They are used as the foundation for soups, stews and sauces.

CATEGORIES AND TYPES OF STOCKS

White Stock

It is made from the bones of veal, beef, poultry, some types of game, and fish. The bones should be cleaned properly and are first blanched in hot water to remove any impurities that might cloud or discolor the finished stock. Ordinary white stock is classically prepared from veal meat and bones, with the addition of poultry carcasses.

A white beef stock (sometimes referred to as a "neutral stock") is often prepared by first simmering the stock at higher temperature than would be used for most stocks for several minutes. The aim is to produce a stock with a nearly neutral flavour. It is often flavored with mire poix and bouquet garni for use in vegetable soups or bean dishes. White beef stock can contribute a significant body to these dishes, while still allowing the flavour of the major ingredient to predominate.

Brown Stock *(fond de brun)*

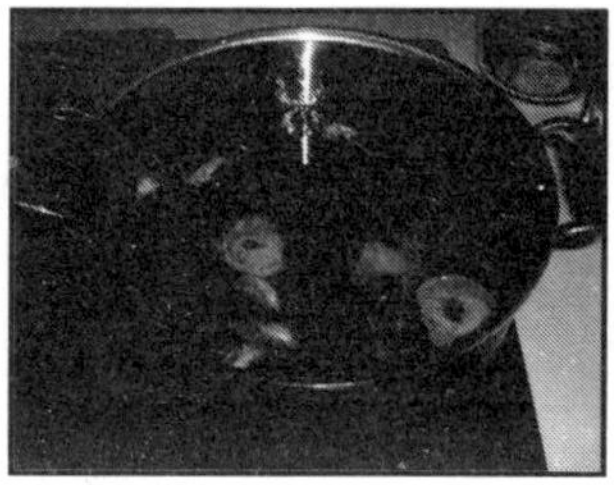

Brown stocks are prepared by first cooking meaty bones and mirepoix to a deep brown colour by heating till it gets the brown colour. This changes both the flavour and colour of the finished stock. Brown stocks are especially valuable in sauce cookery, as they are used as the foundation for brown sauce, demi-glace and pan gravies.

Broth (or Bouillon)

They are prepared by meat, bird or fish are long simmered in stock along with a variety of vegetables and other aromatic ingredients. Many meatless dishes are prepared with a vegetable broth. Those stocks made from meat or fish bones will reach a state of clarity and body through the extraction of proteins found in bones and meat. Vegetable broths vary greatly in the degree of body and clarity that they may achieve.

Fumet (or Essence)

The most common fumet is one prepared by sweating fish bones along with vegetables such as leeks, mushrooms and celery, then simmering these ingredients in water, perhaps with the addition of a dry white wine. The end result is generally not as clear as a stock, but it is highly flavored. Fumets and essences can be prepared from such ingredients as wild mushrooms, tomato, celery or celery root, ginger and so forth. These essences, nothing more than highly flavored infusions made from especially aromatic ingredients, can be used to introduce flavour to other preparations, such as consommés or broths and a variety of "small sauces".

Estouffade

The classic formula for estouffade set down by Escoffier .Estouffade is prepared by simmering together browed meaty veal bones, a piece of fresh or cured pork, and the requisite vegetables and other aromatics. Contemporary kitchens tend to prepare a brown stock that does not include pork. Today, estouffade is less widely used as a basic preparation, although it is still regarded as a classic preparation.

Court Bouillon

Cooking liquid for fish or vegetables. The basic components of a court bouillon include aromatic vegetables and herbs, an acid such as vinegar, wine or lemon juice, and water. Mainly used for poaching fish.

Glaze

To make glaze, reduce brown stock to 1/3.

Recipe

White Chicken Stock (for 02 lts)

Ingredients Ingredients

2kg chicken bones including carcass

400 gm mirepoix

30 gm bouquet garni

2 bay leaves

8 to 10 peppercorns

2 whole cloves garlic, peeled

4 liter cold water

Method

Place chicken bones, mirepoix, and bouquet garni with spices stockpot. With water. Cook on high heat until liquid starts boiling. Turn heat down to medium low so that stock maintains low, gentle simmer. Skim the scum from the stock with a spoon on every 10 to 15 minutes for the first hour of cooking. Simmer uncovered for 4 to 6 hours.

Strain stock through a muslin cloth. Cool immediately-Place in refrigerator. Prior to use, bring to boil for 2 minutes. To Use as a base for soups and sauces remove fat from top.

Note

It is better to blanch the bones to clear fat and impurities before using. Same recipe can be used for white beef, fish stock except bones and ingredients quantity needs to change. Cooking time for beef stock is 6-8 hr Cooking time for fish stock is 30 minute

For vegetable stock except bone rest is same. One can use the trimming of vegetables like carrots, celery, leeks, beans, mushroom etc.

Brown beef stock (for 01 litre)

Ingredients

- ½ kg meaty beef bones (shank, short ribs, shin bones)
- ½ kg cracked beef bones (knuckle)
- 300 g mirepoix
- 20-30 g bouquet garni
- 1 ½ litre water
- 350 g chopped tomatoes,
- 1-1/2 tsp. salt

Preparation

1. Place all bones in a large roasting pan and roast at 200 degrees centigrade for 30 minutes. Stir well, then add mire poix and chopped tomatoes ,roast for 30-45 minutes longer, until bones are very deep brown, stirring mixture occasionally. Be careful not to burn the bones.
2. Place roasted ingredients into a stockpot. Remove fat from liquid in the roasting pan, then add 2 cups water to the drippings in roasting pan and heat and scrape to loosen any browned drippings. Add to pot along with remaining 8 cups water. Bring to a boil. Reduce heat and simmer partially covered for ½ hour. Add bouquet garni. Skim off any impurities to the surface. Add remaining ingredients and simmer partially covered for minimum 6-8 hour.
3. Strain and Cool uncovered. Skim fat from broth before using. This stock will keep for 3 days in the refrigerator, or will freeze up to 6 months.

SAUCE

"A sauce is to the culinary art, what grammar is to language".

The use of sauces has changed dramatically during the past few years. It has brought great changes in our eating habits and has made a huge impact in the way we now view, create and use sauces in the modern kitchen.

The old thought of heavy cream sauces and thick, rich gravies are slowly being replaced by lighter versions of highly flavoured glazes and sauces acting much more as a final seasoning agent than anything else. However, to learn the newer ways of making sauces, one must first have a good grasp of the basics of sauce making to understand where the differences lie. Sauce-making is definitely an art that, once learned, gives endless possibilities to any dish.

Sauces are liquid or semi-liquid mixtures. A keen sense of smell, delicate sense of taste, a light, strong hand for the blending all contribute to the perfect sauce.

- It also helps in digestion, e.g. mint sauce, apple sauce.
- It gives moistness to the food, e.g. white sauces.
- It enhances flavours.
- It adds colour to the food, e.g. hollandaise sauces.
- They give contrast taste to another food.
- Sauce also denote the name to the dish, e.g. Madeira wine.
- It enhances nutritional value of the dish.
- it makes the food more palatable

The Mother Sauces

Mother sauces are the basic sauce formed thc foundation of other sauces used in continental cuisine.

Béchamel, the classic white sauce, was named after its inventor, Louis XIV's steward Louis de Béchamel. The king of all sauces, it is often referred to as a cream sauce because of its appearance and is probably used most frequently in all types of dishes. Made by stirring milk into a butter-flour roux, the thickness of the sauce depends on the proportion of flour and butter to milk.

Béchamel Sauce

1. 1 cup white roux
2. 10 cups milk
3. 1 small onion studded with 2 to 3 cloves,
4. 1 small bay leaf
5. salt and white pepper to taste
6. nutmeg, to taste

Heat milk below boiling point. Slowly add roux and keep on stirring to avoid the formation of lumps. Simmer, stirring gently with a wire whisk or wooden spoon. Add studded onion and bay leaf. Cook, stirring, over low heat, 15 to 20 minutes, until smooth and thickened. Strain sauce through fine-mesh strainer. Add salt, white pepper and nutmeg to taste. Makes about two cups.

TRADITIONAL DERIVATIVES OF BECHAMEL SAUCE

Avignon Sauce

Cream Sauce Flavored With Garlic, Seasoned With Grated Parmesan Cheese, Finished With An Egg Yolk Liaison, And Garnished With Chopped Parsley.

Brantome Sauce

Cream Sauce Flavored with a Reduction Of Shallot, White Wine, And Oyster Liqueur, Mounted With Crayfish Butter, Seasoned With Cayenne Pepper, and Garnished with Grated Truffle.

Cream sauce - white sauce with cream

Cardinal Sauce (Sauce Cardinal)

White Sauce Flavored with Fish Stock and Truffle Essence, Seasoned with Cayenne Pepper, and Mounted with Lobster

Butter Cardinal Sauce is typically served with shellfish.

Mornay sauce/cheese sauce

Cheese added 2/3 and mix thoroughly but do not cook. Used in augratin and cheese baked dishes.

Mustard sauce

White sauce cooked with English mustard.

Velouté is a stock-based blond sauce

It can be made from chicken, veal or fish stock. Enrichments such as egg yolks or cream are sometimes also added. For making of veloute sauce replace milk with stock. Also no need of studded onion. Sauce can be finish with cream.

1. *Allemande sauce* - Veal velouté with egg yolk and cream liaison.
2. *Caper sauce* - lamb stock mix with capers
3. *Supreme sauce* - Chicken velouté reduced with heavy cream.
4. *Mushroom sauce* - chicken velouté cooked with mushrooms.
5. *Supreme sauce* - chicken veloute with mushrooms and cream.
6. *Vin Blanc sauce* - Fish velouté with shallots, butter, and fines herbs.
7. *Aurora Sauce (Sauce Aurore)* – chicken veloute sauce blended with tomato puree.

Aurora sauce is typically served with poached, soft-boiled, and hard-boiled eggs (served hot).

8. *Bercy sauce* - fish veloute mix with mushrooms, shallots, white wine and butter.

Espagnole or Brown Sauce

Espagnole or brown sauce is traditionally made of a rich brown stock, mix with nicely browned roux, herbs and sometimes tomato paste. Makes about 4 cups

20 g bouquet garni.

1 clove garlic.

1/8 cup brown roux.

2 tablespoons additional butter.

6 cups beef stock.

2 ounces tomato purees.

1/8 teaspoon salt.

$1^1/_8$ teaspoon ground white pepper.

1. Sauté garlic in pan for 1 to 2 minutes. Add the brown stock.
2. Gradually, add cooked roux and stir slowly then add the tomato puree. Bring to a boil, skimming off any impurities from the surface, as needed. Add bouquet garni.
3. Reduce heat and simmer, uncovered, for about 2 hours, skimming the surface occasionally, until the sauce is reduced to 2/3.
4. Season to taste with salt and white pepper, if desired. Apply butter on top to avoid scum formation.

Demi-glace

To make 500 ml demi glace Place 01 liter Brown Stock and 01 lt Brown Sauce/Sauce Espagnole in a heavy saucepan. Bring to a boil over medium heat, stirring occasionally. Reduce heat and simmer, uncovered, for 15 to 20 minutes or until the sauce is reduced by one-half. Remove from heat. And strain through a fine.

DERIVATIVE OF BROWN SAUCES

- DEMI-GLAZE (equal quantity of brown sauce and brown stock, reduce to half)
- RED WINE - demi glaze with reduce red wine and chopped shallots
- MADEIRA - demi glaze and Madeira wine
- PIQUANT- demi glaze with vinegar, gherkins, capers and shallots
- DIABLE- demi glaze with white wine, shallots and cayenne pepper
- BROWN CHOUD FROID SAUCE- demi glaze with Madera, truffle essence and aspic jelly.

- CHASSEUR - demi glaze with shallots, mushrooms, dry white wine and tomato concasse
- LYONNISE - onion slice cooked in butter and demi glaze.

Egg base sauce - Hollandaise and Mayonnaise are two sauces that are made with an emulsion of egg yolks and fat.

Hollandaise is made with butter, egg yolks and lemon juice, usually in a double boiler to prevent overheating, and served warm. It is generally used to embellish vegetables, fish and egg dishes, i.e. Classic Hollandaise Sauce.

[HOL-uhn-dayz] A rich egg based sauce flavored with a bit of lemon or vinegar, butter and a hint of cayenne pepper. The sauce is served over vegetables, fish, or eggs benedict.

The most important aspect of a successful sauce is to use a double boiler and make sure not to allow the water in the bottom of the double boiler to boil, just remain, hot and lightly simmering. You can add a tablespoon of cold water if needed to reduce the heat of the water if it starts to boil. The sauce should be served immediately upon completion.

Makes: 1 cup

Ingredients

2 tablespoons white-wine or tarragon vinegar or fresh lemon juice

4 tablespoons boiling water

3 large egg yolks

1/2 cup unsalted butter

1/4 teaspoon cayenne

1/2 teaspoon salt

Method

Melt the butter and keep it warm.

Heat the vinegar or lemon juice until just warmed. Have small saucepan with boiling water and a measuring tablespoon ready.

Place the top of a double boiler over (not in) hot water. (This means the bottom of the top of the double boiler sound not make contact with the water heating in the bottom half of the double boiler.)

Place the egg yolks in the top of a double boiler and whisk until they begin to thicken. Now add 1 tablespoon of the boiling water. Continue to beat the sauce until it begins to thicken. Repeat with the remaining water, one tablespoon at a time, beating the mixture after each addition.

Now add the warmed vinegar or lemon juice. Remove the double boiler from the heat. Beat the sauce briskly with a wire whisk. Continue to beat the mixture as you slowly pour in the melted butter. Add the salt and cayenne and beat the sauce until it is thick. Serve immediately.

DERIVATIVE OF HOLLANDAISE

- BEARNAISE-Hollandaise with, tarragon vinegar and chopped chervil and tarragon.
- NOISETTE-Hollandaise finish with hazelnut butter.
- MOUSSELLINE-Hollandaise mix with whipped cream
- MALTAISE-Hollandaise mix with orange juice and sauté zest
- PALOISE-as in Béarnaise sauce replace tarragon with mint.
- CHORON-in Béarnaise replace chopped tarragon with tomato puree.

Mayonnaise is a thick, creamy dressing that's an emulsion of vegetable oil, egg yolks, lemon juice or vinegar and seasonings. It is widely used as a spread, a dressing and as a sauce. It's also used as the base for such mixtures as Tartar Sauce, Thousand Island Dressing, Aïoli, green sauce, cocktail sauce and Remoulade. Method to make mayonnaise sauce is given below:

Method

- Place 01 yolks of eggs, vinegar, and seasoning in a clean bowl and whisk well.
- Add 120 ml. oil slowly, a little at a time, whisking continuously, until all the oil is incorporated.
- Finish the sauce by adding the juice of lemon and warm water.

Rectification of curdled mayonnaise

- Add a drop of water while whisking
- Take fresh egg yolk and whisk the curdled sauce slowly in it.

Derivates

- TARTARE - Mayonnaise with chopped pickles, gherkins, olives, lemon juice, chopped egg white and parsley
- VERTE - Mayonnaise with finely chopped and blanched spinach, tarragon, chervil, chives and watercress
- COCKTAIL - Mayonnaise with tomato ketchup, Worcestershire sauce and Tabasco sauce
- REMOULADE - Tartar sauce with anchovy essence

- THOUSAND ISLAND - Cocktail sauce with chopped pickles, gherkins, olives, lemon juice, and parsley

TOMATO SAUCES

It is a red kitchen sauce and has some piquancy. It is served with spaghetti, eggs, fish and meat. It adds colour to the dish.

Recipe

1. Melt butter in a pan add mirpoux roughly chopped Vegetables, crushed garlic and sauté, till slightly brown.
2. Mix in flour and fry till it gets a sandy texture and gets a slightly brown colour.
3. Add tomato puree and chopped tomatoes and stir.
4. Add cold vegetable stock, and bring it to boil.
5. add seasoning and cook for one and half hour

Derivatives

- Provencale - tomato sauce with castor sugar, garlic and parsley
- Portugaise - meat glaze and tomato sauce

BUTTER SAUCES

They are served melted, in a liquid form or as hard butter sauces. Butter is mixed with different ingredients, set and cut in fancy shapes and served with food items.

Derivatives

- Anchovy - Butter with Anchovy Essence
- Colbert - Butter with Meat Glaze
- Shrimp Butter - Butter with Shrimp fine paste
- Garlic Butter - Butter with chopped garlic
- Brown Butter - Butter lightly brown and serve

OTHER SAUCES

- *Bread sauce* - it is like white sauce except instead of flour bread is thickening agent
- *Apple sauce* - apple cooked in butter with sugar and purred, sdeason with cinemon powder
- *Cranberry sauce* - cranberry cooked with sugar and pureed

White Stock

Brown Stock (*fond de brun*)

Court Bouillon

Soup

Mulligatawny

SOUP

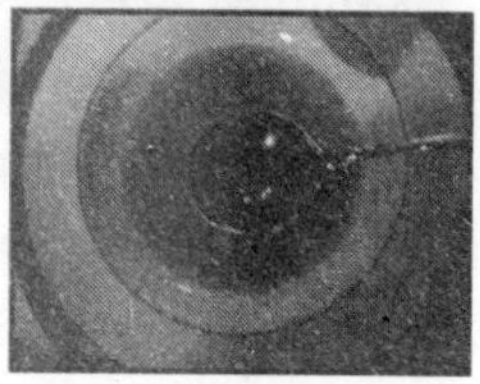

Soup is the extract of solid in a liquid form after long and careful simmering. The word soup is derivied from Sanskrit '*supa*'.

Su-good, po-to nourish

Soup is an appetizing, nourishing, digestible and flavoured extract of solid, Prepared by using a good stock

Types of Soup

1. Thin soup,
2. Thick soup,
3. International soup.

Thin soups do not carry any thickening agent. They are served in natural form or they can be assume as a flavoured stock.

They have two types:

Consommé – Thin Clear soups are called consommé. An egg white is used to clarifies these soups. These are transparent, amber colour, non greasy clear soup. it can be prepared from mince meat or chicken.Name of the soup denotes the garnish used in the soup like juliennes, royals etc. Other ingredients used for making consommé are egg white, vinegar, vegetable trimmings

Different types of consommé with garnishes:

Consommé Colbert - consommé with sauté vegetables and poached egg

Consommé royal - consommé with savory egg custard

Consommé princess - consommé with asparagus tips and chicken quenelles

Consommé Xavier - consommé with egg drop while serving

Consommé Celestine - consommé with juliennes of herbs pancake.

Double Consommé - consommé reduce and serve cold

Broths/bouillon: Broth is unpassed soup simmered and served with dices of vegetables, meat and barley. It should be amber in colour and clear in appearance. Examples are scotch - broth and bouillabaisse

Bouillon

It is unclarified meat or poultry stock or a combination of two. It should be amber in colour and clear in appearance e.g. Petite Marmite (marmite is a type of earthenware pot) - consommé simmered with beef, celery, carrots, cabbage, leeks, winglets of chicken etc. These soups are garnished with beef marrow. Served in marmite. Accompanied by Parmesan cheese and grilled flutes.

Thick soup carry thickening agent like puree, roux, beurre manie and starch etc. Examples are:

1. Cream soup – stock + roux + cream
2. Puree soup/coulis - stock + puree of vegetables
3. Veloute'- stock of base + blond roux + cooked pieces of base
4. Bisque - shell fish thicken stock+ shellfish butter + brandy + tomato sauce + shell fish piece + cream
5. Chowder - shell fish stock thicken with potatoes flour + bacon+ dice vegetables cream

Cream Soup

1. Thick passed soup are generally made with stockmilk. Like cream of tomatoes and cream of mushroom. They can also be finish with a Liaison of egg yolk and cream.
2. Puree soups are naturally thickened by the puree of main ingredient generally served with croutons. Examples are puree of celery or potage St. Germaine.
3. Velouté are made with white stock and blond roux (velouté sauce).

   Garnished with dices of main ingredient. Example like chicken velouté soup.Liaison of cream and yolk is finally used.
4. Chowder is an American soup made of meat, fish and vegetables. Can be thicken by potato and Usually served with a crackers.

   New England clam chowder and Manhattan are the most famous chowder.
5. Bisque is the thickened fish or shellfish base soup. It is cooked with tomato puree, shallfish stock and finish with cream.

International soup are special soup and do not come in any of the above-mentioned category. They can be:

1. Hot,
2. Cold and
3. Fruit base.

Some of them are:

Minestrone: Italian soup, vegetable payssane soup with pasta. Traditional accompaniments are grated Parmesan cheese and grilled flutes.

Green Turtle Soup: England, beef, poultry and turtle consommé garnished with diced turtle meat.

French onion soup: France

Petite marmite: soup from France, beef and chicken flavoured soup garnished with turned root vegetables and dices of beef and chicken.

Scotch Broth and Cock-a-leekie: Scotland, Scotch broth is soup made of barley, carrot, turnip, celery, and leek and chopped parsley. Cock-a leekie is thick soup include chicken, leeks and barley.

Mulligatawny: South Indian /Srilankan base lentil soup.

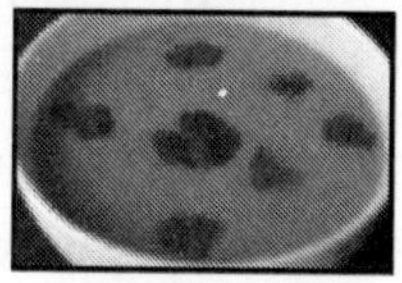

Bortsch polonia: From Poland, Duck flavoured consommé.

Gazpacho: from Spain a cold soup made by liquidizing tomatoes, cucumber, onion, garlic, green pepper and finished with lemon juice with oil and water. Garnished with diced cucumber green pepper and can be chilled with tomato juice ice cubes.

Manhattan clam chowder: From America.

Labernoedel: From Germany.

Paprika and Hungarian Goulash: From Hungary.

Batwinia: From Russia, puree of spinach, beetroot, white wine with small ice-cubes served separately. Served very cold.

Bouillabaisse: From France, it's a type of fish stew.

COLD SOUP

1. **Vichyssoise** - Made from leek and potato and served pureed and finished with ice cubs, cream and chopped chives.
2. **Gazpacho** - a Spanish soup prepared by tomato, cucumber, onion, garlic and finished with lemon.
3. **Fruit soups** - are famous in the Scandinavian countries and can be taken in dessert and breakfast. Like cold cherry soup.

QUESTIONS

1. How and why are bones blanched and browned?
2. What is the difference in techniques used to produce white and brown stock?
3. What is clarification of a consommé?
4. What is the difference between a stock and a broth?
5. Explain the difference between bisque and a cream soup?
6. Explain mother sauce with derivatives.
7. How many types of stocks are there? Give a recipe of brown stock.
8. Differentiate between hollandaise and mayonnaise.
9. What are the international soups? Give examples.
10. explain following terms:
    a) Estouffade,
    b) Glaze,

c) Fumet,
d) Bouillon,
e) Broth,
f) Gazpacho,
g) Bisque,
h) Chowder,
i) Demi glaze,
j) Brown stock.

8

Indian Cuisine

OBJECTIVES

After reading this chapter students should know:

1. Background of different Indian cuisines.
2. English terms of Indian spices.
3. Some famous traditional culinary terms used in Indian cuisine.
4. Types of gravies/*masalas*.

India is a blend of different cultures and languages. Rarely one can find such a place where so many varieties are available.

There is wide differences in Indian regional food are found in the preparation, service, ingredient and aroma. Indian food provides variety and satisfaction to the palate of each one with different way. It has all that things which may a person look for like dry, spicy, nutritional, roast and much more. Today Indian cuisine has acquired a top position in international market. Thanks to the globalization and India's growth. Indian chef are the best cook in the world because they know how to derive the best even from the small ingredient. Many innovations have been done regarding improving the flavour or inserting aroma like dhumr.

India's cuisine is as rich and diverse as its people. The spectrum of Indian cuisine can be said to lie between two dietary extremes: vegetarianism and meat-eating.

THE ROLE OF SPICES IN INDIAN CUISINE

Spices in Indian food are not heavy and although Indian food is not bland, most Indian dishes are delicately spiced to enhance the flavour of the main cooking ingredient.

Curry powder sitting on the grocers shelf may be like saw dust when one compares it to the fine spices roasted, combined and dry ground or wet ground in the traditional Indian traditions. Fresh ground spices are the order of the day in an Indian home and will be chosen according to the nature of the dish, season, individual and family.

The role of spices and herbs has gone beyond just cooking. Ancient ayurvedic texts prescribe the herbs and spices for curative and therapeutic functions. Ayurvedic scripts dating back to 3000 years, list the preventive and curative properties of various spices.

Masala is a word that is often used in an Indian kitchen. It literally means a blend of several spices. *Garam* (hot) *masala* is the most important blend masala and an absolute essential to north Indian preparations, added just before serving the dish to enhance its flavour. The rational garam masala is a blend of cardamom, cinnamon, cloves and black pepper. *Masala* may be in dry, roasted ground or paste form. Each State in India has its own blend and each family is partial to their own blend and each cook is partial to his bend which may be many and which change daily.

South India has a wonderful blend of wet spices where the spices are ground with various combinations of spices, fresh herbs and nuts.

The differences between curry powder and garam masala are vast. *Garam Masala* is a north Indian spice blend. *Garam* means "hot" and *masala* simply means spice or spices. It consists of spices purported to warm the body and digestion. It is often used in all dishes mainly meat and vegetables. It is mostly commonly added to a dish in the last minute or so of cooking as a finishing touch though there are exceptions to this. The usual ones are cardamom, cloves, cinnamon, black peppercorns, cumin, coriander and nutmeg. Bay leaves or the Indian cassia leaves are also considered traditional. Different regions have their own way of making it. It also changes from house to house.

Curry powder is a southern blend with a lot of variations as well. It's primary flavors come from fresh curry leaves (often called *karivepalai*, *meetha neem* or *kari patta*) and fenugreek seeds with support from cumin, coriander and bright yellow colour from turmeric. Maybe a true southern on this list can give you the real lowdown.

Recipe for curry powder:

1 cup coriander seeds

½ cup *chana dal*

½ cup *urad dal*

3 teaspoons oil

¾ cup red chillies

2 tsp *hing* (asafetida)

1) In a heavy sauce pan, dry roast coriander seeds, *chana dal* and *urad dal*, about five minutes.
2) Heat 3 tablespoons of oil in a heavy frying pan. Add the red chillies and fry for another 2-3 minutes.

3) Place all the ingredients in a blender, including hing and salt. Blend to a fine powder.

Garam Masala

Dry roasted aromatic whole spices, powdered and added to a dish for aromatic flavour, a pep up spice.

Ingredients

140 gm coriander seeds
115 gm cumin seeds
55 gm black pepper corns
25 gm cinammon sticks
25 gm black cardamoms
15 gm dry ginger powder
15 gm mace powder
15 gm bay leaves (about 20)

Method

Mix together all the ingredients except the ginger powder. Heat a wok or a heavy non sticky frying pan. Add the mixed spices and stir continuously for a couple of minutes. Remove from the heat and when cool grind to a fine powder. Add the ginger powder and mix well. Store in a airtight container in a dark place.

ENGLISH	HINDI
Spices/Herbs	*Masale*
Turmeric	Haldi
Coriander seeds	Dhania (whole)
Coriander powder	Dhania powder
Cloves	Lavang
Fennel	Saunf
Cinnamon	Tuj/Dalchini
Cardamom	Elaichi
Cilantro, Coriander leaves	Dhania (green)
Ginger	Adrak
Garlic	Lasun
Pepper corns	Kalimirchi

Fenugreek seeds	Methi
Red chili pepper	Lal Mirchi
Poppy seeds	Khuskhus
Asafoetida	Hing
Saffron	Kesar
Aniseed	Sauf
Bay leaf, Cinnamon leaf	Tej patta
Cumin seeds	Sfed Jeera/ Kala Jeera
Mustard seeds	Rai/Sarson
Mint leaves	Podina
Nuts/Dried fruit	
Peanuts, Groundnuts	Moongphali
Cashew nut	Kaju
Almonds	Badam
Pistachio	Pista
Walnut	Akroot
Dates	Kajhoor
Dried Apricot	Khumani
Raisin	Kishmish
Grains/Flours	
Gram flour	Besan
All purpose flour (Maida)	Maida
Wheat flour	Atta/Chappathi flour
Par-boiled rice	Bhat
Semolina	Suji
Lentils	Dal
Vermicelli	Seviyan
Yellow split peas	Toor dal
Bengal gram	Channa dal
Black gram	Urad dal
Green gram	Moong dal
Seasonings	
Tamarind	Imli

Jaggery	Gur
Sesame seeds	Til
Green hot chili	Hari Mirchi
Green pepper, Capsicum	Bari mirch
Curry leaves	Kari Patta
Shrimp, Prawn	Jinga
Vegetables	
Egg plant, Brinjal	Biangan
Okra, Ladies Finger	Bhindi
White Bait	——
Gentleman's Toes, Tindla	tinda
Drumstick	Seeng
Bottle Guard,Opo Squash	Doodhi
Serrated Guard, Chinese Okra	
Amaranth	Chauli, chavleri
Arrowroot	Paniphal, Tikora
Ash gourd	Petha
Asparagus	Shatwar,
	sootmooli, halyan
Asparagus	Musli
Avocado, butterfruit	Makhanphal
Bell Pepper	Simla Mirch
Bengal gram leaves	Chaney ki bhaji (Hummus)
Bitter gourd	Karela
Bottle gourd	Lauki, doodhi
Cabbage	Patta gobhi
Carrot	Gajar
Cauliflower	Phool gobhi
Chilli	Mirchi
Cluster Beans	Gowaar Phali
Colocasia	Arbi
Coriander Cilantro	Dhania
Corn cobs, maize	Bhutta, makka
Corn kernel	Makai

Cowpea	Lobia
Cucumber	Kakdi
Dillweed	Suvabhaji
Drumstick leaves	Muranka bhaji
French Beans	Flas Beans
Gardencress	Halim
Gherkins	Kunthroo, Goli, Tondli
Green chilli	Hari mirch
Indian sorrel	Khatti bhaji
Khesari leaves	Masoor bhaji
Lettuce	Kasmisaag
Lime or Lemon	Nimbu
Lotus Stem	Kamal Kakadior, Bhien
Mushrooms	Goochi
Olives	Zetoon / Zaitoon
Onion	Kanda Pyaaz
Peas	Matar
Potato	Aloo
Pumpkin	Kadhu
Radish	Mooli
Red sorrel	Chukka bhaji Salad leaves, endives Gulsuchal
Spinach	Palak
Sweet potato	Shakarkand
Tapioca	Simla Aloo
Tomato	Tamatar
Vegetables	Sabji
Water Chestnuts	Shingara
Fruit	
Apple	Seb
Bael, Stone apple, Bengal quince	Bel, siriphal
Banana	Kela
Chakothra	Pomelo
Chin fruit, litchie	Lichee

Figs	Amjeer
Grapes	Angoor
Guavas	Amrood
Jackfruit	Kathal
Jambul fruit java plum	Jamoon
Mango	Aam
Mashmelon	Kharbooja
Mulberry	Shehtooth
Muskmelon Cantalope	Kharbooja
Orange	Santra
Papaya	Papeeta
Pear	Nashpati
Pineapple	Ananas
Plum	Aloobukara
Pomegranate	Anar
Sweet lime	Mosambi
Watermelon	Tarbooj, Kalingad
Zizyphus	Ber, Bor

POPULAR INDIAN DISHES

Achar	:	Any kind of pickle
Biryani	:	A flavored rice dish cooked with meat, poultry, seafood or vegetables
Chapati/Roti	:	Thin bread cooked on the griddle
Dal	:	Any kind of legume—beans, peas, or lentils
Dosa	:	Crispy, crepe-like southern Indian specialty filled with potatoes or vegetables
Ghee	:	Clarified butter
Gosht	:	Meat base dish
Korma	:	Braised meats in a thick, mild creamy sauce
Kulcha	:	Tender, pita-like bread cooked in the tandoor
Lassi	:	A refreshing, creamy butter milk that can be sweet or salty
Naan	:	Flat, oval bread cooked made of refined flour in the tandoor
Pakora	:	Meast /vegetables Fritter dipped in a spicy gram flour batter;
Paneer	:	Cottage Cheese
Pappadum	:	Spicy lentil wafers

Paratha	:	Stuffed / Flaky bread shallow fried on the griddle
Poori	:	Airy, deep-fried bread
Pulao	:	An aromatic rice pilaf
Raita	:	A yogurt-based condiment usually containing vegetables
Rasam	:	A thin, spicy broth
Saag	:	Spinach, but can also refer to other greens

SOME INDIAN TERMS

Bhunao (Curry)

This is Indian curry cooking. Oil is added to a pan. To this chopped onion and cumin are added. After the onions are browned then the desired herbs, spices are added (tomatoes may also be added). Small quantities of water, yogurt, and stock are introduced to the pan if and when the ingredients start to stick. After the oil separates from the mixture, the main ingredient (meat or vegetable) is added and cooked

Dhuangar (Smoke Seasoning)

Glowing charcoal is placed in a small *pot*, which is then put in a bigger pot. Cooked meats, are placed around this. Dry spices and *ghee*/butter are poured on top of the coals and a lid is quickly placed over the larger pot. This meats imbibe the fresh smoke taste of *ghee* and cumin. Very popular in the cold months of North India especially in the dessert areas.

Do-Piaza (Cooking with Onions)

There are two theories for the origin of this method.

1. India's great Mughal ruler Akbar the Great had the team of most talented people in their field. He called them his nine gems. *Mullah Do-Piaza*, the legendary cook was one of them. He created a style of his own and items cooked in this style are called *Do Piazza*.
2. The other is cooking with two (*do*) onions (*piaz*).

Potatoes and meats are cooked generally with double of onions, yogurt and spices. Tomatoes are generally not added in this method of cooking.

Dum (Steaming)

This process reflects the art of the Indian chefs. They virtually created a pressure and baking oven cooking with very simple ideas. Food was partially cooked before hand. They then put this in a pot and sealed the cover with *atta* (dough) to capture the moisture within the food as it cooked tenderly and slowly over a charcoal fire. Coals were also placed on the lid to ensure even cooking.

They then added their main ingredients like rice or vegetables or meats or all three with spices, herbs, seasonings, saffron, and tomato and let the food continue to cook in its own steam. The entire dish retained all its flavour and aroma and the slow cooking created perfect foods fit for their emperors and kings and *rajahas*.

The Indian Biryani is one of the most popular dum dishes. Dum means, "to steam". Below is a recipe we make when we entertain.

Pasanda

A special cut of meat with a thick piece of flesh.

Dum Pukht

"Dum Pukht", means 'to breathe' and 'to cook'. The cuisine owes its excellence to the fact that the food, sealed in a dish and slow-cooked in its own juices, retains all its natural aromas and flavours. According to legend *Dum Pukht* cuisine was discovered when Nawab Asaf-ud-Daulah declared that the builders of the Bada Imam Bara Mosque should have access to food day and night. Labours then assembled giant pots, filled them with rice, meat, vegetables and spices and placed them on gently simmering fires for the next shift workers. The lids were sealed with dough and topped with hot coals to ensure the slow-cooking of the food and keep it warm around the clock. As the Nawab tasted the food during an inspection, he was most impressed by the flavour and used the cooking technique in the royal kitchens.

Moin dena

It is a process of kneading dough in ghee (fat) for crispness, like *kachori*, *samosa* dough.

Gile hikmat

To wrap the vegetables in special clay and buried in earth. Keep charcoal on top. Remove after few hours.

Baghar

Tempers the *dal*, meat etc. with ghee, butter, spices and seasoning.

Ghee durust karna

Flavoring the fat with herbs and spices. This is used far topping of Dal & curries.

TYPES OF GRAVIES

Indian foods have following types of gravies:

1. **Shahi gravy** - Gravy is also called Mughlai gravy. This is very rich gravy and is made of cashew nuts, boiled onion paste, *char magaj*, yoghurt and cream.
2. **Makhani gravy**- This is Tomato base gravy and is cooked in white butter and cream. Used for butter chicken, Paneer makhani.
3. **Kadhai gravy** - This is cooking of Onion with double quantity of tomatoes and finish with capsicum and coriander. Used for kadhai chicken, Paneer kadhai.
4. **Hariyali gravy** - This is green colour gravy and is made of puree of spinach and coriander like Palak chicken,
5. **Vegetable gravy** - this is yellow colour gravy made of cashew nut paste, onion and tomato e.g. Matar Paneer gravy.
6. **Kofta gravy** - this is made from brown onion paste and is used widely for the mutton and chicken dishes. Like nargisi kofta, chicken curry.

TANDOOR

History

The first of all is still to be discovered but as long as the history goes Tandoor has been in existence. It has been found in the Harappan and even Pre- Harappan times and sites. The roots of the name are also interesting like the equipment itself. Some believe it came from KUND from Sanskrit, while some say it is TATA ANDAR which literally means hot inside in Persian. Be it any thing however the ancestors have given us a very useful and charismatic equipment to work with, which produces wonders if used in a proper way.

Tandoor is particularly famous in Indian, Afghanistan, Pakistan, and Persian region of Iran, Iraq and other Middle Eastern Countries. It is now famous all over but known for these areas. In India this was considered as the base of many Cuisines where the delicacies are created in a Tandoor. Awadhi, Hyderabadi, Punjabi, and Kashmiri have a strong influence of Tandoor in their cooking. These have a variety of Breads, Kebabs and Tikkas made in the Tandoor.

Preparation of Tandoor

The Tandoor is constructed, is an art and to perfect this art it takes years of experience. Tandoor can be used for homemade purposes while it could be used for commercial needs also which demands long hours of heat. Tandoor is made from some basic ingredients like

1. Clay which is free of any sand content
2. Munj is a kind of grass mixed with clay and acts as a binder.

3. Animal Hairs used for Binding
4. Hay is used for modelling and ease of drying

There are 2 ways of preparing the Tandoor

1. **Modelling Method**: It is the famous style of making the Tandoor. It is also called the Ring Method. The Clay once ready for use is made into slabs. They are then rolled using some clay and the cylinders are then rolled in semi-circle. Two or three are put together to make the ring for Tandoor. These form the base of Tandoor. This ring is then dried so as to have the weight of the next ring. The ring is pinched to create notches to make the other ring stick in a better way. This acts as a claw to hold the wet ring on top once the lower ring has dried to doneness. These Rings are attached to give the Tandoor the desired height. The last stage involves making the mouth and moulding it with hand like the upper part of a pitcher.
2. **Coiling Method:** As the name suggests the clay is made into long ropes and then it is coiled in circles till the desired height is attained. The Mouth is made in the same fashion as the Modelling Method. The surface is smoothed with hand and left to dry out. A small opening is made when the tandoor is dry to facilitate air circulation and removal of ashes.

Curing of Tandoor

A Tandoor needs curing before it is lit for the first time. Spinach Leaves are used to smooth the inner surface of the Tandoor before it can be lit. After 1 day Butter milk, Oil, and Salt is rubbed in the inner walls. Some even apply a coating of Molasses for the same purpose. After curing the tandoor is lit on Low heat for a short duration for a day or two. On the third day it is ready for use. This curing is also done atleast in a fortnight to keep the surface intact.

Equipments Used

The main equipments used for tandoor are

1. Gaddi
2. Jodi
3. Seekh/ Skewers
4. Hooks.

Fuel Used

Different types of Fuel are used in the modern times as the Tandoor has evolved like

1. **Charcoal:** This is the original fuel used for lighting the Tandoor. KEEKAR is the favourite wood Charcoal used.

2. **L.P.G.:** Propane Gas is used to ignite the Gas Tandoor. It requires low maintenance and is cheaper. It however decreases the taste of the food and does not have the peculiar smoky taste evident for the Tandoor items.
3. **Electricity:** In the modern era this is again used as a substitute for L.P.G. as it works on the same principal but the power consumption is more and has the same advantages and disadvantages of a Gas Tandoor.

Types of Tandoor

Tandoor can be classified in 2 ways

- **Clay Tandoor**: Which has many variations
  1. Clay Tandoor Drum Setting used mainly for home purposes
  2. Under ground Tandoor used in local shops and famous in Afghanistan and Pakistan
  3. Porcelain Chinese Clay which is famous for cooking the Peking Duck, traditionally and has a lid to cover the mouth
- **Gas Tandoor**
- **Electric Tandoor**

Lightning a Tandoor

Home Tandoor takes 20 – 30 Min to heat while the commercial ones take an Hour or two to get to the desired degree. Tandoor should be ignited by 1 type of fuel only. Before lighting one should ensure the base is clear of the previous day ashes and they should be removed from the vent in the bottom. The vent at all times should not be crowded as this will hinder the air flow which is necessary for the charcoal and wood to burn. Heavy woods should find the base and the smaller to the top the charcoal should be in between to facilitate the burning of the wood and remain hot for a longer period thus ensuring the temperature to be stable while busy operations. The vent will help the fire to grow with the air flow and when the desired temperature is attained the vent is closed and the tandoor top is replaced to keep the warmth sustained.

Seasoning of Tandoor

This is done to maintain the quality of Tandoor and its working ability. Seasoning gives the strength, covers the minute cracks, enhances flavour and helps the coating of the inner walls to work efficiently.

Process

Spinach, Jaggery, Curd, sugar, Salt, are all boiled together to form a paste /glue consistency liquid. Even mustard oil is used to this mixture and then the mixture, with the help of a cloth is swapped in the inner walls of the Tandoor. This is done before lighting the Tandoor. The tandoor is then lit for atleast 2 hours.

Spinach is used for binding, salt to retain the heat and add flavour, Mustard oil gives an extra shining to the walls, Jaggery extra strength and Curd gives a different flavour, while the combination of salt and sugar provide the surface a bi of roughness and coarser texture.

Misc en Place for Tandoor Dishes

The different stages of misc- en place for Tandoor dishes include

1. **Making the marination:** This includes preparing the marination for different dishes and according to the recipes.

Marination is used for following purposes

- To prevent the food item from burning
- To enhance the taste
- To prevent the food item to dehydrate.
- To apply a coating to the food item
- To enhance the eye appeal
- To soften the meat tissues for faster cooking

Basic Marination Recipe for Tandoor

- Yoghurt/ hung curd
- Red chilli
- Turmeric
- Ginger garlic paste
- Garam masala
- Salt
- Cooking oil
- Food colour if needed

The marinations include preferably Tenderizers in the recipe. The common ones are Lemon, Yoghurt, Vinegar, Kachari, Raw papaya, Butter milk/ Khatti Lassi, Raw Pineapple, Raw Figs, Tamarind Brown Mustard.

Basic Garam Masala: Peppercorn, Caraway, Cumin, Cardamom Green, Cardamom Brown, Cloves, Cinnamon, Nutmeg, Mace, Pipal, Star anise.

Tandoori Khatta Masala/ Chat Masala: Caraway seeds, Rock Salt, Raw mango powder, citric acid, vegetable charcoal (food grade), ground Black Pepper.

Curry Masala: Coriander, Red Chillies, Turmeric, Cumin, Fenugreek, Mustard, Black Pepper.

2. **Processing the Food Items:** The Ingredients should be processed in proper way and they should be cut in a size which is suitable for cooking in a faster mode. This is planned before cutting the vegetables, Fruits and Meats for Tandoor.
3. **Checking the temperature of Tandoor**: The temperature of tandoor has to be checked before it is used. Different temperatures are suitable for different ingredients and preparations

REGIONAL CUISINES

AWADH CUISINE

History

It was 137 years ago that the last of the kings of Avadh walked on the land of their beloved Lucknow. While these monarchs sat on the throne of Avadh, there was nothing that they left untouched, thankfully, for their touch was like the well known magic wand. It could raise the most ordinary of activities into the Kingdom of art and to unattained heights of excellence.

Under the patronage of Awadhi ruler, developed a cuisine which did not remain the privilege of royalty alone. Recipes traveled from the royal kitchens of the Maharajas and from there, to the kitchens of ordinary people.

All the while, research and innovation preceded regularly in the bawarchi khanas of the royalty and aristocracy where money was no constraint neither was time. In the mid 18th century, in the personal bawarchi khana of Nawab Shuja-Ud-Daula, R60000 was spent per month or R7.2 lakh per year on the preparation of dishes. The dishes which decorated his **Dastarkhwan** did not come from the kitchen alone but from five other **Bawarchikhanas,** including that of his mother Nawab Begum and his wife Bahu Begum. These ladies separately spent R9000 per every month on the preparation of food. The staggering salaries of the hierarchy of cooks and other kitchen staff came from a separate budget.

However, high salaries were not the only reason for the excellent performance of the cooks. They were given total freedom to pursue their work their own way. Examples of cooks laying down conditions of employment before crowned heads, and the latter humbly accepting them, would only be found in Lucknow. And in Lucknow alone would you find cooks showing frustration if the king did not sit down for a meal, then told to do so by the cook because the food was hot. A cook employed only to prepare mash ki dal (arhar ki dal) on a monthly salary of R500. The dal was not cooked daily but once in a while, and the king was condition bound to sit down at the dastarkhwan when the cook announced that dal was ready. The king once delayed, so the cook left. Before leaving, he emptied the contents of the dish at a place where stood a stalk of a dead tree.

It was unwritten law that the master would sanction whatever quantity of ingredients the cook demanded. No questions were asked nor doubts expressed. A popular story goes that king Ghazi-ud-din Haider slapped his vazir Agha Meer for reducing the quantity of ghee used by the cook in preparing parathas. The king was no fool. He said that even if the cook pilfered some ghee, so what? The parathas he made were excellent, while you rob the whole monarchy and think nothing of it."

It was not royalty alone who pampered their cooks. The nobility, aristocracy and people of lesser means too maintained well stocked and well staffed kitchens from where were turned out the most exotic of dishes. Begums and ordinary housewives too preserved in their kitchens and acquired an excellence that could match the skills of a professional bawarchi.

Broadly, there are three categories of cooks in Lucknow. The **Bawarchis** cook food in large quantities. The **Rakabdars** cook in small gourmet quantities. Rakabdars also specialize in the garnishing and presentation of dishes. The **Nanfus** make a variety of **roti, chapattis, naans, sheermals, kulchas and taftans**.

Normally, one cook does not prepare the entire meal. There are specialists for different dishes and also a variety of helpers like the **Degbos** who wash the utensils, the **Masalchis** who grind the masala and the **Mehris** who carry the **khwan** (**tray**) to be spread on the dastarkhwan. The wealthy always had their kitchens supervised by an officer called **Daroga-e-bawarchi khana or Mohtamim**. It was this officer's seal on the khwan that guaranteed quality control.

The Lucknow dastarkhwan would not be complete unless it had the following dishes. Qorma (braised meat in thick gravy), salan (a gravy dish of meat or vegetable), qeema (minced meat), kababs (pounded meat fried or roasted over a charcoal fire), bhujia (cooked vegetables), dal. Rice is cooked with meat in the form of a pulao, chulao (fried rice) or served plain. There would also be a variety of rotis. Deserts comprise, kheer (milk sweetened and boiled with whole rice to a thick consistency), muzaffar (vermicelli fried in ghee and garnished with saffron).

The Lucknowi's menu changes with the seasons and with the festival which mark the month. The severity (harshness) of winters is fought with rich food. Paye (trotters) are cooked overnight over a slow fire and the shorba (thick gravy) eaten with naans. Turnips are also cooked overnight with meat koftas and kidneys and had for lunch. This dish is called shab degh and a very popular in Lucknow.

Peas are the most Regular vegetable in Lucknow. People never tire of eating peas. One can spot peas in salan, qeema, pulao or just fried plain.

Activity in the kitchen increases with the approach of festivals. During Ramzan, the month of fasting, the cooks and the ladies of the house are busy throughout the day preparing the iftari (the meal eaten at the end of the day's fast), not only for the family but for the friends and the poor.

Id is celebrated with varieties of siwaiyan (vermicelli) – Muzzaffar is a favorite Lucknow. Shab-e-barat is looked forward to for its halwas particularly of semolina and gram flour. Khichra or haleem , a delicious mixture of dals wheat and meat, cooked together.

There are dishes which appear and disappear from the Lucknow dastarkhwan with the season and there are those which are a permanent feature, like the qorma, the chapatti and the roomali roti. The test of a good chapatti is that you should be able to see the sky through it.

Utensils are made either of iron or copper. Meat kababs are cooked in a mahi tawa (large, round shallow pan), using a kafgir which is a flat, long handled ladle for turning kababs and parathas. Bone china plates and dishes were used in Lucknow since the time of Nawabs. The seating arrangement, while eating was always on the floor where beautifully embroidered dastarkhwans were spread on white sheets. Sometimes this arrangement was made on a takhat or low, wide wooden table.

Kebab

Kebabs are an important part of Awadhi cuisine

Lucknow is proud of its Kebabs. The Kakori Kebabs, Galawat ke Kebabs, Shami Kebabs, Boti Kebabs, Patili-ke-Kebabs, Ghutwa Kebabs and Seekh Kebabs are among the known varieties.

The Seekh Kebab has long been considered a piece de resistance in the Awadhi dastarkhwan. Introduced by the Mughals it was originally prepared from beef mince on skewers and cooked on charcoal fire. Now lamb mince is preferred for its soft texture.

The 100-year old **Tunde ke Kebab** in Chowk is the most famous outlet for choicest Kebabs even today. Tunda Kebab is so named because it was a specialty of a one-armed chef. This restaurant's signature dish is its masala which is a zealously guarded family secret and prepared by women in the family. It is said to incorporate 160 spices.

Kakori kebab is considered blessed since it was originally made in the place by the same name in the dargah of Hazrat Shah Abi Ahder Sahib with divine blessings. Kakori Kebab is as far as perfection could go. The mince for the kebab is to be obtained from no other part but the "raan ki machhli" (tendon of the leg of mutton) other ingredients include khoya, white pepper and a mix of powdered spices which remains a closely guarded secret adds to the perfect blend.

The Shami Kebab is the most important of them all. Made from mince meat, with chopped onion and coriander and green chillies usually added to the mixture, the kebabs are round patties filled with spicy surprises and the tangy raw green mango. The best time to have them is May when the fruit of the mango tree is in its infancy. When mangoes are not in season, kamrakh or karonda may be substituted for kairi, as both having a tart flavour reminiscent of the raw mango.

A variant made without any admixture or binding agents and comprising just the minced meat and the spices is the **Galawat kebab**.

An unusual offering is the **Pasanda Kebab,** piccata of lamb marinated and then sautéed on a griddle.

Boti kebab is lamb marinated in yoghurt and skewered, then well cooked. Traditionally, Boti Kebab (Lamb) is cooked in a clay oven called a tandoor. You can achieve an authentic tandoor flavor using your own barbecue grill.

Vegetarian kebabs include Dalcha Kebab, Kathal ke Kebab, Arbi ke Kebab, Rajma Galoti Kebab (kidney bean kebab cooked with aromatic herbs), Zamikand ke Kebab (Lucknowi yam kebabs), etc.

Curry Preparations

Korma is actually the Indian name for the technique of braising meat. It originated in the lavish Moghul cuisine wherein lamb or chicken was braised in velvety, spiced sauces, enriched with ground nuts, cream and butter. While kormas are rich, they are also mild, containing little or no cayenne or chillies. There are both vegetarian (navratan korma) and non-vegetarian (chicken, lamb, beef & fish korma) varieties of korma. Murgh Awadhi Korma is a classic from Lucknow.

Kaliya is a mutton preparation with Gravy along with the complusory inclusion of turmeric or saffron.

Rice Preparation

Biryani derived from the Persian word 'Birian', which means 'roasted before cooking', biryani is a mixture of rice (basmati), meat/vegetables, yogurt and spices.

Lucknow Biryani or **Awadh Biryani** is a form of Pukki Biryani. Pukki means 'cooked'. Both the meat and rice are cooked separately and then layered and baked. The process also lives up to the name Biryani in Persian meaning 'fry before cooking'.

It basically has three steps. First, the meat is seared in ghee and cooked in water with warm aromatic spices till meat is tender. The meat broth is drained out. Second, the rice is lightly fried in Ghee, and cooked in the meat broth from the previous step. Third, cooked meat and cooked rice are layered in a Handi. Sweet flavors are added. The Handi is sealed and cooked over low heat. The result is a perfectly cooked meat, rice, and a homogenous flavor of aromatic meat broth, aromatic spices and sweet flavors.

Haji Wahid Qurash's 'Wahid ki biryani' of Aminabad and Idris Biryaniwala's 'Idrisi biryani'of Patanala, Chowk are most famous for delicious biryani in Lucknow. Among various Biryanis the Lucknow and Hyderabad style are dominant with a friendly rivalry. The vegetarian version of biryani might have some textured vegetable protein based protein balls to present the impression of a meat-based dish for vegetarians.

The difference between biryani and pullao is that while biryani may be made by cooking the items together, pullao is used to denote a dish where the rice is cooked separately from the other ingredients.

Tehri is the name given to the vegetarian version of the dish and is very popular in Indian homes.

Bread Preparations

Naan is one of the staple breads of Awadh. As wheat is the staple food of the state, breads are very significant. Breads are generally flat breads; only a few varieties are raised breads. **Tawa roti** is bread made on crude iron pans. Improvisations of the roti (or bread) are of different types and made in various ways and include the *rumaali roti, tandoori roti, naan (baked in a tandoor), kulcha, lachha paratha, sheermaal and baqarkhani.*

Breads made of other grains have descriptive names only, thus we have *Makai ki roti, Jowar ki roti (barley flour roti), Bajre ki roti (bajra is a grain only grown in India), chawal-ki-Roti (roti of rice flour).*

Chapati: It is the most popular roti in India which is eaten for breakfast, lunch or dinner.

Puri: It is small and are deep fried so they puff like balloons.

Paraatha: A very common variant of roti is the celebrated and immensely popular, cooked in the same way as a regular roti, stuffed with fillings of vegetables, pulses, cottage cheese, and even mince meat and fried in ghee or clarified butter. This obviously heavy and scrumptious round bread finds its way to the breakfast tables of millions.

Rumaali Roti: elaborately and dexterously prepared ultra thin bread made on a huge and hot convex metal pan from finely ground wheat flour. It is a treat to watch one of these being prepared with great flourish by skilled cooks. The Urdu word rumaali literally means a kerchief.

Tandoori Roti: Relatively thick bread ranging from elastic to a crispy consistency, baked in a cylindrical earthen oven at a sometimes amazing speed by aggressively fast cooks at roadside restaurants and eateries. The Urdu word tandoor means an oven.**Naan:** This is a thick bread, softer and richer in texture and consistency than the tandoori roti. It is made from finely ground wheat flour kneaded into a very elastic mass. The roghni is a special treat for lovers of awadhi cuisine. This extraordinary bread is prepared with a rich mixture of cream, sugar, wheat flour, butter, and essence. The taste is rich and elegant— just perfect for the curries of the awadhi cuisine.

Sheermaal: It is sweet bread that accompanies the rich and filling aromatic quorma (gravied chicken or mutton). Sheermal is a sweetened Naan made out of Maida (All-purpose flour), leavened with yeast, baked in Tandoor or oven. In the olden days, it was made just like Roti. The warm water in the recipe for Roti was replaced with warm milk sweetened with sugar and flavored with saffron. Nowadays, the restaurants make it like a Naan and the final product resembles Danish pastry.

Baqarkhani: It is a naan which is an elaborate variation of the sheer-maal except that it is fried on a griddle rather than baked in a tandoor.

Desserts

Winters are dedicated to halwas of all kinds which came from Arabia and Persia to stay in India. There are several varieties of these, prepared from different cereals, such as gram flour, sooji, wheat, nuts and eggs. The special halwa or halwa sohan which has four varieties, viz Papadi, Jauzi, Habshi and Dudhiya is prepared especially well in Lucknow.

The Jauzi Halwa Sohan is a hot favorite even today, but the art of preparing it is confined to only a few households. Prepared for the most part from germinated wheat, milk, sugar, saffron, nuts etc., it has love and patience as its vital ingredients.

Difference between Awadhi and Mughlai Cuisine

Awadhi cuisine has drawn a considerable amount of influence from Mughal cooking style and bears resemblance to those of Hyderabad and Kashmir. The cuisine consists of both vegetarian and meat dishes which employs the dum style of cooking or cooking over slow fire which has become synonymous with Lucknow.

- ❖ Mughlai food is known for its richness. It is famous for the exotic use of spices, dried fruit and nuts. The Mughals did everything in style and splendor. Since they ate very rich food they reduced the number of intake during the day. Mughlai dishes as they are called have lots of milk and cream with spices to make rich and spicy meal that is the reason why Mughlai recipes are rich in fat, carbohydrates and proteins.
- ❖ As opposed to conventional thought, Awadhi food does not make use of hundred-odd spices to produce each dish but a blend of handful but not so common spices. The truth lies in the manner in which the food is cooked on a slow fire. This process allows the juices to be absorbed well into the solid parts. All nutrients are retained in the food through this process. In addition to the major process of cooking food in Awadhi style, there are also other important processes such as marinating meats in order to produce a delightful taste. This is especially the case with barbecued food that might be cooked in a clay oven of over an open fire.

Fish, red meats, vegetables and cottage cheese may be marinated in curd and spices. This helps to soften the taste and texture of them as well as remove any undesired odors from the fleshy materials. They were often cooked on tawa, the flat iron griddle, as opposed to Mughlai influence and bear a testimony to the local influence and convenience. Some of the tawa preparations are, in fact, equally, if not more, famous like tandoori kebabs and tikkas.

Difference between Awadhi and Mughlai kebabs is that, while the former is usually cooked on the tawa, the latter is grilled in a tandoor. This is gives the difference in flavour.

CULINARY TERMS

Dhungar

This is a quick smoke procedure used to flavour a meat dish, dals or even raita. The smoke very effectively permeates every grain of the ingredients and imparts a subtle aroma, which enhances the quality of the dish. The procedure may be carried out either at the intermediate or the final stage of cooking. This is a common technique employed while making kababs. The method is as follows. In a shallow utensil or a lagan in which the meat or mince has been marinated, a small bay is made in the center and a katori or onion skin or even a betel leaf (depending on the dish) is placed. In it a piece of live coal is placed and hot ghee, sometimes mixed with aromatic herbs or spices, is poured over it and covered immediately with a lid to prevent the smoke from escaping. The lid is not removed till about 15 minutes, so as to allow the smoke to work on the ingredients inside. The coal is then removed from the utensil and the meat put through further cooking processes.

Dum Dena

This is a frequently method used in Awadh cooking. 'Dum' literally means 'breath' and the process involves placing the semi-cooked ingredients in a pot or deg, sealing the utensil with flour dough and applying very slow charcoal fire from top, by placing some live charcoal on the lid, and some below. The Persian influence is most evident in this method though in Awadh it has acquired its own distinct character. The magic of dum' is the excellent aroma, flavor and texture which results from slow cooking. This method is followed for a number of delicacies such as the Shabdeg, Pulao and Biryani. Any dish cooked by this method is 'Dum Pukht' or 'Dum Bakht'.

Galavat

This refers to the use of softening agents such as papain (from raw papaya) or kalmi shora to tenderise meat.

Baghar

This is a method of tern pering a dish with hot oil / ghee and spices. It may be done either at the beginning of the cooking as in curries, or at the end as for (pulses). In the former, the fat is heated in a vessel to a smoking point and after reducing the flame, spices are added to it, when they begin to crackle, the same process is carried out in a ladle which is immersed in the cooked dish and immediately covered with a lid, so that the essence and the aroma of the spices, drawn out by the hot ghee are retained in the dish giving it their flavour.

Gile Hikmat

Talking of Persian influence on Awadh cuisine one cannot ignore this interesting method adopted for cooking. 'Gil' in Persian is earth or mud and 'Hikmat' implies the procedure of the Hakims. This method is generally followed to prepare 'Kushtas' which are the ash-like residue of substances which cannot be consumed in their natural form as they are toxic, for instance gems or metals. But when adopted for cooking purposes the method is as follows. The meat or vegetable to be cooked is generally taken whole and stuffed with nuts and spices, It is then wrapped in a banana leaf or cloth and covered completely with clay or 'Multani Mitti' (Fuller's Earth) so as to seal it. It is thereafter buried about 4-6 inches deep. A slow fire is then placed on top for 6–8 hours after which the food is dug out and is ready to be served!

Loab

This is a term which refers to the final stage in cooking when the oil used during cooking, rises to the surface. giving the dish a finished appearance, This occurs mostly when slow cooking of gravy dishes is involved.

Moin

It is the shortening of dough. In this process fat is rubbed into the flour and made into dough for kachoris or pooris or parathas. This makes the final product crisp, flaky and crumbly.

Ittr (Perfumes)

The use of perfumes plays an important role in Awadh cuisine they are used to enhance the aroma of the dish and make it delicate. Most commonly they are made from musk deer, hunting of which is now banned worldwide.

Yakhni Cuts (Mutton)

The cuts for Yakhni are generally bony pieces with flesh on them. These cuts are usually taken from the joints and the ribs of the animal. The basic purpose of meat in preparing Yakhni is to derive the juice and flavour and hence the shape of the meat does not count much.

Chandi Warq

This is the process in which small pieces of silver are placed. between two sheets of paper and then patted continuously with a hammer till it becomes papery thin. These are used in decorating the dishes before presentations, e.g. Chandi kaliya, Moti pulao.

Zamin Doz

This is a style of cooking in which a hole is dug in the ground and the ingredients are placed and covered with mud. Then burning charcoal is placed over it. The cooking process takes about 6 hours.

Utensils Used

Bhagona/Patili

It is generally of brass with a lid. It is used when a great deal of 'bhunna' or saute is required. or even for boiling and simmering. It is also used for preparing Yakhni or Salan, Korma or Kaliya.

Deg/Degchi

This is a pear-shaped pot with a lid of either brass, copper or aluminium. The shape of this utensil is ideally suited for the 'd:Jm' method and is used for cooking Pulaa, Biryani, Nehari or Shab Deg.

Kadhai

This is a deep, cancave utensil made afbrass, iron or aluminium and is used far deep frying paoris and the like.

Lagan

This is a round and shallow copper utensil with a slightly concave bottom. Used for cooking whole or big cuts of meat or poultry especially when heat is applied from both the top and bottom.

Lohe ka Tandoor

It is an iron tandoor as distinct from the clay tandoor more common in Delhi. It is a kind of dome-shaped iron oven used for making most bread such as the Sheermal. Taftan, Bakarkhani etc.

Mahi Tawa

It is the Awadhi version of the griddle shaped like a big round, flat bottomed tray with raised edges, used for cooking kababs. Also used for dishes where heat is applied from both ends, when covered.

Seeni

This is a big thali (round tray) usually used as a lid for the lagan or mahi tawa when heat is to be applied from the top. Live charcoal is placed on it and the heat is transmitted through it to the food. Thus the indirect heat has the desired effect of browning and cooking the ingredients. All the copper and brass utensils are almost always used after 'kalai' or tin plating the insides.

FAMOUS DISHES

Thandai	Laccha Paratha
Papari	Kuttu Ke Parathe
Amoa	Roomali
Paneer Tikka	Naan
Shammi Kebab	Kachori
Dahi Vada	Methi Ke Parathe
Boondi Raita	Matar Paratha
Machi Ke Kebab	Almond Kulfi
Galouti·Kebab	Almond Seera
Kanji ke Vade	Badam Halwa
Kathi Kebab	Carrot Halwa
Kofta Curry	Gujia
Khaja	Gulab Jamun
Lauki Lajees	Gulkand Peda
Machi zameen doz	Imarti
Malai Kofta	Jalebi
Adraki Murg	Kaddu Ki Kheer
Chicken Korma	Kurmura Ladoo
Dahi Gosht	Aam Ki Burfi
Murg Mussalam	Moong Dal Halwa
Nargisi Kofta	Motichoor Ladoo
Navratan Korma	Phirni
Palak Paneer	Rabdi
Nawabi Curry	Til Papari
Shahi Paneer	Zafrani Kheer
Biryani	Kala Jam
Tahari	
Kichdi	

BENGALI CUISINE

Bengali cuisine is a style of food preparation originating in Bengal, a region in the eastern South Asia which is now divided between the independent country of Bangladesh and the Indian state of West Bengal. Bengali cuisine is well-known for the vast range of rice dishes and various preparations of freshwater fish. Bengali cuisine is rich and varied with the use of many specialized spices and flavours.

Influence

Spread of Islam

The Islamic influence came to Bengal a few hundred years after its arrival on the western borders of India. While the religion propagated in the populace, the region remained isolated from the political and religious centres of Muslim India. This meant that people retained many of their local customs and especially food habits.

Influence of the Widows

In medieval Bengal the treatment of Hindu widows was much more restrictive than was common elsewhere. They led very monastic lives within the household and lived under strict dietary restrictions. They were usually not allowed any interests but religion and housework, so the kitchen was an important part of their lives; traditional cuisine was deeply influenced by them. Their ingenuity and skill led to many culinary practices; simple spice combinations, the ability to prepare small quantities (since widows often ate alone) and creative use of the simplest of cooking techniques. Since widows were banned 'impassioning' or aphrodisiac condiments such as onion or garlic, most traditional Bengali vegetarian recipes don't use them; this is in stark contrast to the rest of the Indian subcontinent where almost every dish calls for onions and garlic. This has led to a definite slant towards ginger in Bengali vegetarian food, and even in many common fish dishes. This treatment of widows in Bengal continued until fairly recently; the effect on the cuisine was to preserve many of the dishes and techniques of the old in purest form — well removed from the influence of Mughal or Western methods.

European and Other Outside Influences

The Europeans came to modern Bengal soon after the Mughals, but in small numbers. The Europeans brought cooking techniques, but also new ingredients and food items. In addition, cities developed population centres of Europeans; this in turn encouraged foreign purveyors to set up locally, such as Jewish bakeries and English sausage vendors.

Partition of Bengal

The partition of India from the British in 1947 separated West Bengal from the present-day Bangladesh, causing a significant change in demographics. The newly formed

West Bengal was a small state in India dominated by the mega city of Kolkata, which was already one of the largest cities in the world and about a quarter of the population of the state. Kolkata naturally came to dominate the food habits of the state. The city was India's richest city until the late seventies, attracting people from all over India and building a cosmopolitan culture that both incorporated influences from the rest of India and propagated many trends outwards. On the other side of the border, Bangladesh was isolated by the international boundary and continued to develop a distinct cuisine of its own. Today, three generations later, Bangladeshi and Kolkata cuisines are quite distinct.

Islamic Influence

Islam arrived in Bengal probably around the mid-thirteenth century, coming into force with the penetration of the Muslim rulers from the northwest. The influence on the food was more gradual than in many other parts of India. This led to a unique cuisine where even the common man ate the dishes of the royal court, such as biryani, korma and bhuna. The influence was reinforced in the Raj era, when Kolkata became the place of refuge for many prominent exiled Nawabs, especially the family of Tipu Sultan from Mysore and Wajid Ali Shah, the ousted Nawab of Awadh. The exiles brought with them hundreds of cooks and masalchis (spice mixers), and as their royal patronage and wealth diminished, they interspersed into the local population. These highly accomplished cooks came with the knowledge of a very wide range of spices (most notably jafran saffron and mace), the extensive use of ghee as a method of cooking, and special ways of marinating meats. The Mughal influence is most distinct in preparations involving meat especially mutton. However, even chicken and other meats became more prevalent. The influence was also seen in desserts; traditional desserts were based on rice pastes and jaggery but under the Mughal influence moved towards significantly increased use of milk, cream and sugar along with expensive spices such as cardamom and saffron.

Ingredients Used

The traditional society of Bengal has always been heavily agrarian; hunting, except by some local tribals, was uncommon. The rearing of animals was also not popular. This is reflected in the cuisine, which relies on staples like rice and ðal, with little place for game or meat.

Fish is the dominant kind of meat, cultivated in ponds and fished with nets in the fresh-water rivers of the Ganges delta. More than forty types of mostly freshwater fish are common, including carp varieties like rui (rohu), katla, magur (catfish), chingºi (prawn or shrimp), as well as shuþki (dried sea fish). Salt water fish (not sea fish though) Ilish (hilsa ilisha) is very popular among Bengalis, can be called an icon of Bengali cuisine. Almost every part of the fish (except fins and innards) is eaten; the head and other parts are usually used to flavor curries. Khashi (referred to as mutton in Indian English, the meat of sterilized goats) is the most popular red meat.

Other characteristic ingredients of traditional Bengali food include rice, moshur ðal (red lentils), mug ðal (mung beans), shorsher tel mustard oil, mustard paste, posto (poppyseed) and narkel (ripe coconut). Bengal is also the land of am (mangoes), which are used extensively—ripe, unripe, or in pickles. Ilish machh (hilsa fish), which migrates upstream to breed is a delicacy; the varied salt content at different stages of the journey is of particular interest to the connoisseur, as is the river from which the fish comes - fish from the river Pôdda (Padma or Lower Ganges) in Bangladesh, for example, is traditionally considered the best. To some part of the community, particularly from West Bengal, Gangatic Ilish is the best. The pãch phoron spice mixture is very commonly used for vegetables. A touch of gôrom môshla or hot spices (elachi-cardamom, Dalchini-cinnamon, long-clove, tej pata-bay leaves, and peppercorn) is often used to enliven food.

Another characteristic of Bengali food is the use of a unique cutting instrument, the *bothi*. (This instrument is also used in Maharashtra, where it is known as *vili*). It is a long curved blade on a platform held down by foot; both hands are used to hold whatever is being cut and move it against the blade. The method gives excellent control over the cutting process, and can be used to cut anything from tiny shrimp to large pumpkins. Traditional cuisine is very demanding in the kind of cuts of vegetable used in each dish.

In western parts of Bengal, more connected with the rest of India and dominated by the megacity of Kolkata, a separate culinary style emerged. The delta is thinner there, with fewer rivers and more open plains. There is significant commerce with the rest of India, leading to a flow of spices, ingredients and techniques. The food is much richer with various spices, the presentations are more elaborate and a significant feature of the cuisine is a vast array of sweets based on milk and sugar - the result of both better supply and the influence of traders from the milk belts of Gujarat and Benares. While fresh-water *fish is still common, mutton is more common among the Muslim population than beef and dried fish.* Wheat makes its appearance alongside rice, in different types of breads such as **luchi, kochuri** and **poroþa.** Though mustard paste is extensively used, mustard oil is abandoned in favour of groundnut oil or refined vegetable oil. There's a greater use of coconut, both in cooking and in desserts.

The snack foods are most often consumed with evening tea. The tea-time ritual was probably inspired by the British, but the snacks bear the stamp of the substantial Marwari population in Kolkata - *chaþ, kachori, samosa, phuluri and the ever-popular jhal-muri.*

Eating Habits

Courses in a Daily Meal

The foods of a daily meal are usually simpler, geared to balanced nutrition and makes extensive use of vegetables. The courses progress broadly from lighter to richer and heavier. Rice remains common throughout the meal until the chaþni (chutney) course.

The starting course is a bitter. The bitter changes with the season but common ones are kôrolla (bitter gourd) which is available nearly throughout the year, or tender nim leaves in spring. Bitters are mostly deep fried in oil, or steamed with cubed potatoes. Portions are usually very small - a spoonful or so to be had with rice - and this course is considered to be both a palate-cleanser and of great medicinal value.

Another bittersweet preparation usually eaten in summer, especially in West Bengal, is a soupy mixture of vegetables in a ginger-mustard sauce, called **shukto.** This usually follows the dry bitters, but sometimes replaces it, and is eaten in much bigger portions. Shukto is a complex dish, a fine balance of many different kinds of tastes and textures and is often a critical measure of a Bengali housewife's abilities in the kitchen

This is followed by **shak** (leafy vegetables) such as spinach, palong chard, methi fenugreek, or amaranth. The shak can be steamed or cooked in oil with other vegetables such as begun (eggplant). *Steamed shak is sometimes accompanied by a sharp paste of mustard and raw mango pulp called Kasundi.*

The **Dal course** is usually the most substantial course, especially in West Bengal. It is eaten with a generous portion of rice and a number of accompaniments.

A common accompaniment to Dal is Bhaja (fritters). Bhaja literally means 'deep-fried'; most vegetables are good candidates but begun (aubergines), kumra (pumpkins), or alu (potatoes) are common. Machh bhaja (fried fish) is also common, especially rui (rohu) and ilish (hilsa) fishes. Bhaja is sometimes coated in a beshon (chickpea flour) and posto (poppyseed) batter. A close cousin of bhaja is bôra or deep-fried savoury balls usually made from posto (poppyseed) paste or coconut mince.

Another accompaniment is a vegetable preparation usually made of multiple vegetables stewed slowly together without any added water. Labra, charchori, ghonto, or chanchra are all traditional cooking styles. There also are a host of other preparations that do not come under any of these categories and are simply called **tôrkari** - the word merely means 'vegetable' in Bengali. Sometimes these preparations may have spare pieces of fish such as bits of the head or gills, or spare portions of meat. A charchori is a vegetable dish that is cooked without stirring, just to the point of charring.

The next course is the fish course. Common fish delicacies include machher jhol, tel koi, pabda machher jhal, Doi machh, Chingri machh (shrimp) malai curry, and bhapa ilish (steamed hilsa).

The meat course is the next course. Khashi mutton or goat meat is traditionally the meat of choice, especially West Bengal, but murgi chicken and ðim eggs are also commonly consumed.

Finally comes the chutney course, which is typically tangy and sweet; the chutney is usually made of am mangoes, tomatoes, anarôsh pineapple, tetul tamarind, pepe papaya, or just a combination of fruits and dry fruits. Papo°, a type of wafer, thin and flaky, is often made of ðal or potatoes or shabudana (tapioca) and is a usual accompaniment to the chutneys.

Mishþi (Sweets)

Sweets occupy an important place in the diet of Bengalis and at their social ceremonies. It is an ancient custom among Hindus to distribute sweets during festivities. The sweets of Bengal are generally made of sweetened cottage cheese (chhena), khoa (reduced solidified milk), or flours of different cereals and pulses. Some important sweets of Bengal are:

Shôndesh

Made from sweetened, finely ground fresh chhena (cheese),

Rôshogolla

Rôshogolla is one of the most widely consumed sweets. The basic version has many regional variations.

Pantua

Pantua is somewhat similar to the rôshogolla, except that the balls are fried in either tel (oil) or ghi (clarified butter) until golden or deep brown before being put in syrup.

Chômchôm

Chômchôm (especially from Porabari, Tangail District in Bangladesh) goes back about 150 years. The modern version of this sweet was inspired by Raja Ramgore of Ballia district in Uttar Pradesh in India. Granules of maoa or dried milk can also be sprinkled over chômchôm.

Piþha

In West Bengal, the tradition of making cakes, locally known as piþha, still flourishes. They are usually made from rice or wheat flour mixed with sugar, jaggery, grated coconut etc. (dumplings), among others. The other common pithas are chandrapuli, gokul, pati sapta, chitai piþha, muger puli and dudh puli.

SNACKS

Muri

Muri (puffed rice) is made by heating sand in a pot, and then throwing in grains of rice. The rice can have been washed in brine to provide seasoning. The rice puffs up and is separated from the sand by a strainer. Muri is very popular and is used in a wide variety of secular and religious occasions, or even just munched plain.

Jhal-Muri

One of the most popular and iconic snack foods of Bengal, jhal literally means 'hot' or 'spicy'. Jhal-muri is puffed rice with spices, vegetables and raw mustard oil. Depending on what is added, there are many kinds of jhal-muri but the most common is a bhôrta made of chopped onion, jira roasted ground cumin, bitnoon black salt lôngka / morich chilis (either kacha 'ripe' or shukna 'dried'), mustard oil, and dhone pata (fresh coriander leaves).

Moa

A moa is made by taking muri with gur (jaggery) as a binder and forming it into a ball. Another popular kind of moa is Joynagorer moa, a moa particularly made in Joynagor from a district of West Bengal which uses khoi and a sugar-milk-spices mixture as binder.

Glossary

- **Ambal:** A sour dish made either with several vegetables or with fish, the sourness being produced by the addition of tamarind pulp.
- **Biryani**: Fragrant dish of long-grained aromatic rice combined with beef, mutton, or chicken and a mixture of characteristic spices. It is sometimes cooked in sealed containers (dum biriyani).
- **Bhaja or Bhaji**: Anything fried, either by itself or in batter.
- **Bhapa:** Fish or vegetables steamed with oil and spices. A classic steaming technique is to wrap the fish in banana leaf to give it a faint musky, smoky scent.
- **Bhate:** ('steamed with rice') Any vegetable, such as potatoes, beans, pumpkins, or even dal, first boiled whole and then mashed and seasoned with mustard oil or ghee and spices.
- **Bhôrta:** Any vegetable, fish, or shrimp boiled and coarsely mashed, mixed with spices, mustard oil, and onions.
- **Bhuna:** A term of Urdu origin, and applies to meat cooked in spices for a long time without water. The spices are slow-cooked in oil (bhunno). The spices first absorb the oil, and when fully cooked release the oil again.
- **Chacchari:** Usually a vegetable dish with one or more varieties of vegetables cut into longish strips, sometimes with the stalks of leafy greens added, all lightly seasoned with spices like mustard or poppy seeds and flavoured with a phoron. The skin and bone of large fish like bhetki or chitol can be made into a chachchari called kanta-chachchari, kanta, meaning fish-bone.
- **Chhanchra:** A combination dish made with different vegetables, portions of fish head and fish oil (entrails).

- **Dalna:** Mixed vegetables or eggs, cooked in medium thick gravy seasoned with ground spices, especially garom mashla and a touch of ghee.
- **Dam or Dum:** Vegetables (especially potatoes), meat or rice (biriyanis) cooked slowly in a sealed pot over a low heat.
- **Ghonto:** Different complementary vegetables (e.g., cabbage, green peas, potatoes or banana blossom, coconut, chickpeas) are chopped or finely grated and cooked with both a phoron and ground spices.
- **Jhal:** Literally, 'hot'. A great favorite in West Bengali households, this is made with fish or shrimp or crab, first lightly fried and then cooked in a light sauce of ground red chilli or ground mustard and a flavoring of pãch-phoron or kala jira.
- **Jhol:** A light fish or vegetable stew seasoned with ground spices like ginger, cumin, coriander, chili, and turmeric with pieces of fish and longitudinal slices of vegetables floating in it. The gravy is thin yet extremely flavorful. Whole green chilis are usually added at the end and green coriander leaves are used to season for extra taste. This term is also used to refer to any type of stew in meat, fish or vegetable dishes.
- **Kalia:** A very rich preparation of fish, meat or vegetables using a lot of oil and ghee with a sauce usually based on ground ginger and onion paste and garom mashla.
- **Khichu°i:** Rice mixed with vegetables and in some cases, boiled eggs, usually cooked with spices and turmeric powder.
- **Kofta:** Ground meat or vegetable croquettes bound together by spices and/or eggs served alone or in savory gravy.
- **Korma:** Another term of Urdu origin (literally 'braised with onions), meaning meat or chicken cooked in a mild onion and yoghurt sauce with ghee.
- **Luchi:** Small round unleavened bread fried in oil.
- **Pôroþa:** Bread made from wheat flour and fried in the oven until golden-brown.
- **Paturi:** Typically fish, seasoned with spices (usually shorshe) wrapped in banana leaves and steamed or roasted over a charcoal fire.
- **Polau**: Fragrant dish of rice with ghee, spices and small pieces of vegetables. Long grained aromatic rice is usually used, but some aromatic short grained versions such as Kalijira or Gobindobhog may also be used.
- **Pora:** The word literally means charred. Vegetables are wrapped in banana leaves and roasted over a wood, charcoal or coal fire. Some vegetables with skin such as baigun, are put directly on the flame or coals. The roasted vegetable is then mixed with onions, oil and spices.
- **Ruþi:** Unleaved bread made in a tawa and puffed over an open flame.
- **Tôrkari:** A general term often used in Bengal the way 'curry' is used in English (it is speculated to be one of the origins of curry). Originally from Persian, the

word first meant uncooked garden vegetables. From this it was a natural extension to mean cooked vegetables or even fish and vegetables cooked together.

GUJARATI CUISINE

Gujarati cuisine is in many ways unique from other culinary traditions of India. It is one of the few cultures where a majority of people are vegetarians. This vegetarianism may have originally sprung from religious ideologies and beliefs of the region.

Gujarati cuisine is a blend of exquisite flavours and textures. A wide range of foods are cooked in Gujarati homes, and a variety of typical traditional recipes come from different regions of Gujarat.

In short, Gujarati meal is a great deal more than the ordinary rotli, daal, bhaat ane shaak!

Thali

Typical Gujarati Thali (plate) consists of Rotli (wheat bread), Daal (pulses), Bhaat (rice) and Shaak (vegetables). Although Gujaratis are fond of food, and there are thousands of recipes to add to the Thali. Gujarati cuisine refers to the cuisine of the people from the state of Gujarat in the West region of India. It is predominantly vegetarian. The typical Gujarati Thali consists of Rotli (a flat bread made from wheat flour), daal or kadhi, rice, and sabzi/shaak (a dish made up of different combinations of vegetables and spices, which may be stir fried, curry-like, or even dry boiled). Cuisine varies in taste and heat, depending on a given family's tastes and caste. Mainly vegetarian, energy-efficient, environment-friendly, and highly nutritious with many subtle tastes, it is also very hygienic and high in food safety. Mainly gujurati dishes have a beld of sweetness. Dishes are not too sweet but those are bit sweeter then other other parts of India.

Staples include salad, homemade pickles, Khichdi (rice and lentil or rice and mung daal), and chhaas (buttermilk). Main dishes are based on steamed vegetables and dals that are added to a vaghaar, which is a mixture of spices sterilised in hot oil that is adjusted for the digestive qualities of the main ingredient. Salt, sugar, lemon, lime, and tomato are used frequently to prevent dehydration in an area where temperatures reach 50C (120F) under the shade. It is common to add a little sugar or jaggery to some of the sabzi/shaak and daal. The sweet flavour of these dishes is believed to neutralize the slightly salty taste of the water.The cuisine changes with the seasonal availability of vegetables and, in knowledgeable families, the spices also change depending on the season. Garam Masala and its constituent spices are used less in summer. Regular fasting, with diets limited to milk and dried fruits, and nuts, are commonplace. A very healthy meal popular in the villages near Saurashtra during the cold winters consists of thick Rotis, termed Bhakhri, made of Wheat flour, garlic chutney, onion pieces and Buttermilk. It is a good source of energy which suits low-income villagers working on their fields in the cold days. Sweets made from such ingredients as local sugar cane, jaggery, milk, almonds, and pistachios were originally served at weddings and family occasions as an instant energy booster for relations travelling long distances to attend. They are now being enjoyed every day by those with sedentary occupations. Gujaratis will often refer to Daal-Bhaat (rice)-Rotli-Shaak as their standard, no-frills, everyday fare. For special occasions, this basic quartet is supplemented with additional shaak, sweet dishes and Farsan. A festive Gujarati Thali can easily contain a dozen or more separate items.

Mithai (Sweets)

- Sutarfeni
- Kansar
- Halvasan
- Malpua
- Keri no ras
- Basundi
- Ghari (sweet from Surat)
- Ghebar or Ghevar (sweet from Surat)
- Son Papdi
- Sukhadi
- Mohanthal
- Gud papdi (Gol papdi)
- Shiro: roasted semolina/flour/dal with milk, butter, sugar, nuts and raisins
- Ghooghra
- Shrikhand, a thick yogurt-based sweet dessert garnished with ground nuts, cardamom, and saffron
- Laapsi, coarse ground/ broken wheat cooked with butter and sugar
- Doodhpak, a milk-based sweet dessert with nuts
- Shakkarpara, a deep fried snack made out of sugar and wheat
- Copra paak - Coconut halwa/barfi: Halwa is soft, barfi more like cake
- Gajar Halwo - Carrot Halwa
- Dudhi no Halwo - Bottle Gourd Halwa

Daal (Soups)

- Moong Daal
- Meethi (Sweet) Kadhi

Diwali Special Snacks

- Cholafali
- Mathia
- Soonvali
- Ghooghra

Farsan (Snacks)

- Hahdwoh
- Muthia
- Dhokla
- Khandvi
- Patra
- Khichu
- Fafda
- Khakhra
- Sev Khamani
- Ganthia
- Khaman
- Lilva Kachori
- Pani Puri

Shaak and Daal (Subzee/Vegetables/Curries)

- Undhiyu, a combination of eggplant, tubers, slow cooked with special spices traditionally in a clay pot
- Sev Tameta nu Shaak (Sev Tomato Curry)
- Bateta nu Shaak (Potato Curry)[2]
- Bateta Sukhi Bhaji (Dry Potato Curry)
- Ringan nu Shaak (Eggplant Curry)
- Dudhi nu Shaak (Bottle Gourd or Squash Curry)
- Ganthiya nu Shaak
- Guavar nu shaak
- Tindola nu shaak
- Bhinda nu shaak (Okra Curry)
- Kobi Bataka nu shaak (Cabbage Potato vegetable)

- Dudhi Mag ni dal nu shaak
- Dudhi Ganthia nu shaak
- Dudhi Bataka nu rasawalu shaak (Bottle Gourd & Potato curry in a gravy)
- Chola nu shaak (lentil curry)
- Mag-Math nu shaak (lentil curry)
- Mag nu suku shaak (dry Mung curry)
- Tameta Bataka nu rasawalu shaak (Tomato Potato gravy vegetable)
- Kantola nu shaak (one type of slight bitter tasting vegetable)
- Karela nu shaak (Bittergourd vegetable)
- Ringna no oolo (meshed Eggplant curry)
- Methi nu shaak
- Parwal Bateta nu shaak
- Fansi nu shaak (French beans vegetable)
- Palak Bateka or Palak Paneer nu shaak
- Suva ni bhaji nu shaak
- Kanda Bateka nu shaak (Onion Potato vegetable)
- Gajar no sambharo (Stirred Carrot vegetable)
- Fansi ma Dhokli nu shaak (delectable combination of french beans and spiced dumplings)
- Panchkutiyu shaak (Five vegetables curry)

Breads

- Thepala
- Dhebara
- Fulka rotli
- Bhakhri
- Bajri no rotlo
- Puri (food)
- Parotha

Other

- Khaman Dhokla
- Kachori
- Khandvi
- Daal Dhokli
- Farsi Falafel

HYDERABADI CUISINE

Hyderabadi cuisine is a princely legacy of the Nizams of Hyderabad. Hyderabad, a city created by the Nawabs of Golconda, has developed its own cuisine over the centuries. It is heavily influenced by North Indian cuisines like Awadh, Mughlai and Tandoori, with considerable influence of the spices and herbs of the native Telangana and Marathwada cuisine.

Hyderabadi Cuisine could be found in the kitchens not just in Hyderabad city, but areas belonging to the former Hyderabad State that includes Telangana region, Marathwada region and Hyderabad Karanataka region. Hyderabadi Cuisine also contains city specific specialities like Aurangabad (Naan Qalia), Gulbarga (Tahari), Bidar(Kalyani Biryani) etc.

Hyderabad is never complete without the mention of the "Shahi Dastarkhan". The Dastarkhan is the Dining place where the food is served and eaten. It is normally a low chowki for the dining table and cotton mattresses for squatting and bolsters for the back rest. The Dastarkhan holds a place of reverence in every household.

The Cuisine of Hyderabad has been influenced by various regional and religious cuisines, both Indian and Foreign, despite which it has been able to create an identity of its own. It has also been able to contribute towards making Indian cuisine popular world wide. The "Biryani" from this cuisine is one such example.

What makes the Hyderabadi Cuisine special is the use of special ingredients, carefully chosen and cooked to the right degree. The addition of a certain Herb, Spice, Condiment, or an Amalgam of these adds a unique taste and texture to the dish. The herbs and spices used and the method of preparation gives the dish its name. "Murgh do pyaza" gets its name from the onions that are added twice to the dish in two variations. The key flavours are of coconut, tamarind, peanuts and sesame seeds which are extensively used in many dishes. The key difference from the North Indian cuisine is the presence of coconut and tamarind in its cuisine.

The Masalas or the rich blend of herbs, spices and condiments give the dishes a base, or what is popularly known as "Gravy". Some of these blends are a well-kept secret that pass only down the family line or from the Ustad(Teacher) to his Shagird(Pupil). The head cooks or the "Khansas" were an asset to the house hold, and were treated with due respect.

The word "Nawabi" is as synonymous with the Hyderabadi cuisine as "Shahi" is with Luknowi. These terms conjure delicacies that are rich in taste and texture with mouth-watering aromas. The "Kebabs" in Hyderabad need a special mention, the "ShammiKebab" is one such popular dish. The Kebabs are originally from Greece!!

The Hyderabadi meal is never complete without the bread from the kilns of the local bakers. The breads from this cuisine are equally popular, be it rich "Sheermal" or "lukmi" (bread stuffed with savory mince meat). Bread is not only an accompaniment to the meal but also forms a base for a popular sweet dish "Double Ka Meetha".

The mouth watering Shahi cuisine of Hyderabad; as soon as a person hears the mention of Hyderabadi Biryani, he starts whetting his appetite! The wafting aroma hits you before you set your eyes on the delicious mounds of fragrant, steaming rice with the tempting sight of a traditionally cooked chicken peaking out! It is so popular that it takes a special mention in the world of cuisine. A part from this king of the delicacies, the entire Shahi Nizam cuisine is very popular for its rich and aromatic taste. "The food is a dream of deliciousness", said the Persian Ambassador who came to the Qutub Shahi Kingdom in 1603. The elaborate Dastarkhan, on which are place steaming hot dishes of dum ka murgh, a baked chicken full of savoury herbs and spices. Lagan ke kebab, bhagare bhaingan, machili ka qualiya, mirch ka salan, haleem, and different kinds of Biryanis severed with Bhurani. Even the desserts are world renowned. Khubani ka meeta, badaam ki jaali, hub ke laoz, azam jahi meetha, etc, satiate you beyond imagination.

Another speciality eaten very early in the morning is Nahari, a curried soup of sheep's trotters and tongue. It cooks all night, and a nothing stale is considered edible, it is served up right away in soup bowls, and you drunk in piece of spongy Sheermahal bread. And during the festival day of Id-ul-Fitr, it is traditional to serve sheer quorma, the delicious kheer, made with sevian, dried fruits and dates.

This cuisine owes its origins to the Mughalai style of cooking of the Asaf Jahi period. By carefully mellowing and nurturing the typical Mughalai flavours with a blend of spices, the cuisine of Hyderabad was born.

Variety of Biryanis (a rice and meat preparation, seasoned with spices and flavourings)

Kababs: meat pieces or minced meat cooked in many different style.

- Boti Jhammi
- Kalmi
- Shikampur
- Sheek
- Lagan-ke-kababs
- Dum-ke-kababs

Khormas (either meat or vegetables cooked in a rich creamy gravy) and Lukhmi (pastry)

During the month of Ramzan, one gets to taste Haleem (a pounded wheat and meat preparation). For those who prefer more homely food, there is Kichri (a rice a lentil preparation); Kheema methi (minced meat with fenugreek); Nahari (stew of tongue and lamb trotters); Rumali Rotis (bread as thin as a handkerchief) and Chakna (a spicy dish of meat).

Vegetarians

- Bagara Baingan (a rich spicy preparation of aubergines)
- Mirch-ka-salan (chillies in a creamy gravy)

- Tomato kut (aromatic puree of tomato with flavourings)
- Shahi dahi vadas (lentil dumplings in youghurt sauce).

Curries & Starters

- Boti Kabab
- Bagara khana - Basmati rice delicacy.
- Baghara baingan - Stuffed Eggplants, a delicacy where tender and fresh brinjals are stuffed with grounded peanut-coconut mixture and cooked in a rich and creamy paste.
- Dalcha -Mutton and Lentil delicacy.
- Murghi ka Khorma - Chicken curry
- Hyderabadi Kheema- A popular mutton-mince curry.
- Paaya -
- Chakna - A dish made out of Goat intestines and tripes cooked with flour and other spices.
- Pathar-ka-Gosht - Mutton/lamb deep-fried on a stone slab found in Hyderabad.
- Bina Masale Ka Murgh - chicken done with only curd, turmeric and saffron
- Dum-ka-Kheema
- Muthhi Key Kebab - Meat balls (goat)
- Nizami Murg Handi
- Maghaz Masala (Beja Fry) - A goat's brain deep fried delicacy.
- Dopiaza - A curry made from lamb, onions, butter etc.
- Chugur Gosht- Lamb & Tender tamarind leaves curry.
- Boti Kabab- Minced meat delicacy.
- Bhuna Gosht
- Tamate ka Kut made with tomatoes and often boiled eggs are added to it.
- Katti DalLiquid dal made with Imli.
- Rawghani Roti - A type of Bread.
- Pasande Kabab
- Khagina Made with onions and the fried eggs.
- Khabuli
- Hyderabadi Nihari - A breakfast dish made of Goat's feet.
- Tamatar Ghosht
- Ambade ka Salanmade with a leaves of Ambada and Mutton.

Desserts

- Faluda
- Double ka meetha
- Qubani ka meetha(Khubani-ka-Meetha) - Apricot Pudding, Toppings with almond and cream. The original recipe is a translucent liquid.
- Double ka meetha- Bread Pudding topped with dry fruits, a derivative of mughlai dessert Shahi tukre.
- Gil e firdaus - Kheer made from kaddu.
- Sheer korma- Vermicelli Pudding - Sheer means Milk and Korma is a dry date fruit, is a celebration special dessert, specially made on the Ramzan day.
- Badam-ki-Jhab known as marzipan.
- Gaajar ka Halwa- Carrot Pudding
- Mauz-ka-Meetha- A Banana dessert.
- Firni - A Rice dessert.

Snacks

- Lukhmi
- Chota Samosa - a crispy, onion-filled variant
- Lukhmi A typical Hyderabadi starter and the snack's original and authentic preparation is stuffed with mutton-mince (kheema). "Kheemey ki Lukhmi" is still served as a starter in the authentic Hyderabadi course of meal at weddings, parties, etc.
- Dil khush - A triangular pie, which is bread stuffed with cake leftovers
- Dil pasand
- Chota Samosa - A crispy, onion-filled small samosa.
- Osmania Biscuit - A nice, soft tea biscuit, gets its name after last ruler of Hyderabad, Mir Osman Ali Khan.
- Fine Buiscuit - A multi-layered, oval shaped and sprinkled with sugar.
- Tea Biscuit - A multi - layered, oval shaped and sprinkled with sugar

CUISINE OF PUNJAB

Punjab, the land of milk and honey, boasts of a robust climate where the agricultural revolution has gathered rich dividends. The land has a cuisine which caters to the characteristic needs of the people.

Punjabi cuisine is not subtle (fine) in its flavour. There are no intricate (complex) marinades or exotic sauces but it has full-bodied masalas (spices) cooked with liberal amount of desi ghee (clarified butter) always served with a liberal helping of butter or cream. Milk and its products are an essential part of everyday cookery; curd and buttermilk are also an essential accompaniment with every Punjabi meal.

Predominantly wheat eating people the Punjabis cook rice only on special occasions. It's never eaten plain or steamed, for steamed rice implies that somebody is sick. Rice is eaten always with a bagar (flavouring) of cummin or fried onions with Rajma or Kadhi, Rajma with rice or rice With Kadhi is eaten on holidays or on festive days. In winter rice is cooked with jaggary known as gurwala chawal or with peas called matarwale chawal or as a delicacy called Rao Ki Kheer which is rice cooked on very slow fire for hours together with sugar cane juice.

In Punjab itself, there are differences in flavours and style. For example, people around Amritsar prefer well-fried stuffed paraunthas and milk sweets. The people of Doaba region eat more of them; in the Malwa region Bajra (ground maize) khitchadi (kedgree) is a delicacy. There are of course certain dishes which are part and parcel of Punjab and their very mention calls up the rich flavour of the state. Mah ki Dal, Sarson Ka Saag and Makkee Ki Roti, meat curry like Roghan Josh and stuffed paraunthas can be found in no other state except Punjab. The food is suitable for those who burn up a lot of calories while working in the fields and tilling their small acres. For the urban folk, however, eating even one dish is enough because life in the cities is so sedentary. The main masala in a Punjabi dish consists of onion, garlic, ginger and a lot of tomatoes fried in pure ghee.

Punjabi cuisine can be non-vegetarian or completely vegetarian. The level of spices can vary from minimal to very prevalent. One of the main features of Punjabi cuisine is its diverse range of dishes. Home cooked and restaurant Punjabi cuisine can vary significantly, with restaurant style using large amounts of clarified butter, known locally as desi ghee, with liberal amounts of butter and cream with home cooked concentrating on mainly upon wheat masalas (spice) flavourings; though wheat varieties form their staple food.

Dishes of Punjab

Pulse, bean and / or lentil preparations:

- Dal makhani (ma ki dal)
- Dal maharani
- Dal amritsari
- Lobiya (black eyed bean)
- Rajmah (Red kidney bean)
- Punjabi pindi chholey (Whole Bengal gram)
- Punj ratani dal (mixtures of 5 lentils) etc.
- Saron (sarson) ka saag te makki di roti

These are generally soaked overnight or for at least 8 hours and gently simmered on the embers of a tandoor (A clay oven of the shape of a horizontally sliced pot) along with ginger, garlic and a few other garam masala (whole spices like cardamom, cinnamon, mace, and bay leaf).

These are then combined with a tangy masala base which could include tomato or dried mango (aam choor powder) or even pomegranate seeds (Anar Dana). The character typical to the bean or whole lentil preparation is that the shape is retained intact, but the gentlest pressure would make it into a paste.

Dollops of cream and butter provide for the rich finishing touch. Garnishing is usually with shredded coriander leaves and juliennes of ginger.

Bread Preparations

The Punjabi breads are generally flat breads; only a few varieties are raised breads. The breads may be made of different types of flour and can be made in various ways:

1. Baked in the tandoor like naan, tandoori roti, kulcha, lachha paratha
2. Dry baked on the tava (Indian griddle) like phulka or chapati, jowar ki roti, baajre ki roti and the very famous makke ki roti (these are also smeared with ghee or white butter)
3. Shallow fried like paratha, aloo or mooli paratha
4. Deep fried like puri and bhatoora (fermented dough)

The tandoor also allows for tasty chicken and meat preparations including seekh kebab, tandoori chicken, reshmi tikka and malai tikka.

Meat (Standard English) or Non-Vegetarian (Indian English)

- Chicken - Tandoori Chicken, Butter Chicken, Chicken Tikka, etc.
- Lamb - Rogan Josh, Bhuna Ghosht, Kadhai Ghost, Raan Gosht, Dal Gosht, Saag Gosht, Nihari Gosht, Rara Gosht, Paye da Shorba, etc.
- Beef - Nihari Beef, Beef Pasanda, Kadhai Beef, etc (especially popular in West Punjab).
- Fish - These are all Freshwater fish dishes like Amritsari Fish, Tandoori Fish, Fish Tikka, Fish Pakora, etc.
- Kebabs - Various Lamb, Chicken and Beef Kebabs.
- Biryanis - Chicken Biryani and Lamb Biryani.
- Keema Naans - Chicken mince and Lamb mince stuffed Naans.
- Pickles - Lamb Pickle and vegetable Pickle.

Vegetarian

- Sarron Da Saag: A dish prepared from green mustard leaves and eaten with Makki Roti (bread made by flour of Corn)
- Mushroom & Beans Sabzi
- Dal makhani/ Dal Handi Pulses with butter.
- Rajma (Red kidney bean) and Rice
- Dal Amritsari
- Rongi (Black eyed bean)
- Choley (eaten with Naan or Kulcha)
- Punj ratani dal: A 5 lentil dish; the lentils are soaked for at least 8 hours and then cooked in a tandoor along with ginger, garlic, garam masala, tomato or dried mango
- Kadhi-Pakora (Traditional curry with Pakoras) and Rice: Kadhi (Curry) is made by cooking gram-flour with curd or buttermilk. Fried lumps (Pakoras) of gram-flour with salt, chillies are also added. It is eaten with Rice.
- Kadhai Paneer
- Shahi Paneer
- Phirni
- Jalebi
- Malpua
- Sheer korma (also called Seviyan)
- Pakoras
- Samosas

QUESTIONS

1. Write a detail note about Indian dian cuisine.
2. What are the different spices used in Indian cookery?
3. What are the various gravies used in north Indian cuisine?
4. Differentiate between the food of north India and south India.
5. Explain the contribution of mughals on the food.
6. explain following terms:

- Dum pukht,
- Dhuangar,
- Do-Piaza,
- Moin dena,
- Gile hikmat.

7. Fill in the Blank:

1. Pasanda is a special kind of ————————.
2. Makhani is ————————base gravy.
3. ———————— is the most richest gravy.
4. Dum Pukht is the food from ———————— state.
5. In north India dried and grounded mixture of spices is called————————.
6. Curry powder is prepared by mixing————————.
7. Poriyal means————————
8. Rogan josh is the dish from———————— region.
9. Dastar- khan means————————.
10. Salan is a dish from ————————.

9

Dairy Products and Egg

OBJECTIVES

After reading this chapter student should know:

- Importance and types of milk
- Composition of milk
- What is cheese and making of cheese?
- Different types of cheese?
- How the different types of butter are made?
- What are different types of cream and their uses?
- Composition of eggs and its uses in cookery?
- Checking then quality of egg?

MILK

1. Milk is defined as the lacteal secretion obtained by milking a cow 15 days before and not sooner than 5 days after calving.
2. A normal mammary gland secreting from the female mammals, vary from cow milk to goat milk.
3. Milk has its white colour due to the presence of colloidal calcium.
4. Different types of milks are obtained by the treatment given to them with the help of heat.
5. Milk freshly obtained and not homogenized will form a cream line on the surface if allowed to stand for few hours. This is because the fat particles in milk have a lower specific gravity (0.92-0.94) meaning they are lighter than water.

A fresh milk usually carrying following:

milk fat	3.5%
milk solid	8.5%
water	88.0%

Use of Milk

- Milk is indispensable ingredient in cookery and is essential for many sauces.
- It is also used in soups, gratinate dishes,
- Stock and Court-bouillons for certain fish and even in meat cookery.
- Milk can also be thickened and flavored to produce various deserts like custard
- Milk is require for making of dessert like ice-cream, Indian sweets, batters for pancakes, and fritters.
- Milk is very versatile food, it is the basic ingredient of butter, cheese, buttermilk and yoghurt and it makes a delicious drink either on its own or flavored with, for ex fruits, vanilla or chocolate.
- In Indian cookery used for various gravies and most of sweets are prepared from milk.
- It is stirred into tea or coffee and form basis of many hot drinks notably chocolate.

TYPES OF MILK

1. **Pasteurized milk** – Milk is heated to 71.7° C to cease bacteria growth and then cooled immediately. It contains around 3.9% fats. Most commercial milk and cream are pasteurized.
2. **Homogenized milk** - in this type of milk fat molecules remains suspended in the milk or cream. This is done by forcing the milk through a series of extremely small holes to separates the fat particles into small pieces. So that they Resultant milk does not readily separate. It gives a better quality to use.
3. **UHT (ultra heat treated)** - homogenized milk heated at 172 ° C for 1 sec and then packed in sterilized conditions. It is also bacteria free milk.
4. **Sterilized milk** - Homogenized milk which is boiled at 115° C to 130 ° C and stored at 50 ° C .It is done to make the milk bacteria free.
5. **Fortified milk** - milk with addition of vitamins A and D, and others extra non fat solids.
6. **Skimmed or non fat milk** has a most or all of the fat removed from the milk. It contains 0.5 -2% fat. However it can't be a substitute for whole milk in the making of the soup, sauce, dessert and others culinary preparations.
7. **Flavoured milk** - this type of milk is added with a distinguish flavoring ingredient like coffee, chocolate, vanilla,, cardamom, strawberry etc. they are available in commercially ready to use packs or bottles.

8. **Condensed milk** - the milk boiled and reduces till it achieves the thick consistency usually one third. It contains maximum percent of milk solids
9. **Dry milk powder** - It contains all the necessary milk solids and contents. It has 5% of moisture in it. It is the costliest one from all the above mentioned types of milk.

CHEESE

Cheese is the solid or casein part of milk separated from the whey. Casein is curdled due to the presence of the acetic acid. In cheese Rennet is used to curdled the cheese.

Sequence of making cheese:

1. Milk is warmed
2. A starter culture or natural souring and coagulant like rennet are added
3. The milk coagulates into a single soft curd
4. The curd is stirred and whey is drain off
5. Sometimes more pressed to remove more whey. Salt is added
6. The curd is molded, pressed and shaped into a cheese.
7. Bandaging means application of the grease to provide fixative and close up to any surface deficiency is done.
8. The cheese is matured under controlled conditions.

Checking the quality of cheese:

- Skin or rind of cheese should never show spot of mildew as this is a sign of improper storage.
- When cut, should not smell over. It should smell fresh.
- When cut, it should not be dry.
- Soft cheese should have a creamy consistency.

The quality of cheese is effected by:

- Type of Milk used
- Method of Curdling and Temperature during the Curdling Process
- How Curd Are Cut And Drained
- The Way Curd are Heated, Pressed Or Handled.

Cheese is consist mainly of fat and milk protein.

Storage and Service of Cheese

Soft cheese should be consumed immediately and hard cheese will long last.

Cheese should be stored in refrigerator.

Oxygen is enemy of the cheese.

Wrap cheese tightly in a heavy plastic wrap for storage.

Serve cheese at room temperature.

Cheese should be cut just before the service to prevent getting dry and flavour loss.

Few ingredients used in cheese

Rennet

A substance obtained from the stomach linings of young calves which contains a coagulating enzyme.

Annatto

A colouring agent used to colour a great variety of cheeses ranging from English Cheddar to the French Maroilles. Annatto is a dye obtained from a South American plant

Casein

The element of milk which solidifies when coagulation takes place.

TYPES OF CHEESE AS PER TEXTURE

Fresh/Soft cheese

They can be unripened fresh cheese Like Paneer (cottage cheese), mozzarella, cream, *Neufchatel ricotta* cheese or soft ripened soft cheese like camembert, brie, double cream cheese.

It has 80% of water content. They are freshly prepared and stored for a short period.

Fresh cheese are of creamy consistency and can be use directly or mixed with others.

Semi-hard Cheese

They are pressed and kept for few weeks in the store under control conditions.

Feta, provolone, emmenthal, Roquefort, port de salute,

Hard Cheese

They are pressed and kept for very long period (up to 10 year). They are usually grated and used in cooking for various purposes. Like parmesan, cheddar, gruyere.

Blue Cheese

Blue cheese is blue due to a type of fungus in the cheese. These are edible cheese. There are two ways to prepare the blue cheese

1. By keeping the blue cheese in contact with white cheese to react the white cheese with blue cheese.
2. By inserting a copper wire into the white cheese to enable the bacteria reaction into the cheese.

Ingredients used for Making of Blue Cheese

Pasteurized cow's milk/non-fat dry milk

salt

cheese cultures

enzymes

penicillium.

Types of Blue Cheese

Stilton – king of the cheese. It has semi hard texture and is found in 2 colours - blue and white. It has 55% fat.

Gorgonzola - is smooth in taste and can be used for making of sauce.

Blue vein - has a strong tangy taste with a pungent taste. It carry a network of green bluc vcins of mould.

Danish blue - made from cows milk and is of mallow texture. Ripening period is 2-3 month and is also called Marmora.

Checking the Quality of Cheese

Skin or rind should never show spot of mildew as this is a sign of improper storage.

When cut, should not smell over. It should smell fresh.

When cut, it should not be dry.

Soft cheese should have a creamy consistency.

Some Facts about Cheese

Ratio of cheese from the milk usually is 10:1.

Blue veined cheese is prepared from the skimmed milk.

Quality of cheese depends upon the breed, animal & feed.

Processed cheese is made by grinding the cheese and then cooked in a vacuumed cooker. After they are poured into mould and then wrapped in tin.

- Cheese is used for flavored like parmesan is used in pasta or cheddar in Welsh rarebit. Gruyere is used as a cooking cheese. As protein get toughened on high heat, cheese should be cooked on a very slow fire for short period. Cheese sauce is common derivative for white sauce.
- Cheese should never be overcooked otherwise it will be indigestible and will be split.
- High protein cheese will be tough and stringy when expose to excessive heat or cooked for long Period. Therefore Use only low protein cheese for cooking purpose.
- Cheese can be used for the topping of many excited dishes like pizza, open sandwich. To colour the topping it is served on top and then browned under the salamander. This adds a shine and provides a particular flavour.
- Cheese can be used for stuffing in pastas, poultry and appetizer. Camembert can be fried and served as appetizer.
- Some Cheese can be used in making of various desserts like tiramisu, cheese tart, cheesecake etc.
- On the table cheese can be presented on cheese basket with grapes, dry fruit and celery stick on the bed of vine leaves. Whole meal breads or savory bread and biscuit can be served with cheese.

Storage of Cheese

- Soft cheese should be consumed immediately and hard cheese will long last.
- Cheese should be stored in refrigerator.
- Oxygen is enemy of the cheese. Therefore wrap cheese tightly in a heavy plastic wrap for storage.
- Serve cheese at room temperature.
- Cheese should be cut just before the service to prevent getting dry and flavour loss.

BUTTER

The word *butter* comes from *bou-tyron,* which means "cow cheese" in Greek. It takes 21 pounds of fresh, wholesome cow's milk to make each pound of butter like the pat of butter on waxed paper (at right) at a French farm in Brittany.

Butter is produced by churning the dairy cream and then solid part is separated from whey.

It is one of the two main types of butter sweet and other is lactic butter. Ratio of butter from milk is 22:1.

Butter is one of the most popular cooking fats, providing rich flavour to foods, but due to its low smoke point, it can burn on high heat or frying. To prevent the butter from burning, one should add an oil with a higher smoke point.

Butter is used as a glaze on topping for breads, rolls and vegetables, and is added to many types of sauces to provide a rich, smooth flavour. It is also used as an ingredient in hundreds of baked goods such as breads, rolls, cakes, and pastries

Butter is perishable so it should be stored in the refrigerator. It should be tightly wrapped because it will absorb odors and flavors quite easily. Unsalted butter may be kept in the refrigerator for 2 or 3 weeks and salted butter may be kept somewhat longer (4 or 5 weeks) because the salt acts as a preservative. Butter freezes extremely well and may be kept in the freezer for long-term storage for at least

Lactic Butter

One of the two basic types of butter is lactic butter (the other main type is sweet cream butter), which is produced by adding a culture to pasteurized cream. The culture ripens the butter and at the appropriate time, it is pasteurized again to stop the ripening process.

Clarified Butter

Also called "ghee" in India. Clarified butter is produced by melting normal butter over low heat or double boiler and removing the milk solids and impurities that rise to the top. The golden yellow clarified layer is then strained off, leaving only sediments in the bottom of the pan like salt and milk solid. Clarified butter has a rich buttery flavour and is excellent for cooking because it has a higher smoke point than regular butter due to the non milk protein.

Butter is a rich source of vitamin A. It also contains all the other fat-soluble vitamins E, K and D. It is rich in trace minerals especially selenium, a powerful antioxidant. It supplies iodine and vitamin

CREAM

The amount of butterfat contained in the cream will determine how well cream will whip and how stable it will be.

Types of Cream

Half Cream, 10½ to 12%, not used for whipping. Generally used in beverages.

Single Cream 20%, Not used for whipping. Used in both sweet and savory dishes.

Light Cream, 18 to 30%, Will whip if it contains 30% butterfat but will not be very stable. Generally contains only 20% butterfat.

Whipping Cream, 30%, Does not whip as well as heavy cream but works well for toppings and fillings.

Heavy Cream, 36 to 40%, Whips up well and holds its shape. Doubles in volume when whipped.

Double Cream, 48%, Whips up very quickly and is easy to overwhip. Also used in custard, pies and sauces.

Clotted Cream, 55 to 60%, Does not need whipping, use as is. Found in specialty food stores.

Pasteurized and Ultra-pasteurized

Creams will generally be labeled pasteurized or ultra-pasteurized. Ultra-pasteurized creams will remain fresh longer but pasteurized will provide a better flavour, will whip up fluffier, and will hold up longer. If pasteurized cannot be found, ultra-pasteurized will work

EGG

Few Points for egg:

1. The normal egg shell may have around as 17,000 tiny pores over its surface. Through them, the egg can absorb flavors and odors. Therefore they should be Stored separately.
2. Egg can be cooked in various ways. It can be treated as complete food.
3. Eggs should be kept in refrigerator at cooling temperature (3-5°C).
4. To check if an egg is raw or hard-cooked, it should be spin, if the egg spins easily, it is hard-cooked but if it wobbles, it is raw.
5. Only the shell part contains calcium.
6. Egg yolks are one of the few foods that naturally contain Vitamin D.
7. Yolk colour depends on the diet of the hen. Natural yellow-orange substances such as marigold petals may be added to light-colored feeds to enhance colors.

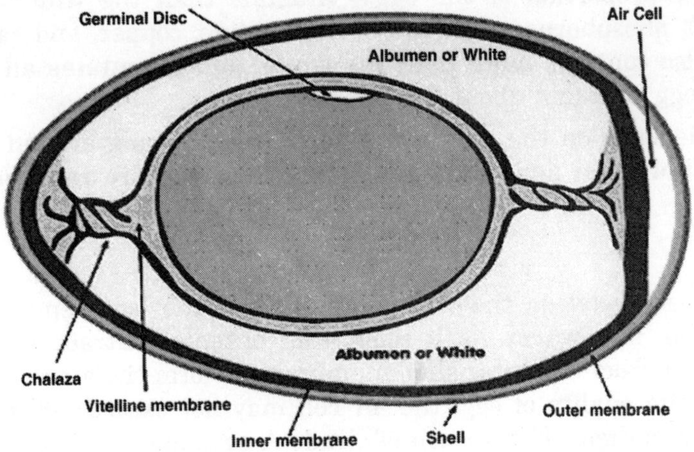

Cooking Functions of Egg

While eggs are widely known as breakfast entrees, they also perform in many other ways for the knowledgeable cook. Their cooking properties are so varied, in fact, that they have been called "the cement that holds the castle of cuisine together."

Shell

It is outer covering, and is about 12% of its total weight depending on egg size. The shell keep the egg's safe from bacterial contamination. The shell is largely composed of calcium carbonate (about 94%) with mall amounts of magnesium carbonate, calcium phosphate and other organic matter including protein.

The colour comes from pigments in the outer layer of the shell and may range in various breeds from white to deep brown.

White

Egg albumen in raw eggs is opalescent and does not appear white until it is beaten or cooked. A yellow or greenish cast in raw white may indicate the presence of riboflavin. Cloudiness of the raw white is due to the presence of carbon dioxide which has not had time to escape through the shell and thus indicates a very fresh egg. White part carries a huge amount of protein thus it expands when whisked.

The Yolk or Yellow Portion

The yolk or yellow portion makes up about 33% of the liquid weight of the egg. It contains all of the fat in the egg and a little less than half of the protein. The yolk contains a higher proportion of the egg's vitamins than the white. All of the egg's vitamins A, D, E, phosphorus, manganese, iron, iodine, copper, and calcium are in the yolk. The yolk also contains more than the white, and it contains all of the zinc. The yolk of a large egg contains about 59 calories

Yolk colour depends on the diet of the hen. Greenish ring around hard-cooked egg yolks is the result of sulfur and iron compounds. When eggs are overcooked it may occur.

Air Cell

The empty space between the white and shell at the large end of the egg. When an egg is first laid, it is warm. As it cools, the contents contract and the inner shell membrane separate from the outer shell membrane to form the air cell. The Candle test is done to check the quality of egg; the air cell may not exceed 1/8 inch in depth and is about the size of a dime. The air cell of Grade A eggs may exceed 3/16 inch in depth. For Grade B eggs, there is no limit on air cell size.

Chalaza

Ropey strands of egg white which anchor the yolk in place in the center of the thick white. The more prominent the chalazae, the fresher the egg.

Use of egg in cookery

Eggs are widely used in breakfast in different shapes like omelet, scrambled, fried, poached, boiled etc. Their cooking properties are so varied, in fact, that they have been called "the cement that holds the castle of cuisine together."

1. Eggs can bind ingredients as in kebab, croquettes.
2. They can also leaven such soufflés and sponge cakes.
3. Their thickening agents seen in custards and sauces.
4. They emulsify mayonnaise, salad dressings and Hollandaise sauce and are frequently used to coat or glaze breads and cookies.
5. They clarify soups like consommé is clarified by egg white. Also used In boiled candies and frostings,
6. They retard crystallization in case of sugar as for candies. As a finishing touch, they can be hard cooked and used as a garnish.

Name of Type of Cooked Eggs

- **A La Coque**: Soft boiled eggs in the shell.
- **Mullet**: Soft cooked without shell.
- **Dur**: Hard-boiled eggs.

Cheese

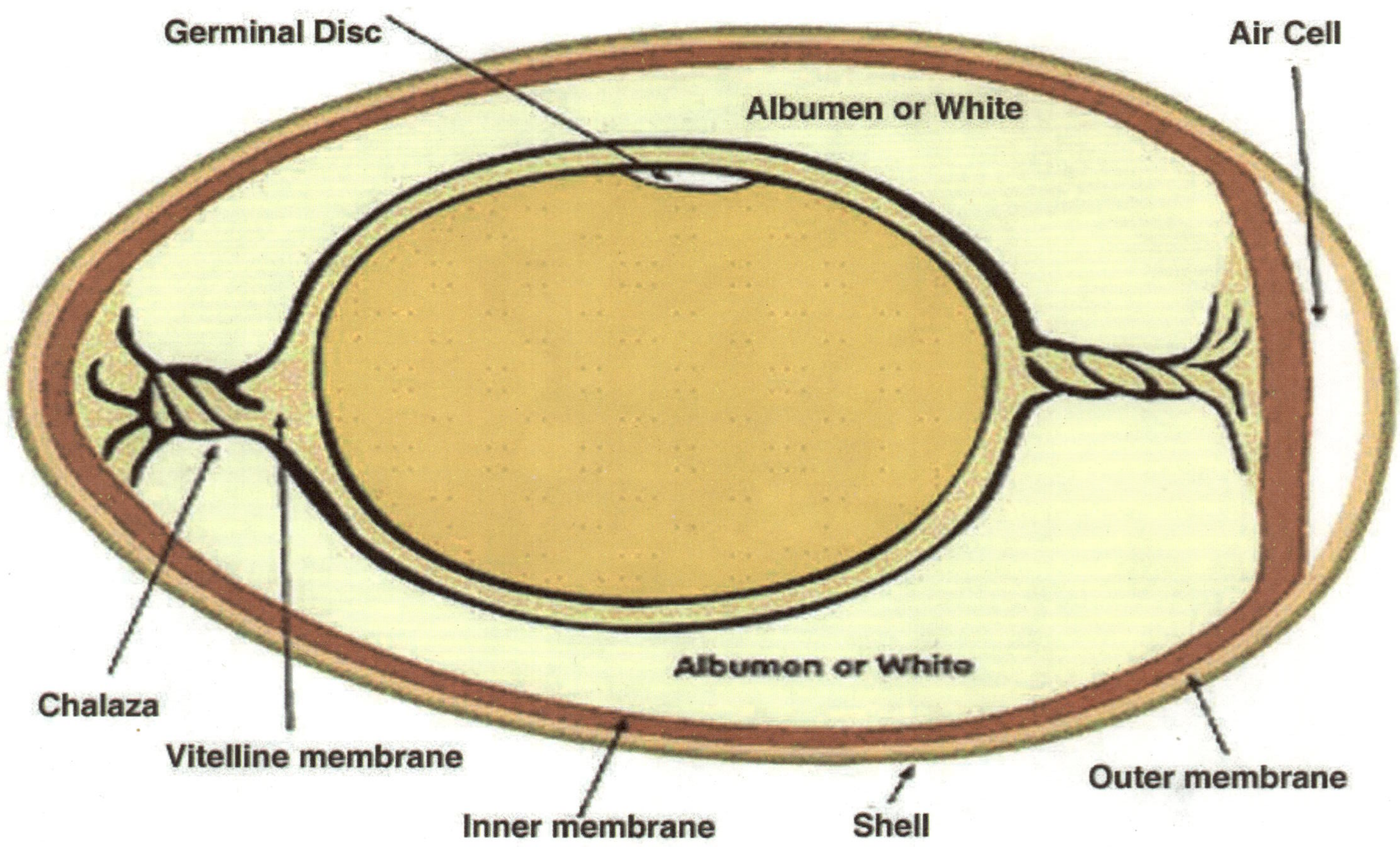
Germinal Disc
Air Cell
Albumen or White
Albumen or White
Chalaza
Vitelline membrane
Inner membrane
Shell
Outer membrane

Egg

- **Brouilles**: Scrambled eggs
- **Poche**: Poached egg.
- **En cocotte**: Eggs cooked in small fireproof dish.
- **Sur le Plat**: baked and served in the same dish.
- **Omelette**: Omelet, accompanied by grilled tomatoes, hash brown potatoes, saute mushroom, baked beans, ham, bacon and sausages
- **Frit**: Fried

Types of Egg Dish

- **Oeuf Espagnole**: Omelets with onions, pepper and tomato. Garnished with half stoned olive and anchovy strips.
- **Omelet aux tomates au champignon**: Tomato or mushroom omelette.

QUESTIONS

1. What are the different types of milks are available in the market and state their use?
2. How the butter and cream is made and what is the use of butter?
3. Explain the manufacturing process of cheese. State different type's of cheese with example.
4. Draw a diagram of egg with the explanation of its parts.
5. Explain the role of egg in cookery.
6. How will you check the quality of egg.
7. Explain following terms:
   - U.H.T.,
   - Double cream,
   - Clarified butter,
   - Rennet,
   - Coagulation,
   - Blue cheese,
   - Albumin,
   - Egg yolk,
   - Air cell.
8. Differentiate the following:
   a) Egg yolk and egg white.
   b) Bind and Thickening of egg.
   c) Blue cheese and Soft cheese.

d) Single cream and Double cream.
e) Lactic butter and Clarified butter.
f) Rennet and Bandaging.

10

Fat and Oil

OBJECTIVES

After studying this chapter students should know:

1. Types of fats
2. Different types of fats and composition of them
3. Use of fat in cooking
4. Storage and care
5. Precaution to be taken while using fats

FATS AND OIL

Fats are solid at room temperature and melt when heated, chemically they are made up of one glycerin molecule and three molecules of fatty acids, that is why they are called 'triglyceride'

Fatty Acids

- Made up of two types of molecules – 'Carbon and Hydrogen'.
- Each of these molecules has eighteen Carbons each attached to something else in Four positions.
  - Degree of saturation of Fatty acids in a fat determines some of its properties and uses in the kitchen.
  - A Fat high in saturated fatty acids is solid at room temperature and the one high in Unsaturated Fatty acids is Liquid at room temperature.

Types of Fatty Acids

1. **Saturated Fatty Acid** - These fats are found in meat and other animal products, such as butter, cheese, and all types of milk. Saturated fats are also found in palm and coconut oils. Saturated fat can raise blood cholesterol levels and increase the risk of heart disease
2. **Unsaturated fatty acids (Stearic acid),** the carbon atoms are attached to as many Hydrogen atoms as they can possibly hold on. These are found in plant foods and fish. These may be good for human health. The best of the unsaturated fats are found in olive oil, peanut oil, canola oil, albacore tuna, and salmon. They have two types
   A. **Monounsaturated Fatty acids** (Oliec acid), two Hydrogen atoms are missing from "Oliec acid' and there is a Double bond between two of the Carbon atoms.
   B. **Polyunsaturated Fatty acid** is the one where there is more than One Double bond in Fatty acid chain and there are more Hydrogen atoms missing at the rate of more than 'Two per Double bond'.
3. **Trans Fatty Acids** are formed when vegetable oils are processed into margarine or shortening. Sources of Trans fats in the diet include snack foods and baked goods made with "partially hydrogenated vegetable oil" or "vegetable shortening." Trans fatty acids also occur naturally in some animal products such as dairy products.

Essentiality of Fat for Human Body

- **Energy.** Fats are the most efficient source of energy. Each gram of fat provides nine calories of energy for the body, while carbohydrates and proteins. Provide four calories per gram
- **Protecting cells.** Fats are a vital part of the membrane that surrounds each cell of the body.
- **Build brains.** Fat provides the structural components to cell membranes and nerve fiber in the brain. That's why they are good for the kids
- **Help the body use vitamins.** Vitamins A, D, E, and K are fat-soluble vitamins, meaning that the fat in foods helps the intestines absorb these vitamins into the body.
- **Hormones making.** Fats are structural components of some of the most important substances in the body, including prostaglandins, hormone-like substances that regulate many of the body's functions. Fats regulate the production of sex hormones, which explains why some teenage girls who are too lean experience delayed pubertal development and amenorrhea.
- **Control temperature.** The layer of fat just beneath the skin acts as the body's own insulation to help regulate body temperature .One of the more obvious signs

of fatty acid deficiency is dry, flaky skin. In addition to giving skin its rounded appeal.

- **Protect organs.** Many of the vital organs, especially the kidneys, heart, and intestines are protected by fat that helps protect them from injury and hold them in place. (True, some of us "overprotect" our bodies.) As a tribute to the body's own protective wisdom, this protective fat is the last to be used up when the body's energy reserves are being tapped into.
- **Pleasurable in cooking.** Besides being a nutritious energy source, fat adds to the appealing taste, texture and appearance of food. Fats carry flavour. Fat is also the reason why cookies melt in your mouth, French fries are crispy, and most of the fast food is prepared from the fat.

Fats are used for various purposes, the major culinary part played by them is as:-

- Spreads
- Shortenings
- Tempering
- Salad Dressing
- Frying Medium

SHORTENING

Any fat is a shortening in baking because it shortens gluten strands and tenderizes the product. Shortening is a type of fat that has additive and enhance its usage in baked goods or as a frying fat

Shortening is the animal or vegetable fat that is used in baking. There are two general types of shortening-solid and liquid. The solid-type shortening is recommended for use in bread dough because it can be more thoroughly distributed through the dough. The reason for this is that it will not saturate the flour it touches. Although the liquid-type shortening can be used effectively, the dough must be well formed before the oil is added. The liquid-type shortening is mainly used in recipes that call for melted shortening, such as some cake and bread recipes.

Frying shortening is hydrogenated vegetable oil to which an anti foaming agent is added

Smoke Point

The smoke point refers to the temperature at which an oil begins to smoke, become discolored, and decompose. Cooking oil should never be allowed to heat to the smoking point because this will cause food to burn and will produce an unpleasant taste in the food.

A **FLASH POINT** "is the temperature where the fat catches a fire"

A number of factors may contribute to a decrease in the smoke point of oil. The length of time the oil has been heated, the number of times the oil has been used, the presence of salt or any other impurities, improper storage, and if the oil is a generic blend of various oils may all contribute to lowering the smoke point.

SMOKE POINT OF VARIOUS OILS AND FATS

Type of Fat or Oil	Smoke Point	Cooking Methods
Refined fat or oil		
Avocado Oil	271°C	Sauté, Pan-fry, Sear, Deep-fry, Stir-fry, Grill, Broil
Safflower Oil	265°C	Sauté, Pan-fry, Sear, Deep-fry, Stir-fry, Grill, Broil, Baking
Almond Oil	257°C	Sauté, Pan-fry, Sear, Deep-fry, Stir-fry, Grill, Broil, Baking
Soyabean Oil	232°C	Sauté, Pan-fry, Sear, Deep-fry, Stir-fry, Grill, Broil, Baking
Corn Oil	232°C	Sauté, Pan-fry, Sear, Deep-fry, Stir-fry, Grill, Broil, Baking
Sunflower Oil	232°C	Sauté, Pan-fry, Sear, Stir-fry, Grill, Broil, Baking
Peanut Oil	232°C	Sauté, Pan-fry, Sear, Deep-fry, Stir-fry, Grill, Broil, Baking
Cottonseed Oil	215°C	Sauté, Pan-fry, Sear, Deep-fry, Stir-fry, Grill, Broil
Type of Fat or Oil	Smoke Point	Cooking Methods
Sesame Seed Oil (Light)	210°C	Sauté, Pan-fry, Sear, Deep-fry, Stir-fry, Grill, Broil, Baking
Olive Oil	210°C	Sauté, Pan-fry, Sear, Deep-fry, Stir-fry, Grill, Broil, Baking
Grape Seed Oil	204°C	Sauté, Pan-fry, Sear, Deep-fry, Stir-fry, Grill, Broil, Baking
Canola Oil	204°C	Sauté, Pan-fry, Sear, Deep-fry, Stir-fry, Grill, Broil, Baking
Walnut Oil	204°C	Sauté, Pan-fry, Sear, Stir-fry, Grill, Broil
Lard	190°C	Sauté, Pan-fry, Sear, Baking
Vegetable Shortening	162°C	Sauté, Pan-fry, Sear, Baking
Butter	148°C	Sauté, Pan-fry, Sear, Grill, Broil, Baking
Unrefined Oil or Fat		
Sesame Seed Oil	176°C	Sauté, Pan-fry, Sear, Stir-fry, Grill, Broil, Baking
Olive Oil (Extra Virgin or Virgin)	160°C	Sauté, Pan-fry, Sear, Stir-fry, Grill, Broil, Baking
Peanut Oil	160°C	Light sauté, Low-heat grilling, Low-heat baking
Soyabean Oil	160°C	Light sauté, Low-heat grilling, Low-heat baking
Corn Oil	160°C	Light sauté, Low-heat grilling, Low-heat baking
Walnut Oil	160°C	Light sauté, Low-heat grilling, Low-heat baking
Sunflower Oil	107°C	Blend it with oils with higher smoke points for low heat cooking
Canola Oil	107°C	Blend it with oils with higher smoke points for low heat cooking
Safflower Oil	107°C	Blend it with oils with higher smoke points for low heat cooking

Storage of Fat and Oils

- Should be kept in cool place
- Go rancid if not kept cool
- Should be free of moisture, otherwise they splutter
- Many compounds that have a strong aroma can dissolve in oils, therefore they must be stored in air tight containers

TYPES OF FAT

Ghee already discussed in previous chapter

Whey Butter

In order to produce whey butter, the whey is drained from the cheese curds during the cheese making process. Any cream remaining in the whey is separated and churned into butter. Whey butter is strong and salty with a cheese flavour and it has limited appeal. It can be found in some specialty shops and farmers markets.

Common Uses: condiment, flavoring ingredient

Cocoa Butter

Cocoa butter is a cream colored vegetable fat that is obtained from cocoa beans, usually as a by-product during the production of chocolate and cocoa powder. It is used as a flavoring for various foods and it is also used in the cosmetic industry for the manufacture of soaps and lotions. It is very high in saturated fat so it should be used sparingly.

Common Uses: chocolate and cocoa powder production, cosmetics

Lard

Lard is pork fat find around the kidneys that has been rendered and clarified to produce a product that is firm and evenly textured with a mild flavour. Lard is a soft, greasy texture and a strong flavour. It produces the most tender and flaky crusts in bakery.

Like butter, lard will absorb flavors and aromas so it should be tightly wrapped when it is stored. The label should be checked for the proper storage method because some types of lard, depending on the processing technique, may be stored at room temperature, while other types require refrigeration.

Common Uses: baking, frying

Suet

Suet is a white, solid fat obtained from the area surrounding the kidneys of beef and sheep. It is a high form of saturated fat. Suet is sold in large chunks or in a shredded form in small packets.

Common Uses: steamed puddings, candles

Vegetable Shortening

Made from vegetable oils, vegetable shortening is a solid fat at room temperature because of a process called hydrogenation in which hydrogen is added to the oils. This changes the chemical characteristics of the oils, making them solid at room temperature. The process also creates trans-fatty acids, which transforms the healthy oils, composed largely of unsaturated fat, into less healthy fats containing mostly saturated fat.

Like lard, vegetable shortening is very useful in baking light and flaky pastries. Some varieties may have butter flavoring added, which improves the flavour and gives the shortening a light golden colour. Vegetable shortening can be stored at room temperature for a year or more if it is tightly covered.

Common Uses: baking, frying

Note: Most solid cooking fats can be called shortening because when they are used for baking, they produce a short, or flaky and crumbly crust. The more fat used in proportion to flour in a recipe, the shorter the crust. If the flour is in a greater proportion to the fat, the crust will be tougher and less flaky.

Margarine

Margarine is made from various vegetable oils such as soyabean and corn. Margarine must contain a minimum of 80% fat.

In order to produce margarine extra hydrogen is added to the oils the process is called "hydrogenation",. This process changes the chemical composition of the oils, causing them to solidify. The hydrogenation process produces trans-fatty acids, which eliminates the unsaturated fats of the vegetable oils and converts them to solid saturated fats. This is it is not good for heart.

Margarine can be used just like butter as a topping for bread, rolls, or biscuits, but it is much more spreadable. Margarine is often used in a variety of baked goods and can be used in any recipe requiring butter. It has a lower smoke point than many cooking oils so for many cooks; it is not the first choice for sautéing or frying.

Margarine should be stored in the refrigerator where it will keep for 2 months or more and for long term storage, it may be kept in the freezer for a half year or longer. Like butter and other solid fats, margarine will absorb flavors and odors so it should be tightly wrapped or covered.

Common Uses: cooking, baking, condiment

QUESTIONS

1. Define different types of fat.
2. What is the difference between saturated and unsaturated fats?
3. What are the smoke and flash points?
4. How will you store the fat?
5. Why the butter is not used for frying?
6. Differentiate between:
   a. Butter and margarine,
   b. Lard and suet,
   c. Fatty acid and Trans fatty acid.
7. Define following:
   a. Fatty acid,
   b. Margarine,
   c. Ghee,
   d. Trans fatty acid,
   e. Hydrogenation,
   f. Lard,
   g. Suet,
   h. Shortening.

11

Vegetables, Fruit and Cereals

OBJECTIVES

After reading this chapter student should know

1. Classification of vegetables and fruits
2. Different types of cuts in which vegetables can be cut.
3. Types of cereals
4. Composition of wheat and rice
5. Use of cereals

VEGETABLES

Vegetables can be served as an appetizer, a side dish, or even a main dish. Health-conscious consumers and the availability of high quality fresh produce have led to increased demand for vegetable menu choices. Students will learn Purchasing, storing, preparing, and cooking fresh and preserved.

In addition to vegetables, fruits also offer health-conscious consumers an alternative when eating in food service operations. Fruit is one of the most versatile and popular foods, providing restaurateurs additional menu options for their customers.

Fruit and vegetables are an important part of daily diet. They contain vitamins and minerals that can help to keep you healthy. They may also help protect you from some diseases. There are many varieties of fruit and vegetables available and, if you buy them in season, they are not expensive.

Fruit and vegetables are available dried, canned, frozen or fresh. They can be prepared, cooked and served in a variety of ways and should be included in every meal.

CLASSIFICATION OF VEGETABLES

Vegetables are classified according to which part of the plant is eaten. Some vegetables may fall into more than one category when more than one part of the plant is eaten, e.g. both the roots and leaves of beet-root can be eaten.

Bulbs	Usually grow just below the surface of the ground and produce a fleshy, leafy shoot above ground. Bulbs usually consist of layers or clustered segments, e.g. onion, shallot, garlic, spring onion, leek, fennel
Flowers	The edible flowers of certain vegetables, e.g. cauliflower, broccoli, gaai laan (Chinese sprouting broccoli), brocco-flower, globe artichoke
Vegtetables fruits	Vegetable fruit are fleshy and contain seeds, e.g. egg plant, capsicum, courgette, okra, pumpkin, tomato, choko, scallopini
Fungi	When referring to vegetables, fungi are commonly known as mushrooms, e.g. button, flats, shitake, oyster, gourmet brown, wood ear, enokitaki, truffle
Leaves	The edible leaves of plants, e.g. bok choy, cabbage, lettuce, silver beet, spinach, mustard leaf
Roots	Usually a long or round-shaped taproot, e.g. carrot, turnip, beetroot, swede, radish, parsnip, celeriac
seeds	Also know as legumes, seeds are usually obtained from pods. The pod is sometimes eaten along with the seed, e.g. broad been, French bean, pea, snow pea, snake beans, butter beans
stems	The edible stalks of plants when the stalk is the main part of the vegetable, e.g. asparagus, celery, kohlrabi
tubers	Vegetables which grow underground on the root of a plant, e.g. potato, kumara, yam, taro, Jerusalem artichoke, Maori potato.

ADVICE FOR COOKING VEGETABLES

To minimise nutrient loss and to retain the flavour when cooking vegetables follow these basic rules:

- Peel the skin thinly or leave it on. Nutrients are often at their highest concentration just beneath the skin. Peeling can mean the best part is thrown away.
- Rinse vegetables in fresh water before using.
- Use a sharp knife when cutting vegetables to minimise cell damage. Damaged cells release enzymes which will destroy Vitamin C.
- Cook vegetables as soon as possible after preparation. Do not soak them. Vitamin C is destroyed when cut surfaces are exposed. Water soluble vitamins (B and C) will be lost in soaking water.

- Use a small amount of water when cooking, or preferably steam vegetables. The water soluble vitamins will leech into the cooking water which is often thrown away. Save vegetable water for use in soups, stocks and gravies.
- Take care not to overcook vegetables. Most vegetables should be tender but still slightly crisp, this will vary with personal preference. Starchy vegetables, such as potatoes and kumara, should be tender throughout.
- When stir-frying, cook at a high temperature for a short time and use as little oil as possible. Try using water in place of oil.
- For storing boiled vegetables always cool by chilled water after boiling them to retain the colour.
- The addition of baking soda to vegetables should be avoided. Whilst it does make green vegetables look 'greener', it destroys valuable vitamins.
- Eat vegetables as soon as possible after cooking. Heat sensitive vitamins will be destroyed if held at a high temperature for prolonged periods.

Boiling of Vegetables

Cut the vegetables into evenly sized pieces. If using whole vegetables select those which are the same size. Place in boiling water 2-3 cm deep. Cover tightly and bring back to the boil as quickly as possible. Boil gently until tender when tested with a fork. Drain and serve immediately. If want to serve later, chill them immediately otherwise pigment will be lost in smoke.

Approximate cooking times for boiling four servings of vegetables

Cabbage, 5-7 minutes, Cauliflower, broccoli 8-10 minutes, Carrots (sliced), Celery 12-16 minutes Potatoes, Parsnips, Pumpkin, Kumara 20-25 minutes

CUTS OF VEGETABLES

Brunoise

This is a very small diced cube, sized between 1-3 mm square. It is often used as a garnish for consommé. Typical vegetables used are carrot, onion, turnip and celery

Dice

All the square shaped cuts end up the same size. These square cuts are known as:

- Fine dice (brunoise), 1/8" square
- Small dice (macedoine), 1/4" square

- Medium dice, 1/3" square
- Large dice, ¾" square
- Cube, greater than ¾" square.

Trim and peel vegetables as needed. Then square the sides. Cut into slices of desired thickness. Stack the slices and cut these slices equal to the thickness of the previous cuts, ending up with stick shaped pieces. Holding the sticks together with your guiding hand, make crosswise cuts through the sticks.

Chiffonade

Finely shredded green leafy vegetables, usually lettuce or spinach, which is used as a base, garnish or in soups.

Jardiniere

A long thin baton, about 2.5 cm long and approximately 0.5 cm wide × 0.5 cm thick.

Julienne (1/8" × 1/8" × 1" to 2" long)

Long thin match-stick shaped pieces about 4 cm in length.

Macedoine

This is diced cube, 0.5 cm (5 mm) square, larger than the brunoise cut. Typical vegetables used are carrot, onion, turnip, beans and celery.

Matignon

Thin even slices of vegetables used as a base to place meat on when roasting. Vegetables normally include carrot, onion and celery.

Mirepoix

A mixture of roughly chopped vegetables which are used as the base of sauces or to enhance the flavour of meat, fish and shellfish dishes. Normally onion, celery and carrot are used and these are slowly cooked in butter until they are very tender. Thyme and bay are often added.

Paysanne

Paysanne cut vegetables may be either squares, triangles, circles or half rounds. In order to cut economically, the shape of the vegetable will decide which shape to choose. All are cut thinly, about 1-2 mm thick.

SOME OF THE FAMOUS VEGETABLES

Cabbage (*Brassica oleracea*)

Popular green cabbages are Polar Green, Green Express, Charmant, Sunup and Belbro. Red types include Ruby Ball, Red Acre and Red Perfection. To buy the cabbage check the firm heads that seem relatively heavy. Leaves should have good colour and be fairly firm, without blemishes or signs of wilting along the edges. Cabbage is a good source of Vitamin C and a source of folacin. Basic ingredient use for salads like green salad, coleslaw and in many hot dishes.

Brussels sprouts (*Brassica oleracea,* var. gemmifera)

Different varieties are Jade E. Lunet, Oliver, Silverstar YT and Valiant. Look for fresh, unfaded green colour with no sign of yellowing. The heads should be dense and firm, the leaves unwilted. Smaller ones are said to have the best flavour. Mainly used in vegetable as side and main dish.

Broccoli

Broccoli is available in different types like broccolini and Italian Green. It is a good source of vitamin C, A and fibres. Always buy the fresh dark green with lots of flower on it.

Radishes (*Raphanus sativus*)

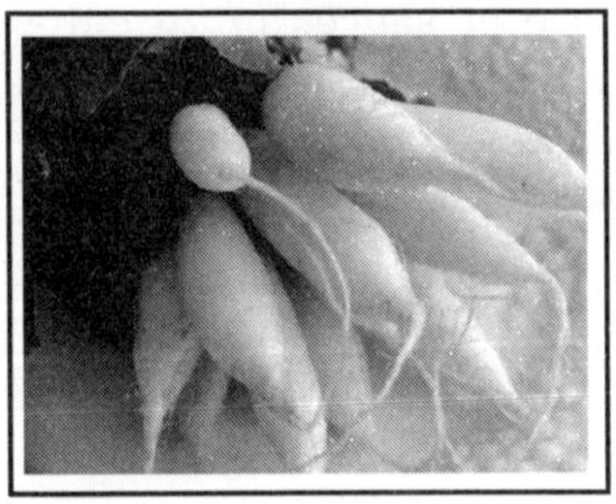

A root vegetable related to the turnip and horseradish family, with a crisp texture and a peppery hot flavour. The most commonly found are the small, round Cherry Belle, the Red Globe radish or the white carrot shaped variety known as Daikon. Can be served as hors d'oeuvres, as complements to salad or sandwiches, or as a garnish, adding a peppery hot flavour. Spring radishes are somewhat milder and are often enjoyed in foods as an ingredient or as a garnish. Winter varieties and are often used as a garnish for food dishes such as fish and poultry, sautéed and braised to be served as a vegetable dish, or diced and added to soups and stews.

When selecting, choose radishes that are firm, crisp, and without blemishes. If the greens are still on the radishes, they should look fresh and green.

Asparagus *(Asparagus officinalis)*

A vegetable with long, tender shoots that are generally categorized as white, purple and green varieties, all belonging to a plant in the lily family. Green asparagus is traditionally the most common variety, while purple or white asparagus is usually available on a limited basis in specialty markets. Asparagus can be boiled, steamed, sautéed, pickled, or served cold. It makes an enjoyable appetizer, or a good complement to salads, vegetable dishes, and soups. Asparagus can also be pureed to be used for soups and soufflés. When selecting asparagus, choose stalks that are firm and crisp with heads that are full and not discolored.

Fresh Beans

Immature and the bean (or seed) and the pod are both very young and tender. This is the stage when the bean and pod are both eaten, either raw or cooked, and they are referred to as fresh, baby or snap beans.

Available in different forms like: Green (French)/Wax/Long Beans. When buying make sure that they are fresh, crispy and raw.

Carrot

This is a plant of the parsley family with feathery green leaves and an orange root that can be eaten raw or cooked. The most commonly found carrots generally have a long, narrow, cylindrical cone shape root. Carrots are high in sugar and fiber and are an excellent source of carotene, which gives the carrots their bright orange colour. Carrots are also a good source of other nutrients, such as potassium, calcium, magnesium, vitamin A, and folic acid. Carrots can be eaten raw or cooked. Raw carrots are eaten as a snack, or an appetizer, and are sliced, chopped, or grated to add to salads. They can be cooked using many different methods, such as boiling, steaming, sautéing, roasting or grilling.

When cooked, carrots are eaten as a side dish on their own or cooked with other vegetables. They are also often added to other dishes, such as stir fries, casseroles, quiches, omelets, soups, and stews. The sweet flavour of carrots also makes them a popular ingredient in baking cakes, muffins, breads, and cookies.

When selecting, look for carrots that are uniform in colour from top to bottom and whose skin is smooth and free of cracks. The carrots may be slightly green at the crown but a dark coloring at the crown indicates that the carrots are getting old. Generally the carrots found readily available are long and slender but there are also varieties that are short and fat. Whatever variety is being purchased, all the carrots should be uniform in size, shape and colour. When selecting carrots that still have the stems attached, select those that have fresh looking greens. Avoid carrots that have begun to sprout, that have blemishes, soft spots, or large green areas at the crown, and any that have become limp.

Various varieties are: Imperator, nantes, danvers, Chantenay, Maroon Carrots, True Baby Carrots.

Cauliflower

Cauliflower consists of undeveloped white florets attached to a single stem that form a compact, cabbage-like head, called a curd. The curd is generally 6 to 7 inches in diameter. The white head is surrounded by long green leaves that are attached to the stem. The leaf, stalk and florets can be eaten raw or cooked. Raw, it is eaten on its own accompanied by a dip or cut up and added to salads. When cooked, it can be eaten as a side dish, alone or topped with a sauce, such as au gratin, hollandaise, or Mornay. It is also often added to other dishes, such as stir fries, pasta, quiches, omelets, soups, and stews. Cauliflower can be interchanged for broccoli in most recipes.

When selecting, look for thick, compact, heads of creamy white florets. The head should be heavy for its size and the leaves surrounding it should be bright green and not be showing signs of wilting. Avoid cauliflower that is blemished or whose florets have started to turn brown, which is a sign that the head is getting old. Check the bottom of the head, if it is soft, it is no longer fresh. If the florets have started to flower they are overripe. Keep in mind that the size of the cauliflower head is no sign of quality.

Garlic (*Allium sativum*)

A bulbous plant consisting of single head containing smaller bulbs or cloves individually wrapped in papery skins, which are all wrapped tightly together with another layer of dry papery skin, forming the bulb head. Garlic, like onions, leeks and scallions, are part of the allium family. Garlic, one of the most important and widely used seasonings for food dishes, is available fresh or dried. Garlic is most often used as a flavoring agent but can also be eaten as a vegetable. It is used to flavour many foods, such as salad dressings, vinaigrettes, marinades, sauces, vegetables, meats, soups, and stews. It is often used to make garlic butter and garlic toast. Store fresh garlic in a cool, dark, dry place that is well ventilated for 4 to 6 months, but is best when used within a few weeks. When the cloves have been removed, they can be stored frozen for several months. If garlic has been chopped, minced, or prepared in any way, it should be refrigerated.

Various types are: green garlic, elephant garlic, Rocambole,

Lettuce

A family of vegetables consisting of five varieties classified according to shape and growth. Vitamin A and potassium are the most notable nutrients in lettuce. The darkest green varieties provide the highest levels of Vitamin A. The five varieties are crisp head, summer head butterhead, leaf and cos or romaine,

used in salads, cooked vegetable dishes, and is commonly used on sandwiches. When purchasing lettuce, look for freshness, selecting lettuce that does not have wilted and discolored leaves.

Crisphead

Crisphead ('cabbage lettuce'), this type is referred to as 'iceberg' lettuce, as it is so crisp and has such a white, crisp, densely packed heart. Varieties are: Great Lakes, Webb's Wonderful, Saladin

Summer Crisp

One of the best lettuce types, Although variable between the various varieties, overall it is perhaps intermediate between the crisphead and the loose leaf lettuce. The outer leaves are thick, crisp and flavorsome. Varieties are: Centennial, Victoria.

Butterhead

This lettuce has thick but soft and tender leaves forming a cream coloured, soft, blanched heart. The outer leaves are large and ruffled.. Butterheads are rarely bitter, quick maturing, more tolerant of less than ideal soil and weather conditions than crispheads,

Example - Buttercrunch, Deers Tongue, Dolly, Merveille Des Quatre Saisons, Perella-Red, Sangria , Tom Thumb.

Lettuce romaine

Summer crisp lettuce

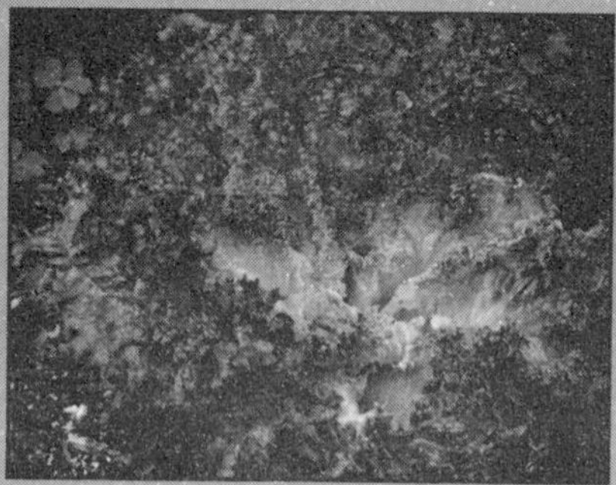

Lollo russo lettuce

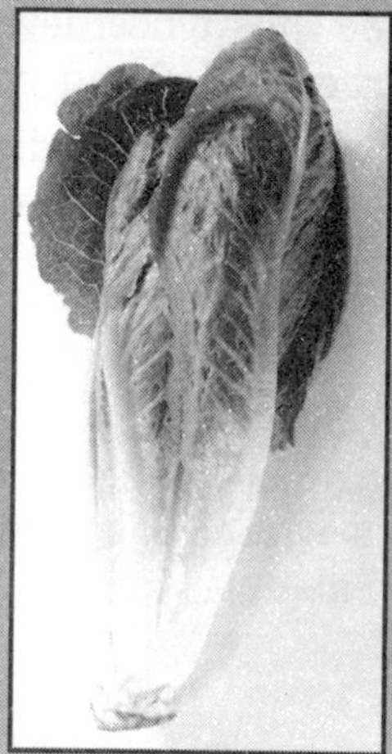

Cos lettuce

Butter crunch

Lettuce leaf

Loose-leaf

These are the simplest form available They form no heart or head, and are, as the name implies, a cascade of loose leaves, which may be picked without cutting the whole plant. They have various shape like thick leaves, thin leaves, savoyed leaves like a silver beet leaf, flat leaves, red, green, frilled, cut, curled, and so on. Others, such as 'lollo rosso', a highly attractive lettuce, looks great as a garnish.

Example - Lollo Rosso, Black Seeded Simpson, Grand Rapids T.B., 'Lovina', Lollo Biondo-A Loma, Oak Leaf, Prize Head, Royal Oak Leaf, Salad Bowl, Simpson Elite, Tango

Cos

Cos (syn 'romaine') originally from the island of Cos in the Mediterranean, this type of lettuce is very upright and columnar, forming a particularly sweet creamy white crisp heart, surrounded by sturdy outer leaves. Fairly demanding to grow, in terms of being unforgiving of poor conditions (a bitter reward), and poorly adapted to hot weather. Some claim this type to be the sweetest and best tasting of all when grown well. All things being equal, in hot weather, the crispheads are the slowest to bolt, then the summer crisps, the bostons, the leaf lettuces and finally the cos types.

Examples - Diamond Gem, Little Gem, Rosalita, Rouge D'hiver, Paris White

Mushrooms

The mushroom is a part of organisms called fungi. It is similar to a plant but lacks chlorophyll, so they cannot produce food for themselves through photosynthesis. The mushroom is a decomposer that absorbs nutrients from materials such as compost, leaves, decaying wood, and soil. There are many types of mushrooms, varying in size, shape and colour, with surfaces that range from smooth and silky to pitted and honeycombed.

Oyster mushroom

Button mushroom

The most common and readily available are the cultivated white mushrooms, which have a mild flavour and can be used in many types of dishes. Wild mushrooms, such as chanterelle, morel, portobello and oyster, will provide a more intense and exotic flavour. Generally, mushrooms contain 90 percent water and have few calories. The fat and carbohydrate content is minimal and they do not contain any cholesterol. They are rich in protein and contain vitamins such as B, C and D, while a few contain vitamin A. Mushrooms can be fried, sautéed, or stir-fried on their own and eaten as a side dish or used to top an entrée. Mushrooms are also popular as an ingredient in salads, soups, sauces stir-fries, meat dishes, and other main dishes.

Morel

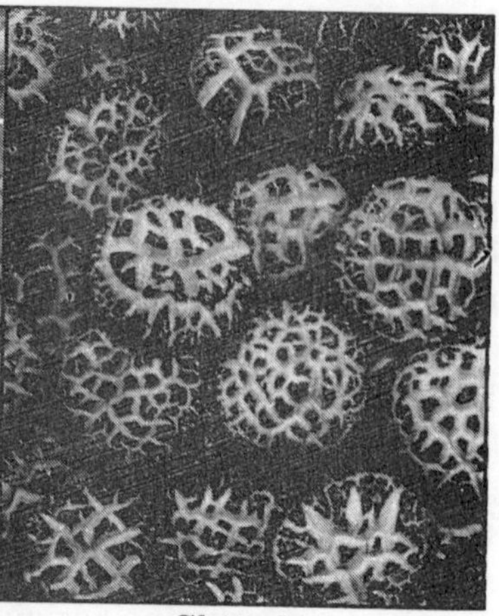

Shiitake

Truffle

When selecting, choose mushrooms that are firm, fresh and free of blemishes. Check underneath their caps for tightly closed brown gills and be sure the surface of the cap is not dried and woody on the edges. Also look for slimy or sticky surfaces and for any coloring that is not normal. When buying dried mush-rooms, check the package and if they are crushed into little pieces, do not buy them

Various types are cremini, button, wild, cup, enoki, morel, oyster and many other

Onions (*Allium cepa*)

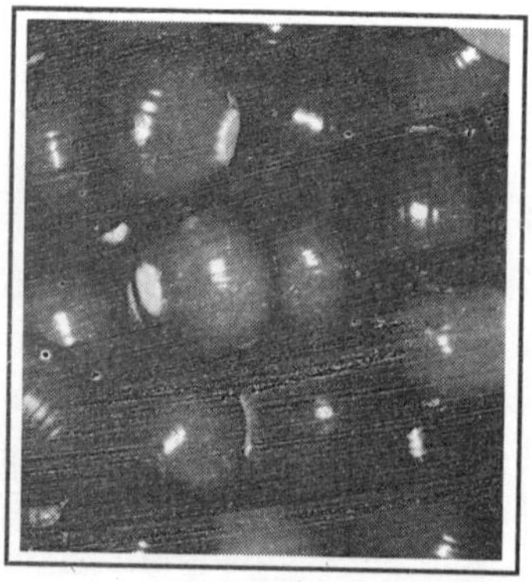

A vegetable, which belongs to the lily family of plants, that is grown for its edible bulb, which most often serves to flavour a variety of foods. Onions are categoriz-ed as being either green or dry onions. Common varieties that are eaten raw or are used to flavour soups and salads include white *Lisbon* and *Ishikura*. There are a wide variety of shapes and sizes, ranging from small round pearl onions to the larger spherical-shaped Spanish onions. The dry onion can be classified as either a sweet or storage onion and are most often sold as a red, yellow or white onion. Sweet onions have higher water content and are served either raw or lightly cooked. Storage onions contain high sulfur content and less moisture, so they can be kept in storage for longer periods of time. The storage onion is used in cooking, providing a sharper and more flavorful taste than sweet onions. Also they play a very important role in Indian Cuisine speciality in the preparation of gravies.

Peas

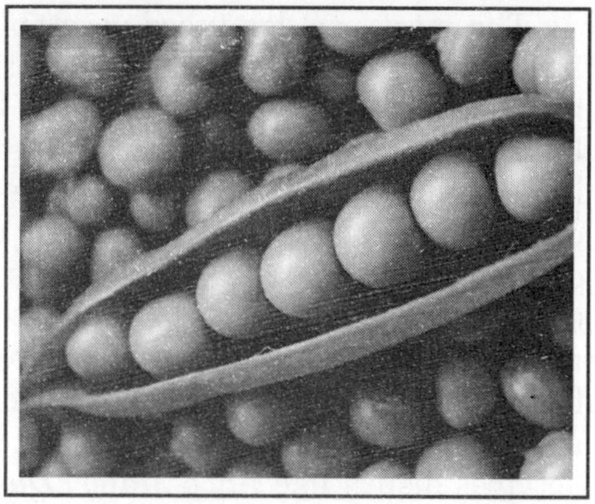

Varieties of small round legumes that are typically classified as fresh, field or pod peas. The fresh pea is a small, round green vegetable, which is grown in a pod and is generally harvested in the early summer. The fresh pea is grown to be removed from the pod and eaten raw or cooked. Field peas, unlike fresh peas, are grown to be dried and then split or used whole for use in purées, soups and food dishes requiring thickening. Pod peas, such as the snow or sugar snap pea are grown to be eaten with both the pod and the pea together, either raw as a fresh pea or cooked. Peas can be eaten raw or cooked, which sweetens them slightly. Peas are eaten on their own as a vegetable dish or added to other vegetables, salads, stir-fries, savory dishes, soups, and stews. Peas can be used as a substitution in most recipes that call for green beans.

Fresh peas: Select peas with smooth, bright green pods that contain a good number of seeds that are small in size.

Pod peas: Select peas with bright green, crisp pods that are not damaged, soft or shriveled. Snow peas should have flat pods with tiny seeds that are barely visible. Sugar snap peas should have mature seeds that are large enough to make the pod appear bumpy.

Capsicum (peppers)

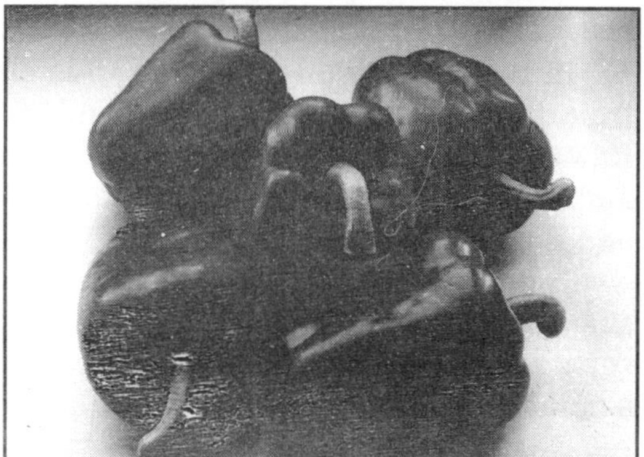

Capsicum (peppers)

A sweet pepper is a mild to sweet flavored pepper that can be eaten raw or cooked. Some varieties have a sweet but bitter taste. The different varieties vary in size, shape, thickness and colour. The most common colour is green at maturity and red when allowed to fully ripen. Some other common maturity colors are ivory, yellow, orange, purple and brown but the majority turn red when allowed to ripen. A pepper has the strongest taste when considered mature, but not fully ripe. If the peppers are not harvested when mature but are allowed to ripen on the vine, their taste will become progressively mild and sweet until they are fully ripened

When selecting, choose those with shiny, even colored skins that are not blemished or bruised. Avoid peppers with shriveled skins.

Potatoes

The most popular tuber vegetable in the world. It is available in hundreds of varieties, which vary in size, shape, taste, colour, and starch content. Potatoes contain 20% indigestible starch, which makes it necessary to cook them in some manner before consuming. Potatoes can be cooked using most any cooking method desired. They are also converted into commercial products, such as potato chips, instant mashed potatoes, canned new potatoes and many frozen products including French fries, hash browns, and stuffed baked potatoes. Indians are also fond of potatoes dishes like *Alloo Mater*, *Dum Alloo*, *Alloo* with vegetables, stuff etc. Potatoes are often served as a side dish to meat and poultry, but they are also used as a significant ingredient in many dishes, such as stew, soups, scalloped potatoes, and other casserole type dishes. They are also converted into commercial products, such as potato chips, instant mashed potatoes, canned new potatoes and many frozen products including French fries, hash browns, and stuffed baked potatoes.

When selecting, choose those that are firm and plump, avoiding those that have shriveled skins, sprouting eyes, soft spots, blemishes and green spots

Types available are long potatoes, round potatoes, russet potatoes, red potatoes, Yukon gold potatoes, creamer, potatoes new potatoes, finger potatoes many more

Tomatoes

In the plant family, the tomato is classified as a fruit (berry), but when eaten it resembles a vegetable. Raw or cooked tomatoes have a sweet, acidic flavour and a juicy flesh. Available in different sizes, shapes and colors, tomatoes can be large and round like, oval shaped as are Roma or plum tomatoes, pear shaped like pear tomatoes, or small and bite size, such as cherry and grape tomatoes. Tomatoes are available in a range of colors, such as green, yellow, red, and purple.

They are often eaten raw as a garnish for salads and appetizers, sliced thinly for sandwiches, or added to various pasta, meat, and vegetable dishes. They are also used in soups, stews, and sauces. When selecting tomatoes, choose those that are brightly colored, plump, heavy and whose skins are not shriveled. Avoid those with blemishes, bruises, or cracks. Ripe tomatoes should yield to light pressure, but not be too soft. If purchasing tomatoes that will not be used for a few days, select those that are a lighter red and allow them to ripen fully by storing them in a cool area out of the direct sunlight. Canned tomatoes that have been processed are available in a variety of flavors and forms. They can be purchased in the can as whole, diced, stewed, chopped, pureed, paste, or a sauce form.

Types: plum, cherry, grape and pear tomatoes.

FRUIT

Fruits are be classified in various ways:

1. citrus fruits-like orange, grapefruit, sweet lime, lemon, Malta etc.
2. stone fruits-like cherry, damson, golden gage
3. berries like strawberry, raspberry, blueberry, cran-berry, black-current, gooseberry, logan berry etc.
4. apple-apple, pear, seckel
5. grapes-like red and white
6. melons-like sweet melon (cantaloupe, honey dew, canary, casaba, galia etc.), sweet melon
7. tropical fruit- like pineapple, papaya, mango, kiwi fruit, , guava, bananas,
8. exotic fruit- custard apple, lychee, loquat, star fruit, rambutan, pepino,
9. others like figs, dates, pomegranate, avocado,

Storing of Fruits and Vegetables

Fruits and vegetables are composed of living tissues and they continue to respire. Vegetables are alive and breathing, with a continued need for oxygen. Although Fruits and vegetables should be purchased fresh and one must try to do the minimum storing as Fruits and vegetables loose their freshness with every hour.

1. **Store Fruits and vegetables correctly.** Storage conditions greatly affect shelf life. As soon as possible after purchase and cleaning the produce should be transferred to the correct storage conditions. Vegetables should be stored between 10-16 °C.
2. **Arrange properly.** Don't overpack the refrigerator, air must be able to circulate effectively otherwise hot spots will develop.
3. **Storage area should be clean.** Decaying or rotting produce releases ethylene. Ethylene hastens both ripening and deterioration.
4. Vegetables such as lettuce, spinach, coriander are best refrigerated in a plastic bag, are most frequently supplied bulk in a crate
5. Vegetables must be handled with care by everyone in the chain from supplier to plate.

6. **Buy produce in plastic crates.** They are generally cleaner and protect the product better
7. All Fruits and vegetables should be stored separately. Special care must be taken for

Apple

A round or oval shaped fruit that is harvested from lower growing trees found in most of the temperate regions of the world. The fruit has a thin skin that may range in colour from shades of green, yellow, and red or any combination of these. The flesh is generally off-white or cream colored and is very juicy. They are generally sweet flavored but may be slightly sour, tart, or even a bit bland depending on the variety. Among the many varieties of common apples are the Braeburn, Cortland, Fuji, Gala, Granny Smith, Golden Delicious, Red Delicious, Jonathan, Jonagold, McIntosh, and Pacific or Southern Rose

Apples can be eaten plain, made into sauce or jelly, or they can be included in a variety of salads, meat dishes, pies, and other desserts. As a dried fruit, apples can be added to a variety of baked goods or in a fresh form, they can be used to produce juice, vinegar, cider, and alcoholic beverages, such as hard cider and apple brandy. To determine the best variety of apple to use for your needs.

Place apples in a perforated plastic bag, sprinkle with water and store in the coldest area of the refrigerator for 2 to 3 weeks. Apples give off a gas called ethylene that speeds up ripening, so they should be kept away from other fruits and vegetables to prevent them from ripening prematurely. Apples can be stored at room temperature for a short period of time but should be checked regularly because they will ripen more rapidly than if stored in the refrigerator. To store fresh picked apples for a long period of time, wrap them in paper and place folded side down in a single layer on a tray. Store in a cool, dark, dry place. The ideal temperature for storage is between 32°F and 40°F. Check frequently to see if any apples have begun to rot. Dried apples can be stored in a sealed plastic bag in the refrigerator for an indefinite period of time.

Apricot

The Apricot (*Prunus armeniaca*, "Armenian plum" in Latin, syn. *Armeniaca vulgaris* Lam., Armenian: *"Tsiran"*) is a species of *Prunus*, classified with the plum in the subgenus *Prunus*. The native range is somewhat uncertain due to its extensive prehistoric cultivation, but most likely is India.

VARIOUS VEGETABLES AND THEIR CUTS

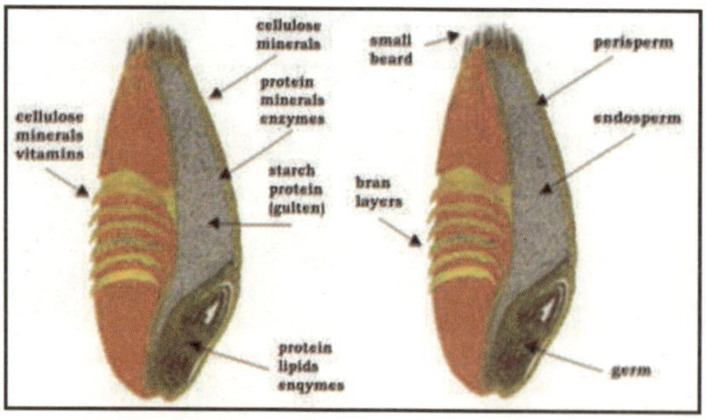
cellulose
minerals
protein
minerals
enzymes
cellulose
minerals
vitamins
starch
protein
(gulten)
protein
lipids
enqymes
small
beard
perisperm
endosperm
bran
layers
germ

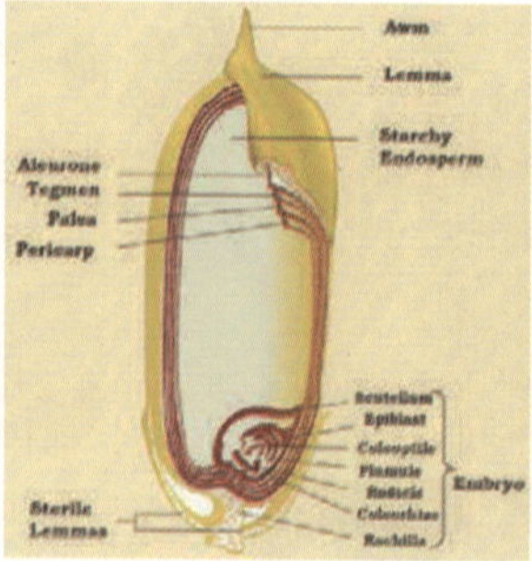
Awn
Lemma
Starchy
Endosperm
Aleurone
Tegmen
Palea
Pericarp
Scutellum
Epiblast
Coleoptile
Plumule
Radicle
Coleorhize
Rachilla
Embryo
Sterile
Lemmas

The fruit is a drupe similar to a small peach, 1.5–2.5 cm diameter (larger in some modern cultivars), from yellow to orange, often tinged red on the side most exposed to the sun; its surface is usually pubescent. The single seed is enclosed in a hard stony shell, often called a "stone", with a grainy, smooth texture except for three ridges running down one side

Grape

A grape is the non-climacteric fruit, botanically a true berry, that grows on the perennial and deciduous woody vines of the genus *Vitis*. Grapes can be eaten raw or used for making jam, juice, jelly, vinegar, wine, grape seed extracts, raisins, and grape seed oil. Grapes are also used in some kinds of candy.

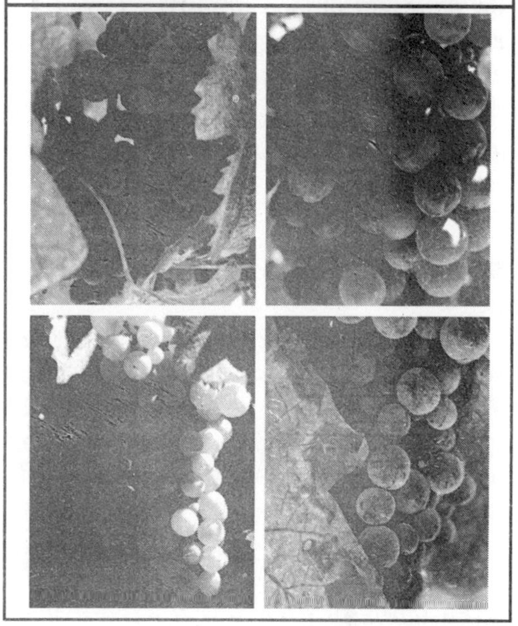

PIGMENTS

Pigment is an enzyme responsible for the colour of meat and vegetables:

1. **Chlorophyll** is the pigment responsible for green colour of vegetables. Vegetables should be cooked with some alkali like soda to retain the colour. High temperature and prolong cooking may cause lightness in colour. That's why green leaf vegetables like spinach, mustard leaf etc. should be blanched uncovered.
2. **Carotene pigment** is responsible for orange colour, i.e. Carrots. Prelong cooking may cause loss of vitamins but colour will retain.
3. **Flavones pigment** is responsible for white colour in cauliflower and radish. Adding lemon will improve the brightness of colour.
4. **Anthocyanins pigment** is responsible for red colour in red cabbage and beetroot.

CEREALS

Key points:

- There are many different types of cereal grains, each having unique properties
- Most cereals are processed to form other foods or ingredients

- Cereals and cereal products are an important source of energy, carbohydrate, protein and fibre. They also contain a range of micronutrients such as vitamin E, some of the B vitamins, sodium, magnesium and zinc.

Cereals are the edible seeds or grains of the grass family. Cereals have been part of the human diet since prehistoric times. Wheat and rice are the most important crops world-wide as they account for over 50% of the world's cereal production. In India wheat and rice are the cereal most commonly used, although many other types of cereals (*e.g.* maize and barley) are used. Each cereal has unique properties which make it suitable for a variety of food products. Cereals require different conditions to grow. For example, rice is grown in damp tropical climates, *e.g.* India and China, and oats in cold temperate climates, *e.g.* Scotland.

Cereals are also known as 'staple foods' as they often make up the bulk of the diet since they are relatively cheap to produce.

TYPES OF CEREALS

Wheat (*Triticum* spp.)

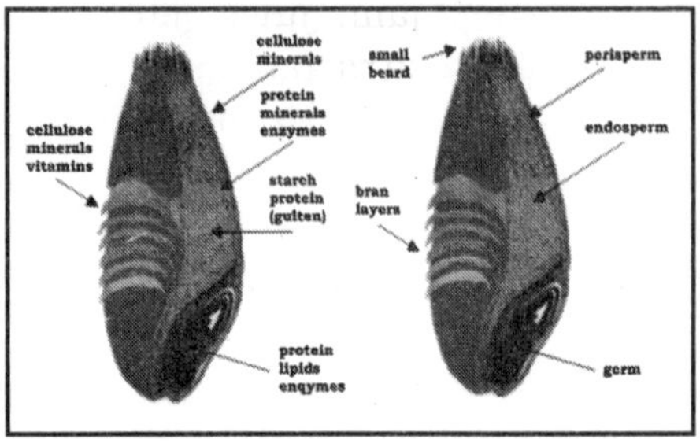

Wheat is grounded to make flour which is used to produce a wide range of flour base products. Wheat, the primary cereal of temperate regions The type of flour produced differs according to the rate of extraction. Semo-lina, whole wheat flour are also made from wheat.

It has various parts (as shown in diagram).

Rice (*Oryza sativa*)

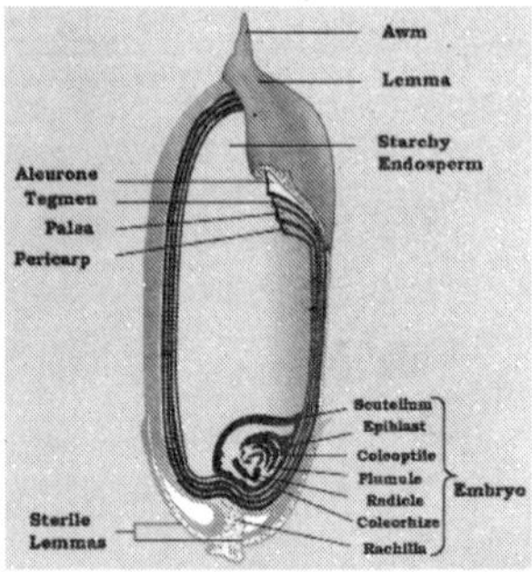

Rice is a plant of the grass family which is a dietary staple of more than half of the world's human population. Rice, the primary cereal of tropical regions and high rainfall, as it is very labor-intensive to cultivate and requires plenty of water for irrigation. In India it is a staple food at many states. The seeds of the rice plant are first milled to remove the outer husks of the grain; this creates brown rice. This process may be continued, removing the germ and the rest of the husk, called bran at this point, creating white rice. The white rice may then be buffed with glucose or talc powder (often called polished rice), parboiled, or processed into flour. The white rice may also be enriched to add nutrients, especially those lost during the milling process.

Brown rice has its outer husk removed, and white rice is milled and polished further to remove the bran and germ. There are many different types of rice, categorised by size, shape and the region where they are grown. Rice can be ground to make flour and is used to make Japanese rice wine (sake).

Maize (or corn) (*Zea mays*)

Maize (or corn) may be processed to make many different food products, corn flour is widely used in Chinese food as thickening agents. It may be milled in a similar process to wheat. Its germ is rich in oil, and can be refined to produce corn oil.

Barley (*Hordeum vulgare*)

Barley is mainly sold as pearl barley, which is the whole grain with its husk removed. It is also used in bread (as flour) and ground as porridge in some countries.

Rye (*Secale cereale*)

Rye contains little gluten, so produces breads with low volume and a dense texture, although in Russia, Poland, Germany and Scandinavian countries it is the major bread grain. Rye is also used to produce crispbread and alcohol.

Oats (*Avena sativa*)

Oats are rolled rather than crushed during processing. Coarse, medium and fine grades of oatmeal are available and are used for porridge and oatcakes, while rolled oats are used for porridge, and oat flour is used for baby foods and for ready-to-eat (RTE) breakfast cereals.

Millet

Millet is the name used for a number of different small-grained cereal grasses, *e.g.* Pearl millet (*Pennisetum glaucum*), Foxtail millet (*Setaria italica*), Proso millet also known as common millet, broom corn millet, hog millet or white millet (*Panicum miliaceum*) and Finger millet (*Eleusine coracana*). These crops are important in parts of Africa and Asia.

Sorghum

Sorghum (also known as great millet, guinea corn, kafir corn, jowar etc. in different parts of the world) is a staple food in many parts of Africa, Asia and parts of the Middle East. It is also used as animal feed in many other countries.

MORE ABOUT CEREALS

Cereals and cereal products are an important source of energy, carbohydrate, protein and fibre. They also contain a vitamin E, some of the B vitamins, sodium, magnesium and zinc. Because of the fortification of some cereal products they also contribute significant amounts of calcium and iron.

They are used in shape of Gelatinization (thickening): When a flour (wheat, corn, rye or rice) is added to a liquid, the starch granules begin to swell on heating. This causes the granules to rupture and starch is released into the liquid. The starch granules absorb liquid, causing the sauce to thicken.

Protein: The amount of protein in each cereal differs (from 6-15% protein) and this affects the final product. Bread, with its characteristic open texture and appearance, relies on high protein flour, *e.g.* strong wheat flour. In products such as cakes, biscuits and pastry, lower wheat flours are used to produce crumbly and light textures.

Storage: Cereals should be kept in a cool dry place. They are prone to infestation by insects if kept for long periods of time.

PASTA

Pasta is an Italian dish made from DURUM flour, egg and oil. Italian food is incomplete without pastas. It can be shaped in many ways-

1. **Spaghetti:** Comes in long straight strands of varying thickness.
2. **Macaroni:** It is a thicker hollow tube, sometimes cut into short lengths. Bucatini, tubetti lunghi, zite & penne are all short macaroni

3. **Lasagne:** It is the widest of ribbon pasta. It comes in flat strips, rectangles or squares with either a smooth or a ridged edge.

4. **Noodles:** Narrow, flat pasta strips that are either straight, ribbon or are folded into a nest shaped mass. Tagliatelli and Fettuccini are the most famous of noodle pasta.
5. **Cannelloni:** These are large hollow tubes that can be stuffed with meat or vegetable mixtures and served with a sauce.

6. **Vermicelli:** Finest ribbon pasta that comes in a nest shaped mass and is mostly used in soups. These are also called Glass Noodles.

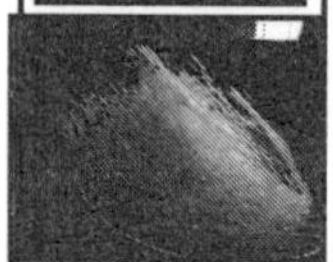

7. **Lumache:** Snail shaped pasta

8. **Conchiglie:** Shells shaped pasta

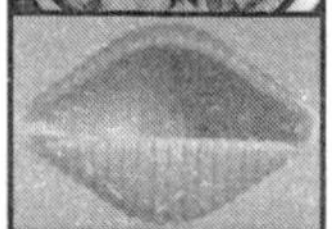

9. **Fussili:** Spiral shaped pasta

10. **Ruotini:** Wheel shaped pasta
11. **Anelli:** Ring shaped pasta

12. **Fiochetti or Farfalle:** Bow shaped pasta.
13. **Ravioli, Cappeletti, Tortellini, Tortelloni or Tortelli are all stuffed pasta**

Styles of Serving Pasta:

(1) **Bolognaise:** Pasta with minced meat sauce.

(2) **Italianne:** Pasta dressed with butter and grated cheese.

(3) **Milanaise:** Pasta with tomato sauce, julienne of ham and tongue.

(4) **Napolitaine:** Pasta with tomato sauce and grated Parmesan cheese (a very hard Italian cheese made from unpasteurized skimmed cow's milk).

(5) **Parmesan, au:** With Parmesan cheese

(6) **Garlic or orange flavour-** sauté in garlic butter or cooked with orange sauce.

Pulses

Pulses are the dried seeds of plants which form pods. They have three types:

1. **Beans.**
   1. Black eyed.
   2. Soya bean.
   3. Red kidncy.
   4. Pinto.
   5. Aduki.
   6. Haricot.
   7. Dutch brown.
   8. Butter.
   9. Soissons
2. **Peas.**
   1. Blue.
   2. Chick.
   3. Split Green.
   4. Split Yellow
3. **Lentils**
   1. Orange
   2. Yellow
   3. Red
   4. Indian brown
   5. Green

QUESTIONS

1. Classify vegetables and explain them.
2. What are the different shapes in which vegetables can be cut?
3. How will you classify fruits?
4. What are cereals and their uses?
5. Explain rice and wheat with diagrams.
6. Explain following terms:
   a) Bulb family,
   b) Endosperm,
   c) Chiffonade,
   d) Tuber,
   e) Juliennes,
   f) Semolina.

12

Fish and Meat

OBJECTIVES

After studying this chapter student should know:

1. Types of fish.
2. Cuts of fish.
3. Shellfish and types.
4. Beef structure.
5. Cuts of beef, pork, veal.
6. Types of chicken and cuts.
7. Games and types.

FISH AND MEAT COOKERY

In this chapter you will learn about the specific cuts of fish beef, veal, lamb, and pork typically used in food service operations, as well as some basic butchering procedures. Recipes using these cuts and applying the various cooking methods are included at the end of each of those chapters.

Fish - Fish is an aquatic creature and around 200, 000 varieties of fish are available in the water. They have two types:

1. finfish
2. shellfish

Mackerel

Pomfret

Prawn

Lobster

Finfish

Finfish are divided into whitefish and oily fish.

Whitefish are sometimes referred to as "lean fish" because all the oils are contained in the liver, which is removed during **gutting** (a process of removing heart and lever of fish after cutting).

Whitefish are further sub-divided into:

Round Whitefish—Examples include cod, haddock, hake and pollock.

Flat Whitefish—Examples include plaice, lemon sole, brill, turbot and black sole.

Oily fish are so called because the oils are distributed throughout the flesh of the fish. Mackerel, herring, salmon and trout are examples.

Shellfish

Shellfish are broadly divided into three catego-ries—mollusks, Cepha-lopods and crustaceans.

Molluscs

Molluscs can be divid-ed into two categories:

Uni-valve molluscs have one shell—periwinkles, whelks and limpets. These molluscs can be found on the seashore.

Bi-valve mollusks have two shells hinged at one end—mussels, oysters and scallops.

Cephalopods have no outer shell, just a single internal one called a pen. Examples include squid, octopus and cuttlefish.

Crustaceans are covered with hard, segmented shells and flexible joints. Examples include prawns, shrimp, crab and lobster.

CUTS OF FISH

Darne

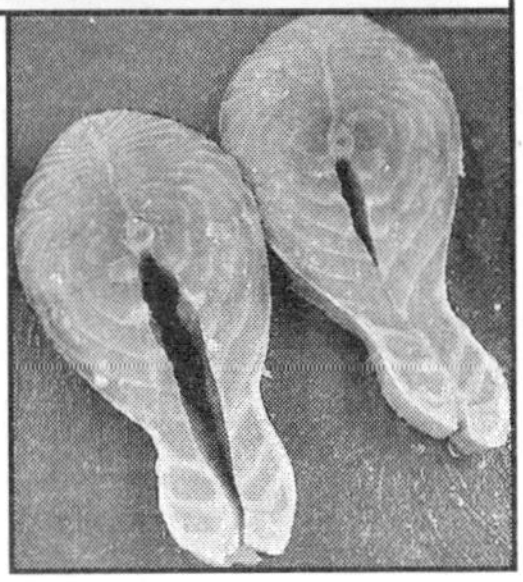

A slice of round fish cut on the bone; they are usually B.B.Q, grilled, pan fry, en papillote, poach, baked.

Tronçon

Slice of (large) flat fish cut on the bone; B.B.Q, grilled, pan fry, en papillote, poach, baked.

Fillets

It is a boneless without skin fleshy part A round fish yields two fillets and a flat fish four, B.B.Q, grilled, pan fry, en papillote, poach, deep fried (with coating).

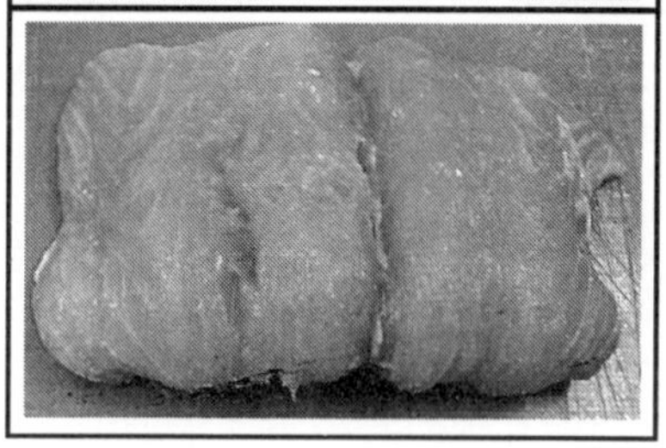

Plaited

This is also known as en tresse; fillet of fish cut lengthwise into three and plaited; Shallow fried, pan fried and deep fried.

Delice

Fillet of fish neatly folded in half; poached.

Paupiettes

Fillet of fish, spread with a farce and rolled; Poached.

Goujons

Goujons and goujon-ettes. Strips of fillet cut 8 ×.5 cm; usually Deep fried (with coating), stir fry.

Goujonettes

As for goujons but half the length; Deep fried (with coating), stir fry.

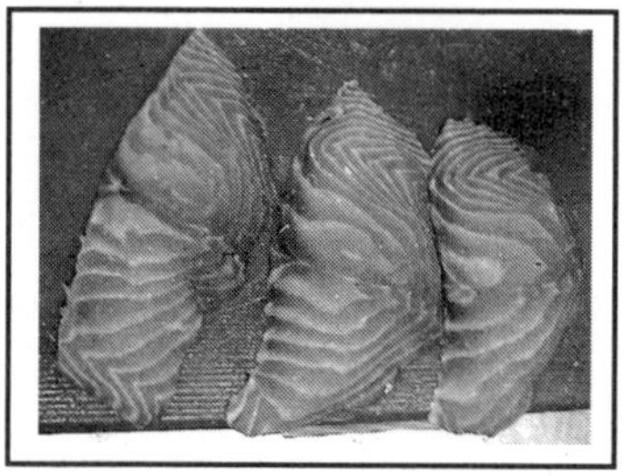

Supremes

Prime cuts of fillet without bone and skin; B.B.Q, grilled, pan fry, en papillote, poach, deep fried (with coating).

NUTRITIONAL VALUE

Fish is rich in protein from 1 to 20% depending upon the species and the season of the year.. Apart from this Fish contains essential minerals, vitamins and fats. Shellfish and salt-water fish are rich in zinc, calcium, iodine and fluorine.

Fish is also a satisfactory source of magnesium, phosphorus, iron and copper. A fatty fish such salmon, mackerel and sardine will supply about 10% of the daily allowance of Vitamin D. Fish and shellfish have high levels of poly-unsaturated fatty acids (PUFA), especially Omega-3 fatty acids, a rare and important for cardiac patient which tend to lower blood cholesterol.

Storage of Fresh Fish

If stored properly as cover with ice/store in chiller immediately the maximum shelf life of fish is up to 10-12 days.. Therefore, it is important to ensure that your suppliers protect and maintain the quality of their product.

The ideal temperature for storage is 0°C or below, this will minimise the activity of enzymes and bacteria. Therefore chiller thermostats should be set at 0°C or -1°C, between -1°C and -5°C fish only partially freezes; this causes a disruption of cell membranes and speeds up enzyme activity and deteriation.

Purchasing

When buying whole fish, it is important to be able to judge which is the freshest fish. The general appearance of the fish, especially the eyes of whole fish and the smell of the fillets are very important. Listed below are the signs to look for that will tell you how long or how well the fish has been stored

- **Eyes** : Black pupil, translucent cornea
- **Skin** : should be covered with fresh sea slime or be smooth and moist, have a good sheen with no abrasions or bruising and no discolouration.
- **Gills** : bright red in colour with no bacterial slime
- **Flesh** : firm, translucent and resilient; so when you apply pressure the impression disappears quickly, the fish should not be limp.
- **Scales** : flat, moist and plentiful
- **Smell** : pleasant and fresh with no hint of ammonia or sourness

The following steps are also recommended for maximum shelf life:

1. Always wash fish to remove scales or foreign matter
2. Always gut fish before storage to avoid the deteriation..
3. Prepare storage container by : place fish on plastic sheeting, cover with another sheet of plastic and cover with ice from the both side.

4. If the fish has been stored on ice for more than two days wash the fillets before cooking.

Freezer Burn

If the temperature fluctuates and there is air present inside the wrapping. Freezer burn or dehydration occurs during frozen storage many times the wrapper may be cooler than the fish and there is no moisture in the fish and condense on the inside of the wrapper. This moisture forms ice crystals in the package and the surface of the fish becomes white and dehydrated. The flesh when cooked becomes spongy and dry.

MEAT

Meat term applied to beef, lamb, pork and others red meat animal. Animal is humanely killed and the meat is prepared in hygienic condition. The skin or hides are removed and innards are taken out. Carcass and offal's are put aside.

Tenderness of meat depends upon meat, age, feeding, hanging and preparation after killing.

Carcass of beef are split into two parts and others are left whole. Lean flesh is composed of muscle, which have numerous bundle of fibers held together by connective tissues. Size of these fiber is extremely small specially in tender cut or cut from young animal.

Size of bundle varies with different muscle and determine to some extent the texture of meat.

Two kind of connective tissue are there-

1. yellow (elastine)
2. white (collagen)

Elastine - thick yellow strip that runs along the neck and back of the animal is an example of elastine. It is found in muscles especially in older animal or receiving considerable exercise. It cannot be cooked and should be broken up mechanically by pounding or mincing.

Collagen- white tissue and can be cooked as it changed in moist heat to form gelatin.

Factors affecting the flavour of the meat

1. Older flesh and strong muscle will be dark, thus less tender
2. Male animal is stronger so it is also less tender
3. Well developed muscle will be strong.
4. Longer the meat is hanged, better the flavour to make it soften. Meat should be hanged for 1-3 days at 1°-3°C. (in hot climate 01 day and in cold climate 03 days). To get the effect of enzymes, veal and pork should be hanged for 3-7 days.

5. Sweetness and saltines of blood effect flavour..
6. Age, Sex, Species and Degree of maturity also determine the taste.
7. Fat is important factor to determine the flavour. It is found in exterior and interior of carcass and in the flesh itself. Fat deposit between muscles or between the bundle of fibers is called **marbling.** It shows tenderness, moistness and better flavour. It comes by good feeding.
8. Extractive ness in meat like shin, shank, neck Impart a good flavour and rich stock.

Process of slaughtering:

- Inspection
- Resting of Animal
- Fasting
- Washing
- Stunning
- Sticking

Method of Killing

1. Knocking
2. Carbon Dioxide Chamber
3. Cartridge Pistols
4. Electric Tongs
5. Bleeding

Rigor Mortis

It is the stiffening of meat after the slaughtering due to depletion of energy reserve in meat protein. It cause meat to loose their extensibility and the muscle became stiff. This condition is referred as rigor mortis.

Resolution of Rigor

The time an animal requires to enter into the rigor mortis is highly dependents on the species, the chilling rate of the carcasses from normal body temperatures the process is slower at lower temperature and the amount of stress the animal experience before the slaughtering. Eventually the stiffness in the muscle tissues begins to decrease owing to the enzymatic breakdown of structural proteins i.e. collagen that hold the muscle fibers together. This process goes for many weeks after slaughtering and is termed as aging of the meat. Aging effect produce meats that are more tender and palatable.

Cooking of Meat

Amount of connective tissues present in the meat determine to a great extent the method of cooking. Large amount of tissue require a moist heat, less can be cooked with a dry heat. Long fibers cuts required long cooking like stewing and braising.

Overcooking can destroy the juices of meat.

To retain the juices one must:

1. Temperature must be constant at 149°C for all types of animal except pork (177° C) or high temperature can be given in beginning for 10 minute and then should be cooked on slow fire.
2. Lower oven temperature (171- 177°C) gives a better result then higher oven temperature (218-232°C). As high temperature denatured the protein.
3. For boiling pressure cooker is better. Frozen food should be thawed before cooking.
4. Tenderizer such as papain can be user for softening of the meat. Acid like curd, vinegar, lemon juice also helps in tenderizing.

	Cooking Temp.
• **Fresh beef**	
• Very Rare (au bleu)	below 51° C
medium rare (Saignant)	51° C - 60° C
Medium (a point)	61° C-70° C
Well done (bien cuit)	70° C and above
• **Fresh veal:**	
• Medium	60° C
Well done	70° C
• **Fresh lamb:**	
• Medium	60° C
Well done	70°C
• **Fresh Pork**	75°C & above
• **Poultry:**	
• Chicken, Turkey, Duck, or Goose	70°C

BEEF

Beef is the meat of steer, ox, or cow, and is the most nutritious and largely consumed of all animal foods. Meat is chiefly composed of the albuminoid (fibrin, albumen, gelatin), fat, mineral matter, and water.

The quality of beef depends on age of the creature and manner of feeding. The best beef is obtained from a steer of four or five years. Good beef should be firm and of

COOKING TIME AND TEMPERATURE

Food	Internal Temp.	Approx. Cooking Time
Chicken, whole (1813 gms.)	82.3°C	70-75 mins.
Chicken, breast (1360 gms.)	82.3°C	30-45 mins.
Chicken, thigh (1360 gms.)	82.3°C	60 mins.
Game Hen (907 gms.)	82.3°C	35-40 mins.
Turkey, whole (4535 gms.)	82.3°C	1½ to 2½ hours.
Pork (roast, chops)	71.11°C	20 mins. per grm.
Spare Ribs	71.11°C	30 mins. per grm.
Beef (roasts, burger, steak)	71.11°C medium	15 mins. per grm.
Lamb (roasts, leg, chops)	71.11°C	20 mins. per grm.
Veal	71.11°C	15 mins. per grm.
Fish	Until opaque and flakey	20 mins. total

fine-grained texture, bright red in colour, and well mottled and coated with fat. The fat should be firm and of a yellowish colour. Suet should be dry, and crumble easily. Beef should not be eaten as soon as killed, but allowed to hang and ripen, from two to three weeks in winter, and two weeks in summer.

Meat should be removed from paper as soon as it comes from market, otherwise paper absorbs some of the juices.

Meat should be kept in a cool place. In winter, beef may be bought in large quantities and cut as needed. If one chooses, a loin or rump may be bought and kept by the butcher, who sends cuts as ordered.

Always wipe beef, before cooking, with a cheese-cloth wrung out of cold water, but never allow it to stand in a pan of cold water, as juices will be drawn out.

TERMS ASSOCIATED WITH BEEF

- **Gelatin** is a transparent, tasteless substance, obtained by boiling with water, muscle, skin, cartilage, bone, tendon, ligament, or membrane of animals and in raw state is termed *collagen. By* this process, collagen of connective tissues is dissolved and converted into gelatin. Gelatin is insoluble in cold water, soluble in hot water, but in boiling water is decomposed, and by much boiling will not solidify on cooling. When subjected to cold water it swells, and is called hydrated gelatin.
- **Fat:** Fat is the white or yellowish oily solid substance forming the chief part of the adipose tissue. Fat is found in thick layers directly under the skin, in other parts of the body, in bone, and is intermingled throughout the flesh. Fat as food is a great heat giver and force-producer. *Suet* is the name given to fat which lies about the loins and kidneys. Beef suet tried out and clarified is much used in cookery for shortening and frying.

Blooming

When beef is first cut, it is purple in colour. Within 10 minutes after exposure to air, the myoglobin protein will capture oxygen and the steak will turn a bright red. This is called "blooming."

WEIGHT OF JOINTS AND THEIR PREPARATION

Sticking Piece	10½ kg	stewing and mincemeat
Chuck Ribs	5 kg	Braising, Small Steaks and Stewing
Mid Rib	8 kg	Roasting and Braising
Foreribs	6¼ kg	Roasting and Braising
Wing Ribs	6 kg	Roasting

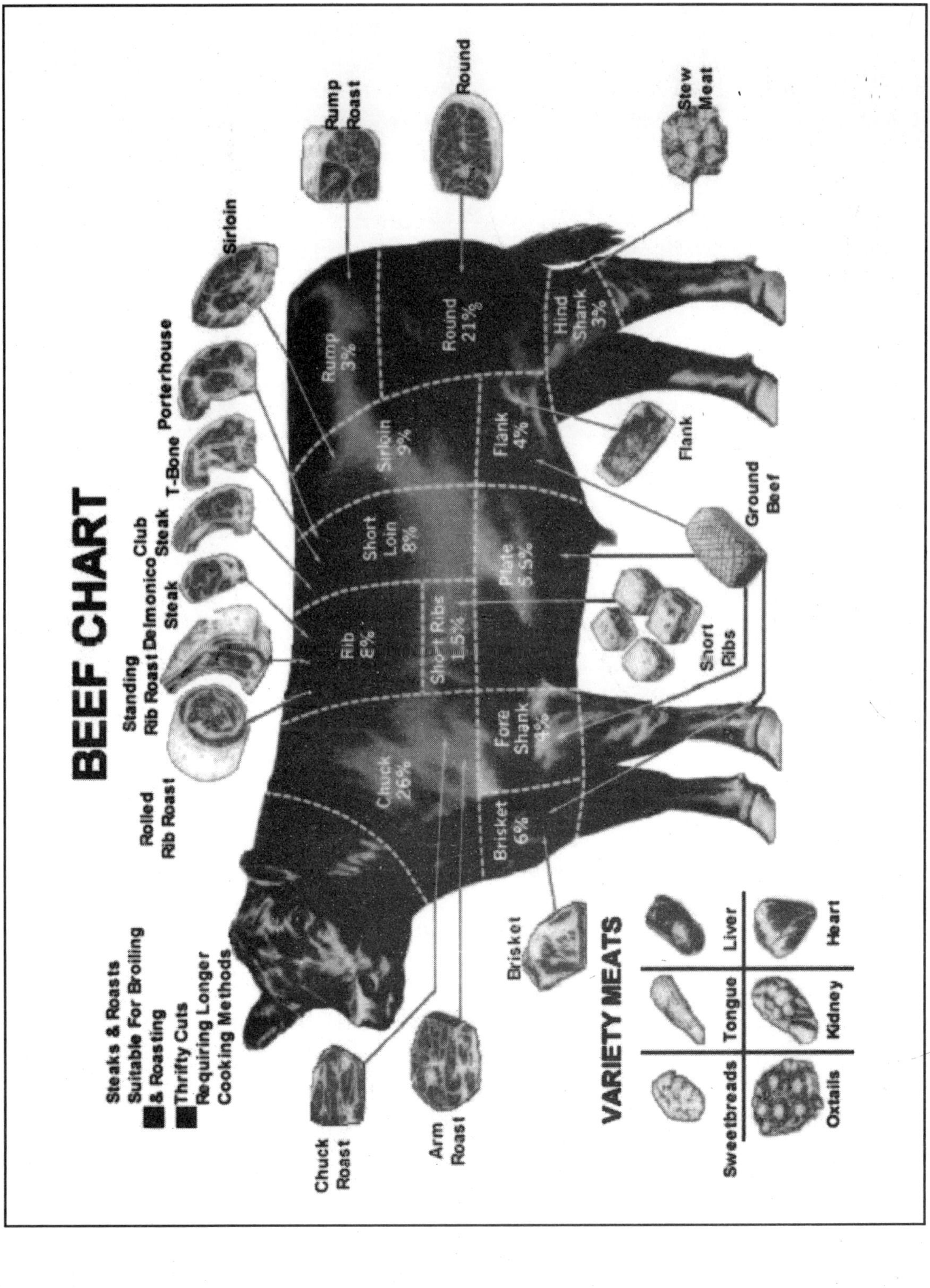
BEEF CHART
Steaks & Roasts Suitable For Broiling & Roasting
Thrifty Cuts Requiring Longer Cooking Methods
Rolled Rib Roast
Standing Rib Roast
Delmonico Steak
Club Steak
T-Bone
Porterhouse
Sirloin
Rump Roast
Round
Stew Meat
Chuck 26%
Rib 8%
Short Loin 8%
Sirloin 9%
Rump 3%
Round 21%
Hind Shank 3%
Flank 4%
Plate 5.5%
Short Ribs 1.5%
Fore Shank 4%
Brisket 6%
Flank
Ground Beef
Short Ribs
Brisket
Chuck Roast
Arm Roast
VARIETY MEATS
Sweetbreads
Tongue
Liver
Oxtails
Kidney
Heart

Sirlion or Half Saddel		9½ kg Roasting Sirloin and Porterhouse Steaks
Fillet	3 kg	Roasting, Grilling
Rump	7 kg	Roasting, Braising steaks gor grilling
Thick Flank	6½ kg	Braising, Steaks prepar-ed for Braising, Stewing
Silverside	10 kg	Braising
Topside	7½ kg	Braising, Stewing, Roast-ing
Thin Flank	4 kg	Stewing
Plate	5¼ kg	Boiling, Stewing
Brisket	6½ kg	Pickling and Pressed Beef Boiling, Finest Pieces are used for corning
Shin and Shank	9 kg	Boiling, Stock and Soup

Other Parts of Beef Creature used for Food

Brains	Stewed, scalloped dishes, or croquettes
Tongue	Boiled or braised, fresh or corned
Heart	Stuffed and braised
Liver	Broiled or fried
Kidneys	Stewed or sautéd as garnish
Tail	Soup and side dish

Suet (kidney suet is the best)—for cooking and tallow

Sign of Quality Beef

1. Fresh beef has a firm cream white colored, brittle in texture fat and older animal should have soft and deep yellow fat. Bright red meat.
2. The best beef is marbled with fine strands of fat, which bastes the meat as it cooks and makes it tender and juicy. Fat should be evenly distributed. Lower grades of beef have thicker marbling or no marbling, so the meat's tougher after you cook it.
3. The colour of meat should be bright red. Cut surfaces that are dull and sticky have been exposed to the air for some time.
4. Lean meat should be firm and elastic to the touch.
5. Any moisture on the cut surface should be watery, not thick and sticky to the touch.

Types of Steaks

Each can be marinated in spices and herbs, acidic fluid, such as Balsamic vinegar or wine, and seasoned with a rub.

1. **Rib steak**: **T-bone steak**: less marbling and less tender than a rib steak.
2. **Strip steak**: tender and lean; can be marinated in both olive oil and an acidic fluid.
3. **Fillet**: lean but very tender. Can be marinated in olive oil because of lack of fat content.

   Fillet or Tenderloin

   This is a very lean and tenderest steak. Full tenderloin runs from the short loin section into the sirloin section. It is found in short loin and sirloin section. This steak is known by a number of names.

   - **Chateaubriand** is head of fillet weigh about 250-900 g. (3.5 cm- 8 cm) long.
   - **Fillet steak** is cut from the upper middle part. Steak is 2 cm. thick and weight around 100- 150 gram.
   - **Tournedos** a round barrel shaped steak cut from lower middle of the fillet and weigh approx 100 g. It is 2.3 cm thick.
   - **Fillet mignon** is tail part of the fillet weigh around 50 gram.
4. **Porterhouse**: a combination of strip and fillet. Can be marinated
5. **Sirloin** and **Flank steak**: tougher than the above steaks. Helps to marinate in an acidic fluid.
6. **Tartar steak** is the finely chopped fillet of beef with chopped onion, parsley and caper and is served with egg yolk in a center.

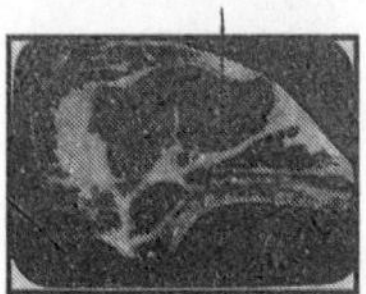
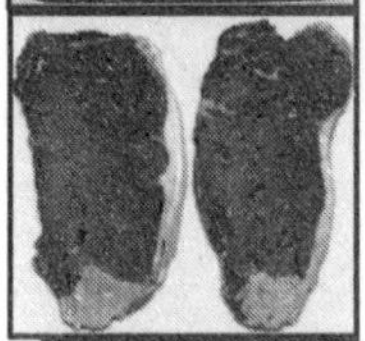

POULTRY

Poultry is the name given to the domestic bird specially bred to be eaten and for their egg.

Food Value

Flesh of poultry is more easily digested then that of the red meat. It contain proteins and is therefore useful for building and repairing body tissues, providing heat and energy. Fat content is low and contains a high percentage of unsaturated fat.

Choosing Poultry

Only young birds are suitable for the roasting, older birds may be boiled, steamed, braised or stewed. For roasting age should be between 9-12 month.

Sign of Young Bird

1. feather especially the quill on wing should be easy to pull out.
2. there should be down all over the body but specially under the wings.
3. no long hair on body.
4. skin should be white, clean and smooth.
5. the feet should be supple (flexible) with smooth even overlapping scale.
6. the comb and wattle should be small.

Quality of Good Chicken

1. Breast should be plum
2. The Vent-end of the breast bone should be pliable.
3. The flesh should be firm.
4. Skin ought to be firm.
5. Skin ought to be white and unbroken with no faint bluish things.
6. The legs should be smooth with small scale and small spur, should be moist.
7. Eyes should be prominent and clean.

Types of Chicken

- **Broiler**: A young chicken usually 6-8 weeks old. A broiler may be of either sex and will be tender - meated. The dressed weight of whole birds will range from 1.3 to 2.0 kg. Broilers are sometimes referred to as fryers.

- **Roaster**: Roasters have the same general characteristics as broilers, except that their dressed weight will range from 2.15 to 3.40 kg. Roasters are processed when they are 8-12 weeks old. Roasters are generally sold as whole birds.

- **Capon**: A surgically castrated male chicken. Capons are grown to the ripe old age of 15 weeks. Dressed weights range from 2.72-4.0 kg. Sometimes called *The Christmas Bird*, capons are meaty, flavorful, tender and highly regarded for holiday meal celebrations. Capons are marketed as whole birds.

- **Rock Cornish Hen**: The offspring of a Cornish chicken or a Cornish chicken crossed with another breed of chicken. The Cornish hen is a young, immature chicken, usually 5-6 weeks old, with a dressed weight of not more than 0.9 grams. (Poussin)
- **Rock Cornish Fryer**: A cross between a purebred Cornish and a purebred Rock Chicken. Rock Cornish Fryers are young, of either sex, and will be tender-meated. The dressed weight will range from 1-2 pounds.
- **Hen**: A mature female chicken. Chickens of this classification are generally spent hens. Referred to as fowl, hens may be further classified as heavy or light depending on their breed or weight. Hens may be used for stewing, baking for use in processed meats.
- **Rooster**: A mature male chicken with coarse skin and toughened, dark meat. Roosters are generally spent breeders that are deboned for use in processed meats.
- **Free range bird** lives a reasonable natural life.
- **Spring chicken** are 4-6 week old also called poussing.

Cuts of Chicken

1. Carcass
2. Drum stick
3. Thigh
4. Wings
5. Winglet
6. Supreme
7. Breast

8 **Piece Cut** - The whole bird is cut into
 2 breast halves with ribs and back portion,
 2 wings,
 2 thighs with back portion and
 2 drumsticks.

The parts may be packaged together and labeled as whole cut-up chicken. These are usually sold without giblets.

PORK

- **Pork:** is meat derived from dressed carcasses of porcine animals. It may be derived from male, female, ridgling or castrated animals.

- **Dressed pork carcass:** means a pork carcass from which the hair, and toenails, developed mammary glands or skin and head have been removed and the carcass has been eviscerated and split.
- **Side of pork:** means one (1) of the two (2) approximately equal portions of a **dressed pork carcass** obtained by a straight cut from the tail to the neck along the median line.
- **Head:** means that portion of the **dressed pork carcass** severed at the atlas joint (first cervical vertebra) and may exclude the **jowl**.
- **Shoulder:** means that portion of the carcass which is separated from the **loin** and **belly** by a straight cut passing posterior to the second (2nd) thoracic vertebra and between the second (2nd) and third (3rd).

HAM AND BACON

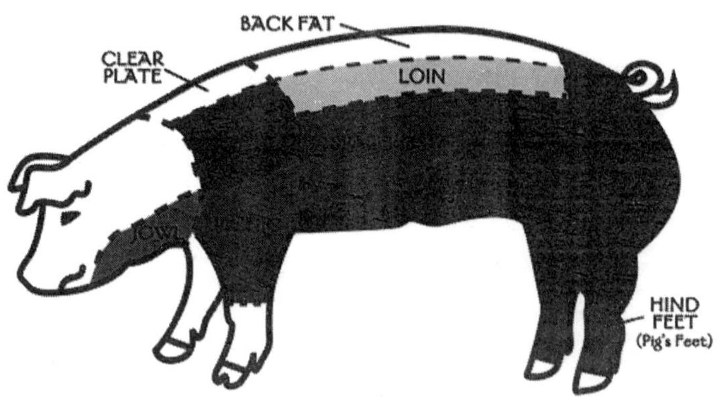

Note: Ham and Bacon (are explained in Chapter Cold

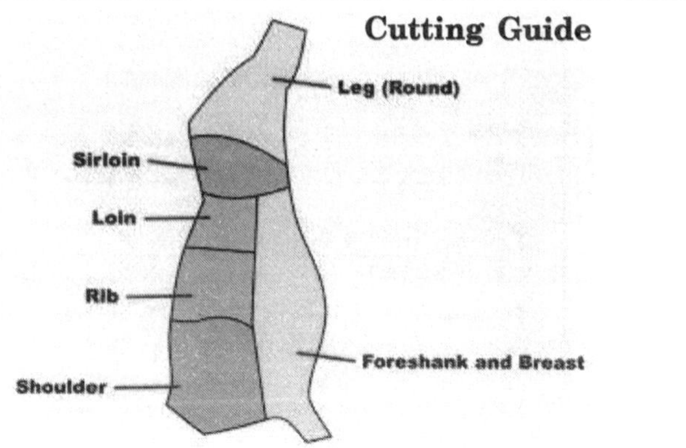

Lamb

Cuts of lamb:

1. Leg
2. Loin (Sirloin Chops)
3. Rib (Rack Or Chops)
4. Breast
5. Neck
6. Shoulder
7. Shank

Veal

Veal is young male animal dairy calves' meat. Male calves purchased by veal farmers are nourished with nutritionally complete milk supplement, until they reach almost five months of age and weigh approximately 250 kg.

Newborn female calves used as future milking cows. However, when male calves are born, since they cannot produce milk, their meat is used for human consumption.

Game

Game refers to animals that are normally raised in the wild. Meat from game tends to be leaner and more flavorful than that from their domesticated counterparts, but it's also much more expensive. It's also tricky to cook well. Tender cuts of game should be cooked very quickly with high heat and served rare, or else the meat will dry out and become tough. Tough cuts should be braised or used as stew meat, and cooked slowly. Most of the game that's available commercially has been ranch-raised, and have a milder flavour than wild game.

Examples are:

Antelope, venison, bear, boar , crocodile, deer meat , grouse, kangaroo, partridge. Pigeon quail and turtle.

Meat Carving

Meat carving is an art which in the past has been quasi-ceremonial and considered to be an integral part of the presentation of a meal

The secret of successful carving lies beneath Good and sharp knives, the proper cutting surface, and knowledge of the anatomy of meat to be carved. Artful carving is the result of experience, knowledge, and good equipment.

The normal thickness of cuts to be carved should be 1/4 to ½ inch for each slice. Some cuts of meat are easier to carve than others.

Degree of cooking also affects the ease of carving. Highly roasted meat due to harder outer crust makes the carving extremely difficult. Poached or braised meat will fall apart when it is carved. Setting of roast meat after cooing will make it firm enough to carve properly.

QUESTIONS

1. What should be checked when evaluating fresh shellfish? Fresh fish/
2. Briefly describe the following terms of fish and shellfish:
   a. Round fish.
   b. Flat fish.
   c. Fish.
   d. Univalves.
   e. Bivalves.
   f. Crustaceans.
   h. Darne
   g. Cephalopods.
3. Explain different cuts of fish.

4. What is the process of aging beef?
5. Explain different cuts of beef, poultry, pork and fish.
6. What is fillet? Describe different parts of it.
7. What is veal? Explain the cuts of veal.
8. What is freezer burn? What precaution you will take while storing the fish and shell fish?
9. Differentiate between:
   a. Capon and free range chicken.
   b. Round fish and flat fish.
   c. Games and domestic animals.
   d. Chateaubriand and fillet steak.
   e. Univalve and bivalve.

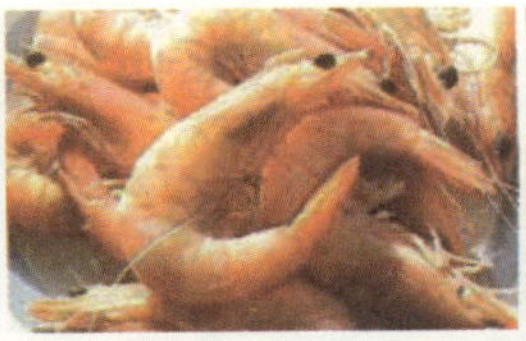

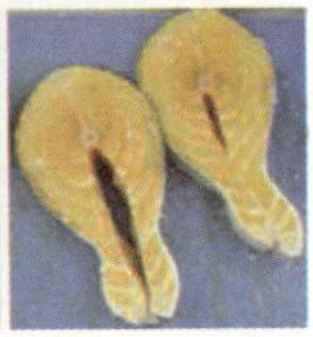
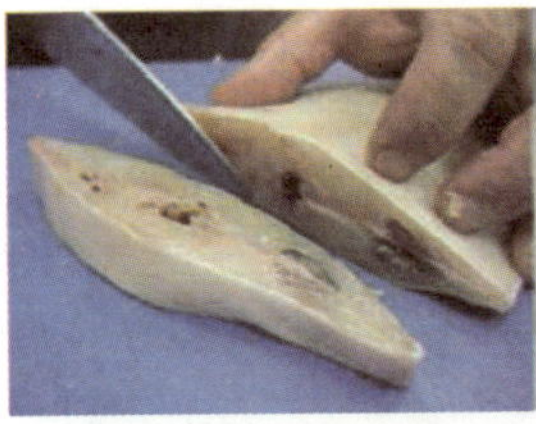

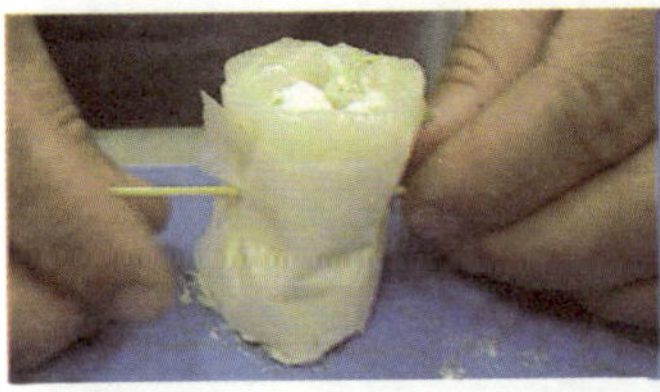
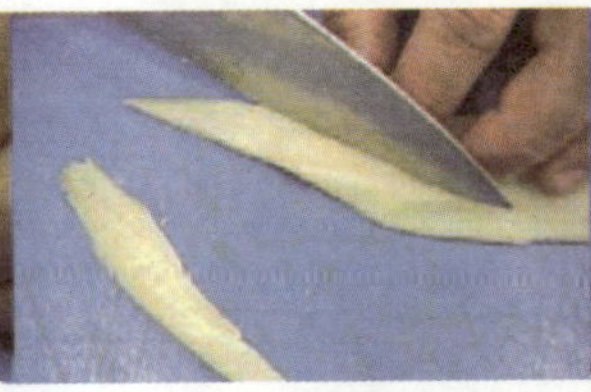

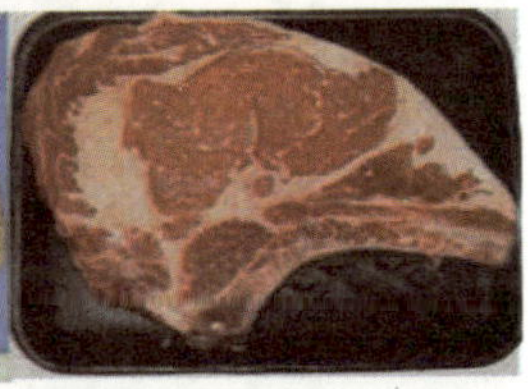
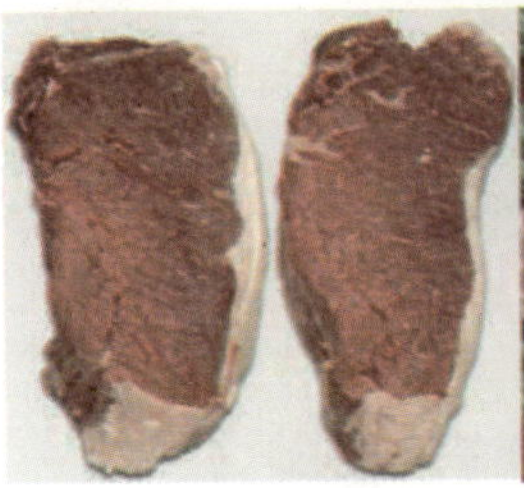

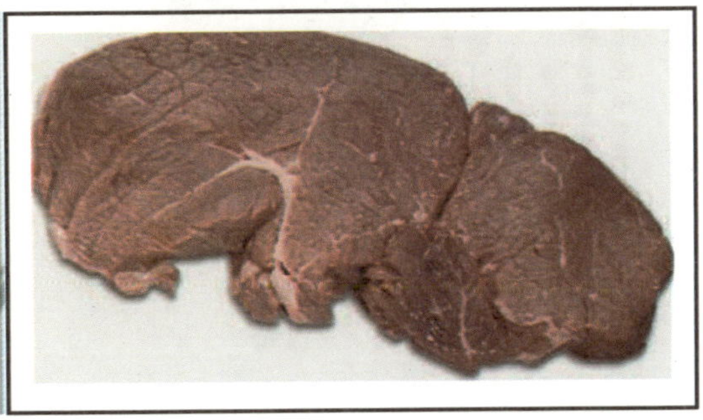

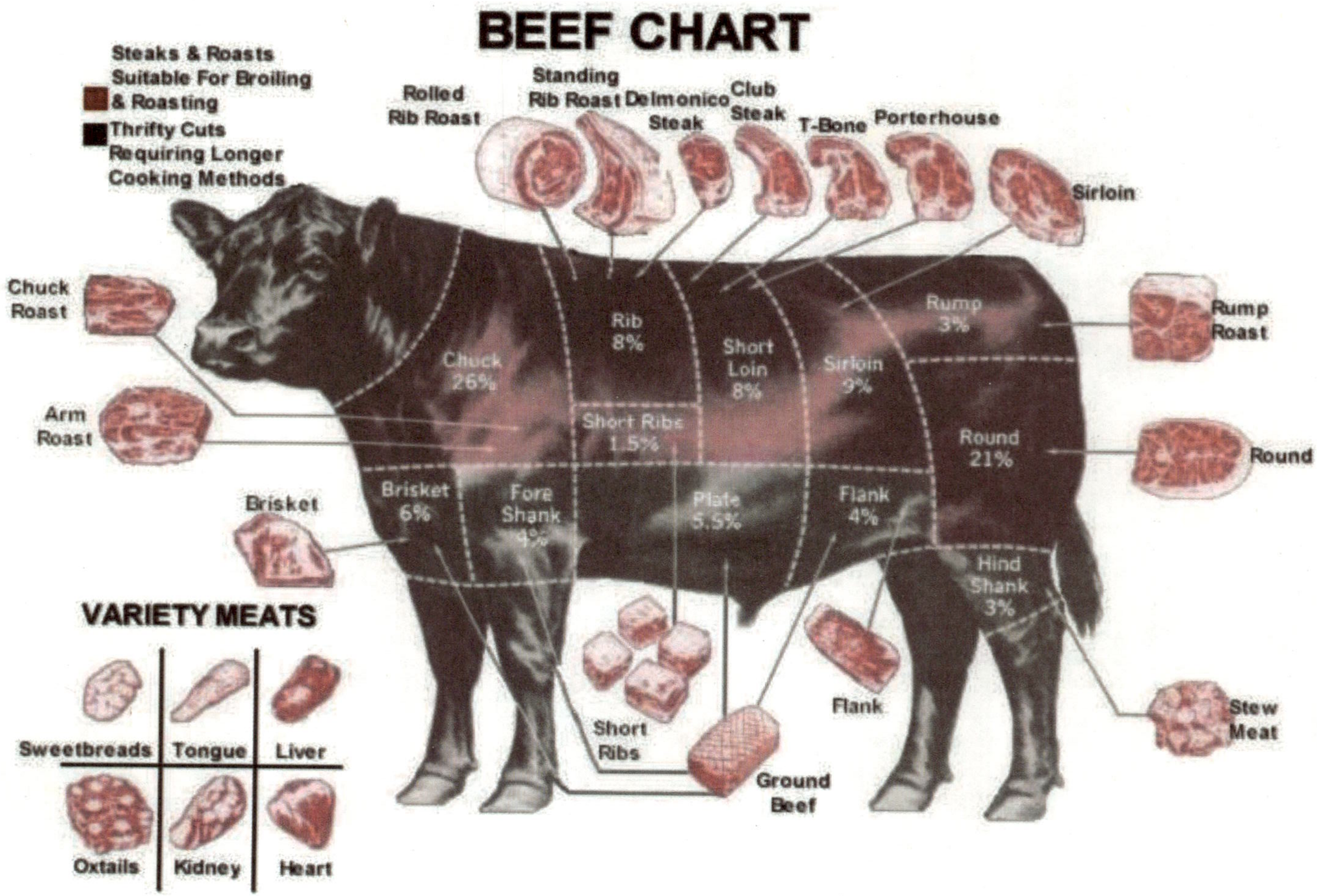

BEEF CHART
Steaks & Roasts Suitable For Broiling & Roasting
Thrifty Cuts Requiring Longer Cooking Methods
Rolled Rib Roast
Standing Rib Roast
Delmonico Steak
Club Steak
T-Bone
Porterhouse
Sirloin
Chuck Roast
Arm Roast
Brisket
Rump Roast
Round
Stew Meat
Flank
Ground Beef
Short Ribs
Chuck 26%
Rib 8%
Short Ribs 1.5%
Short Loin 8%
Sirloin 9%
Rump 3%
Round 21%
Brisket 6%
Fore Shank 4%
Plate 5.5%
Flank 4%
Hind Shank 3%
VARIETY MEATS
Sweetbreads
Tongue
Liver
Oxtails
Kidney
Heart

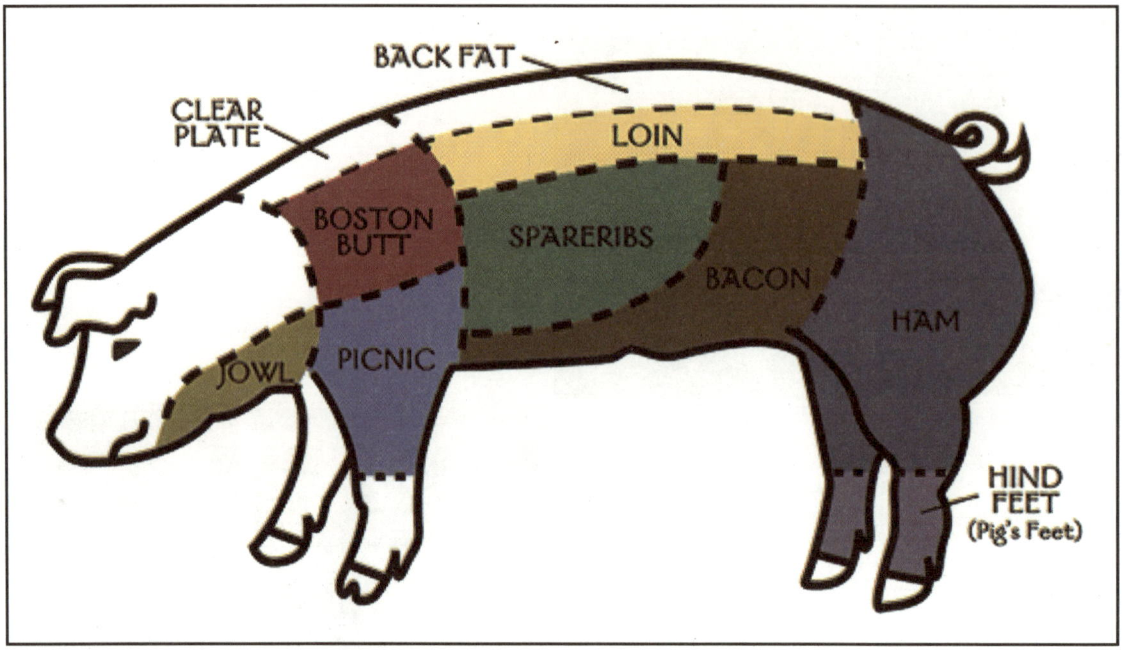
BACK FAT
CLEAR PLATE
LOIN
BOSTON BUTT
SPARERIBS
BACON
HAM
JOWL
PICNIC
HIND FEET
(Pig's Feet)

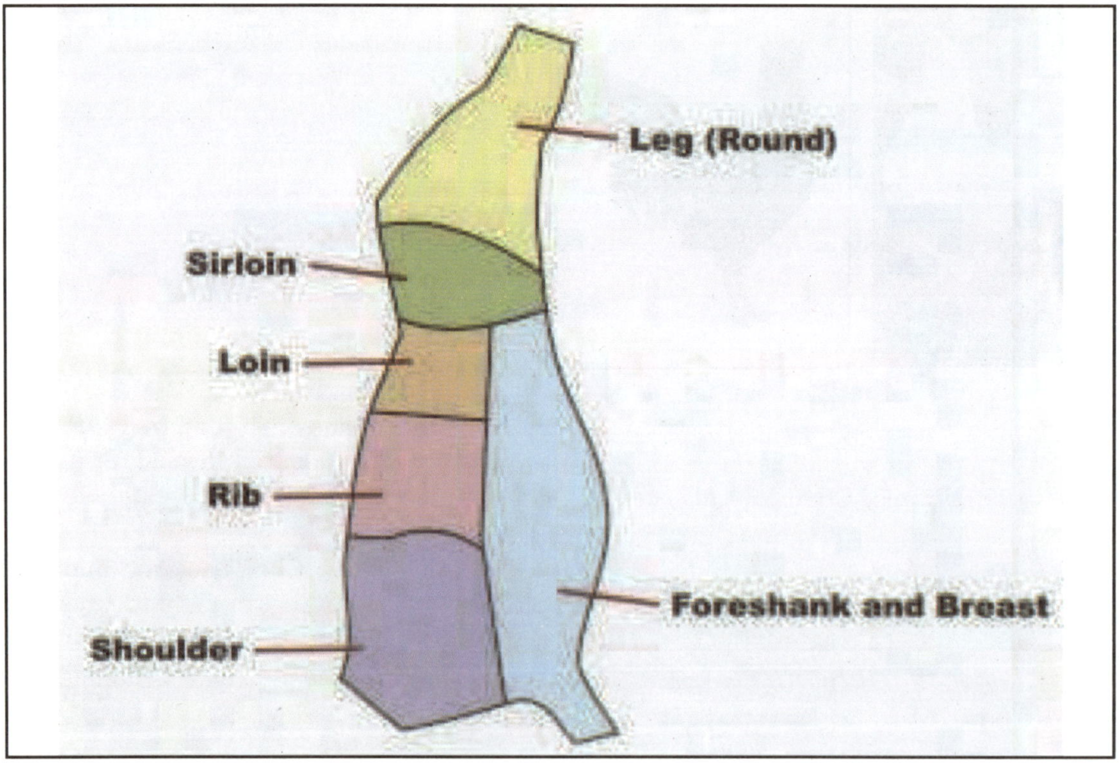
Leg (Round)
Sirloin
Loin
Rib
Shoulder
Foreshank and Breast

13

Cold Food and Larder

OBJECTIVES

After studying this chapter students should know:

1. Definition of garde manger and the type of food prepared in garde manger.
2. Different types of appetizers and salads with marination and dressings prepared in garde manger.
3. Types of sausages, bacon, ham and others cold food display.
4. Different types of sculptures and displays.
5. Definition of garnishes and accompaniments.

Cold food is the as name indicate food which is served cold even if it is cooked. They can be served in the form of hors d' oeuvres or appetizer.

GARDE MANGER

It is a French term for the area where cold buffet dishes are prepared and other foods are stored in refrigerated units. Some of the items prepared in a garde manger are salads, Pates, Chaud-Froids and other decorative dishes can also be called larder or cold kitchen.

In the classic French kitchen using the brigade system, Chef de garde manger is the person responsible for the preparation of all cold foods. This can include appetizers, desserts, pates, cold sauces, salads, dressing and sandwiches. Also known as pantry chef.

Here we are going to discuss some of the preparation done in garde manger as a cold food.

HORS D' OEUVRES/APPETIZER

This is composed of tangy, salty, sour food items aimed to stimulate the appetite. The hors d'oeuvre should have eye appeal and well presented. The term hors d'oeuvre is usually applies to a variety of side dishes offered as an appetizer such as potato salad, seafood, olives, Russian salad, herrings, sardines, artichoke, asparagus etc. An hors d'oeuvre may be a single item served as a preliminary appetizer course before the soup.

The function of this course is to stimulate the appetite by producing more saliva and other digestive juices in our system. Thus to make a way for next dish. So the dishes should be attractive, colourwise and well portioned.

In Russia they are served as 'Zakuski'. In Italy it is known as 'Antipasti'.

Hors d'oeuvres are divided in two main categories:

1. Hot and
2. Cold.

Types of Cold Hors d'oeuvres:

(1) Salads
(2) Seafood and seafood cocktail
(3) Spring vegetables
(4) Pork products like salamis etc.
(5) Pate'
(6) Savory jelly or aspic
(7) Various types of egg
(8) Fruit juices
(9) Fruits
(10) Caviar's
(11) Galantine
(12) Vegetables base terrine
(13) Canapés and sandwich.

Type of Hot Hors d'oeuvres:

(1) Beignet or Fritters
(2) Bouchees/Patties
(3) Brochette or Skewers
(4) Croquette - cooked mixture of meat, fish, poultry or vegetables (especially potatoes) formed into small roll coated with eggs, bread crumbled and deep fried grill

(5) sandwich like croquet monsieur

(6) flambé base dishes.

SALADS

Salad is derived from the Latin word 'sal' means salt. Salad originally meant any food dipped in salt. Basic points while making a salad:

- Only crisp fresh pieces of vegetables and fruits should be used.
- Any ingredient, which is washed in water, should be dried thoroughly. This prevents the risk of dressing being watered down.
- Ingredient should complement each other in flavour, colour and texture.
- Use dressing to enhance the flavour of the salad.
- Arrangement of the salad should be simple.
- If using cooked ingredients it should be ensured that they are not overcooked.
- Salad should be stored in cold places and served on cold plates.
- Garnish should be designed to give an eye appeal.

Basic Ingredients for Making of Salad

Lettuce, cucumber, tomato, capsicum, mushroom, carrots, radishes, onions, beetroot, potato, pickles, olive, caper, cabbages, ham, bacon, beef, types of seafood, boiled chicken, and eggs .almost any thing can be used for making of salad. Like pastas, rice, cous-cous,

Types of Lettuce

Iceberg, cos, romaine, loloroso, endive, cabbage, little gem, butter head, oak-leaf, Webbs.

Salads are further divided into:

a) Simple and

b) Compound.

Salad Simple

Simple salad could be green salads or salads of cooked vegetables consisting of single kind of vegetable. These salads can be of two types:

a) Raw salad - like Fresh garden vegetables and

b) Plain salad - boiled chicken salad

Compound Salad

These salads are made of two or more kind of cooked or uncooked ingredients.

1) **Salad waldorf:** Dices of apple, celery and walnut bound together with mayonnaise sauce.
2) **Salad mimosa:** citrus fruit, banana and grapes mix with the garnish of acidulated cream.
3) **Salad japonaise:** Pineapple, tomatoes cut into square pieces. Orange segments used with acidulated cream.
4) **Salad nicoise:** Dices of potatoes, French beans, dice tomatoes bound with vinaigrette dressing. Decorate with fillets of anchovy or bread croutons (small round oily fish), olives and capers (pickled flower buds).. Sprinkle with chopped chervil and tarragon (herb).
5) **Salad imperial:** White lettuce leaves regular in shape and hollow. Filled with asparagus tips and truffles (tubers which grow near oak and beech tree).

Salad can be served as an accompaniment also with the main course.

DRESSING OF SALAD

Dressings are used to add flavour, improves palatability and act as a binding agent too.

Different Type of Dressing

1. **American:** Salt, pepper, and English mustard. Equal parts of oil and vinegar. Sweetened with sugar. Reason to add sugar offsets the sharpness of vinegar.
2. **Acidulated cream:** Fresh cream and fresh lemon juice seasoned with salt.
3. **English dressing:** Similar to American dressing with two parts of vinegar to one part of oil. Castor sugar is added.
4. **French dressing:** Salt, peppermill, French mustard with one parts vinegar to three parts of oil.
5. **Lemon dressing:** Salt, pepper, lemon juice, and olive oil to taste with castor sugar.
6. **Mayonnaise dressing:** Mayonnaise sauce thinned with vinegar and lemon juice to a dressing consistency.
7. **Vinaigrette dressing:** Salt, pepper, and 1 part vinegar to 2 parts of olive oil. Often blended with French or English mustard.

Thousand Island Dressing

Mayonnaise with little chilli sauce, chopped red pimentos, chives (it is a herb from onion family) and green bell peppers

TYPES OF MUSTARD

1. **English mustard:** Made by mixing mustard powder with water or milk. Leaving it to stand for 10 minutes.
2. **French mustard:** It is made in France. Has a darker colour, a hint of sweetness and often flavoured with tarragon.
3. **Dijon mustard:** The name refers to a style of mustard that is pale, smooth and clean tasting. This is made with brown mustard seeds, water, white wine, salt and spices. Dijon is the mustard capital of **France.**
4. **Other types of mustard:** American, German, Herb, red, champagne mustard, honey, and whole grain mustard.

FORCE MEAT

Seasoned pureed meat or fish emulsified with animal fat made from A mixture of chopped or ground vegetables, meat, poultry, fish or fruit and seasonings bound with eggs, panada or bread crumbs and used as a stuffing. The ingredients used may be raw or cooked.

Forcemeats can be used either to stuff eggs, fish, meat, vegetables, pasta, vols-au-vent or tartlets or as the basis for pâtés, terrines, sausages, quenelles etc.

The preparation should have a mouth melting quality when eaten. This is achieved through:

- Fine pureeing of all ingredients
- Animal fat/butter
- Addition of moisture
- Using right cooking technique
- Stable emulsion.

Different Types of Force Meat

Country Style Force Meat

The meat is cut in strips and marinated along with fat and flavoring. Then grinded and passed through a sieve (tamis) . Panada is added for binding along with the sieved liver.

Gratin Force Meat

Gratin forcemeat is made by partially cooking some of the meats before pureeing. This is done to create a softer texture in the finished product and to improve flavors

Straight Force Meat

Used only with pork fat and a temperature below 10°C to be maintained every time. The finesses depends upon the number of grinds it goes through.

Mousseline Style Force Meat

Eggs and heavy cream is added to it and the fine paste has to be made in cold conditions, while using ice. The mixture is very fine, fluffy and light. Work on the required meat and keep the balance in the refrigerator.

5/4/3/ Forcemeat or Emulsion

The ratio in which the ingredients are added thus the name. 5 parts of meat to 4 parts of fat to 3 parts of ice is added to the emulsion. Maintain the temperature below 10°C at all times. Pass through fine sieves and make a fine paste.

Sausages

A sausage consists of ground meat and other animal parts, herbs and spices, and possibly other ingredients, generally packed in a casing (traditionally the intestines of the animal), and preserved in some way.

The word sausage originally comes from the Latin word 'salsus', which means salted or preserved. In the days of old people did not have refrigeration to preserve their meat and so making sausage was a way of overcoming this problem typical sausage consists of ground meat that's combined with fat, flavorings, and preservatives, and then stuffed into a casing and twisted at intervals to make links. Pork is most commonly used, but butchers also use beef, lamb, veal, turkey, chicken, or game, and some also use fillers like oatmeal and rice to stretch the meat a bit.

Parts of Sausages

The Sausage consists of 2 parts

1. Casing
2. Filling

Types of Casings

Lamb and Sheep Casing

These casings are very tender, and used for sausages such as breakfast sausage, frankfurters, and fresh pork sausage.

Pork Casing

Undoubtedly the most popular casing which can actually be used for almost any sausage. As it is popular it is normally easier for the home sausage maker to find.

Beef Casing

For sausages that require a very thick casing, such as bologna and salami.

Collagen Casing

This casing is made from the gelatinous substance found in the connective tissue, bones and cartilage of all mammals. The substance is harvested from the animals and reconstructed in the form of a casing. Used now a days

Fibrous Casing

This casing is used to make dry and semi dry sausage. The fibrous casing is extremely strong and is used to stuff sausage that is very tightly packed, as it will not break. The inside of this casing is coated with protein that allows it to shrink with the meat as it dries out.

Muslin Casing

This casing is made of muslin, and is used for sausages such as liverwurst, blood sausage, salami's and bologna's.

Synthetic Casing

This casing is made from alginates, and requires no refrigeration. It is used by mass producers and can be made in different colors.

Natural casingsmeans animal made for sausage gives the best flavour and appearance to the final product. A natural casing enhances and complements the natural juices and quality of the meat and spices.

Types of Fillings

The filling is made up of 2 parts:

Meat Component

A variety of meats are used in sausage making. Lean Meat makes up the largest proportion of the component providing the dominant character of the product. It determines the colour, Flavour, Texture and the appearance of the product. Pork is y far the most common and popular meat used in the sausages. Beef , Veal, Lamb and Poultry are also used.

Pork fat adds taste, Flavour and texture to the force meat. Fowl fat, found in the cheeks of the animal, is the most commonly used.

Apart form these Offal's like Heart, Kidney, Tripe, Liver and tongue is also used. They have a very low binding power.

Non-Meat Component

These are added to the filling before the stuffing. They enhance the flavour and the colour, prevent bacteria growth and acts as a preservative and increases the bulk and volume of the filling. There are 6 types of additives:

- Water – Helps in mixing of the ingredients and extract proteins from the meat.
- Curing Agent – They improve the self life. Eg. Sodium Nitrate – dry sausages, Sodium nitrite – Cured, Cooked or Smoked Sausages.
- Curing Accelerators – They speed up the curing process eg. Ascorbic acid, Sodium Erythorbate and Citric Acid
- Sensory Enhancers – Used to enhance the flavour, smell, colour, feel and texture. Eg. Salt, Saccharin, Sorbital, Spices, Milk, Yeast, Mustard flour, Turmeric, Caramel and Smoke are some.
- Binders – They bin d the mixture together eg. Egg, panada, gelatin.
- Stability Enhancers – help in stabilizing the meat and increase the strength of the meat.

Type of Sausages

Cooked Sausage

Made with fresh meats and then fully cooked. The sausage is either eaten immediately after cooking or must be refrigerated and is usually reheated before eating. Examples include Braunschweiger, Veal sausage and Liver sausage.

Cooked Smoked Sausage

Much the same as cooked sausage, but it is cooked and then smoked, or smoke-cooked. It can be eaten hot or cold, but is stored in the refrigerator. Examples include Wieners, Kielbasa and Bologna.

Fresh Sausage

Made from meats that have not been previously cured. This sausage must be refrigerated and thoroughly cooked before eating. Examples include Boerewors, Italian Pork sausage and Fresh Beef sausage.

Fresh Smoked Sausage

This is fresh sausage that is smoked. After smoking, the sausage can then be refrigerated and cooked thoroughly before eating. Examples include Mettwurst and Roumanian sausage.

Dry Sausage

Made from different types of meats. These are the most complicated of all sausages to make, as the drying process has to be carefully controlled. Once produced this type of sausage can be readily eaten, and will keep for very long periods under refrigeration. Examples include Salami's and Summer sausage.

FEW FAMOUS SAUSAGES

1. **Brühwurst** is a German cooked, smoked Brühwurst sausage originally from Bavaria, with a garlicky flavour and dark red colour. It is seasoned with black peppercorns, paprika, and mustard seeds for flavour. The meat is partially cured and then made into the sausage with the other ingredients, after which, the sausage is further cured, smoked and then blanched.
2. **Black Pudding** This large sausage is made of pig's blood, suet, bread crumbs, and oatmeal. Blood Sausage Also known as "blood pudding" and "black pudding".
3. **Bockwurst** is a kind of German sausage, traditionally made from ground veal and pork (tending more towards veal, unlike bratwurst). In modern Germany. A natural casing sausage, it is usually cooked by simmering although it may also be grilled. When thoroughly cooked, its casing usually splits open.
4. **Bologna sausage:** An American sausage somewhat similar to the Italian Mortadella (a finely hashed/ground pork sausage containing cubes of lard that originated in the Italian city of Bologna). It is commonly called bologna and often pronounced and/or spelled baloney. Bologna to be finely ground, and without visible pieces of fat. Bologna can alternatively be made out of chicken, turkey, beef, or pork.
5. **Bratwurst:** A German sausage composed of pork, beef, or veal. The name is German, derived from Old High German brätwurst, from brät-, which is finely chopped meat and wurst, or sausage. Bratwurst are usually grilled and sometimes cooked in broth or beer.

6. **Capocollo:** A Italian sausage prepared with first class meats. After a trimming by hand, the slice of meat called Capocollo is salted and spiced and then left to rest. After some days the Capocollo is made into sausage in a natural gut and stringed by hand. Seasoning of about 3 months. Capocollo is a superior high quality sausage with soft and delicate taste, slightly sweet.
7. **Cervelat:** A fresh, smoked sausage named after the former German region of Thuringia. Coriander. Cervelat, also spelled cervelas, servelat or zervelat, is a type of cooked sausage produced mainly in Switzerland and in parts of Germany. In its modern Swiss variety, it consists of a mixture of beef, bacon and pork rind that is packed into zebu intestines, slightly smoked and then boiled.
8. **Corn Dog:** The corn dog, pogo, dagwood dog, pluto pup or corny dog is a hot dog coated in cornbread batter and deep fried in hot oil, although some are baked. Almost all corn dogs are served on wooden sticks, though some early versions were stickless. The 'korn dogs' were baked in a corn batter and resembled ears of corn when cooked.
9. **Frankfurter:** A smoked and seasoned precooked sausage that is also called the "hot dog", "wiener". Introduced in the United States in about 1900 and quickly came to be considered an archetypal American food. The first so-called hot-dog stand, selling the sausages as a sandwich on what was to become the standard long hot-dog bun, was opened at Coney Island, New York, in 1916. The hot dog remained popular in the United States throughout the 20th century, being especially associated with barbecues, picnics, and athletic events.

   Sold ready-cooked and lightly smoked, either loose, vacuum-packed, or canned, to be heated by grilling, steaming, or gentle, brief boiling (frying makes them tough).
10. **Head Cheese:** Head cheese (AmE) or brawn (BrE) is a cold cut originating from Europe. Head cheese is in fact not a cheese, but meat pieces from the head of a calf or pig (sometimes a sheep or cow), in aspic, with onion, black pepper, allspice, bayleaf, salt and/or vinegar. It may also include meat from the feet, tongue and heart. It is usually eaten cold or at room temperature as a luncheon meat. It is sometimes also known as souse meat, particularly if pickled with vinegar.
11. **Italian Sausage:** A popular pizza topping consisting of pork flavoured with garlic and fennel. In the United States, Italian sausage is a style of pork sausage which is noted for its seasoning of fennel and/or anise, containing at least 85% meat, which can be no more than 35% fat. It is made in sweet and hot styles. It is generally not cured, and is normally grilled and eaten with giardiniera or other vegetables.

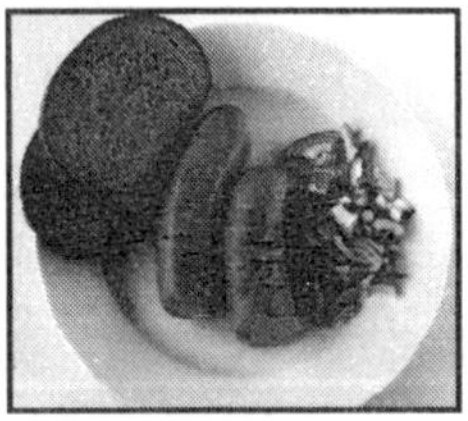

12. **Knackwurst:** A smoked and cooked sausage made from beef and/or pork. **Knackwurst** is a short, plump sausage originating from the Holstein region in Germany. The original recipe for knackwurst is attributed, who stuffed ground veal,

ground pork, and fresh garlic into hog casings, and aged the sausages for a short time over burning oak wood. Knackwurst is often prepared highly seasoned.

13. **Kolbassy:** A highly seasoned smoked sausage of Polish origin made from pork and (sometimes) beef.
14. **Liverwurst:** German for "liver sausage." Liverwurst, also known as Kentucky Paté, is an anglicisation of the German Leberwurst (Dutch leverworst, Hungarian kenQmájas, Serbian dzigernjaca, Slovene jetrnica, Swedish leverkorv, Finnish maksamak-kara), literally meaning "liver sausage". It is a typical sausage served in Germany, Hungary, Serbia, Slovenia, The Netherlands, Finland, and Sweden. Most liverwurst varieties are spreadable. The sausage is usually made with pork. Only about 10-20% of the sausage is actually pork liver, which is enough to give it a distinctive liver taste. Other ingredients are meat, fat, and spices such as ground black pepper, marjoram, allspice, thyme, ground mustard or nutmeg.
15. **Mortadella:** A smoked sausage from Bologna, Italy, the city that brought us "bologna" sausage. Mortadella is a large Italian sausage or cold cut (salume/ sa'lume) made of finely hashed/ground heat-cured pork sausage which incorporates at least 15% small cubes of pork fat (principally the hard fat from the neck of the pig). It is delicately flavoured with spices, including whole or ground black pepper, myrtle berries, nutmeg, coriander and pistachios and/or olives.
16. **Pepperoni:** A highly spiced dry sausage made of pork and beef. **Pepperoni** is a spicy Italian-American variety of salami made from cured and fermented pork. Carrying the title of the literal Italian translation of "peppers", pepperoni is often recognized as the American counterpart to Spanish-style chorizo, which is usually similar in colour and flavour. The term *pepperoni* is a corruption of *peperoni*, the Italian plural of *peperone*.

BACON

Bacon is prepared from the belly of the beckoner pig. Bacon is a fatty slab taken from the belly of a baconiar pig.

The bacon sold in markets is usually cured and which smoked, but it's also possible to buy uncured Smoked bacon is often fried and served with eggs or in sandwiches, or it's sometimes wrapped around lean meats to keep them moist while they're cooking.

Types of Bacon

1. Slab bacon- this is a un-slice bacon (a whole slab).
2. Country cured bacon. This is a salty and strong flavour bacon.
3. Canadian bacon- less fat bacon and smoked
4. Pea meal bacon – this is un-smoked Canadian bacon.

Bacon is a cut of meat taken from the sides, belly, or back of a pig, and then cured, smoked, or both. Bacon may be eaten fried, baked, or grilled, or used as a minor ingredient to flavour dishes. Bacon is also used for barding and larding roasts, especially game birds.

Curing and Smoking bacon

Bacon is cured through either a process of soaking in brine or using plain salt (dry curing). The former may reduce considerably in cooking due to the release of water in the meat. Bacon is usually cured and smoked, and different flavours can be achieved by using various types of woods, or turf. This process can take up to eighteen hours, depending on the intensity of the flavour desired. Un-smoked bacon being referred to as **green** bacon. The leaner cut of Back Bacon is preferred to the bacon from the belly is referred to as *Streaky Bacon* due to the prominence of the bands of fat. While there is a tendency on both sides of the Atlantic to serve belly bacon well done to crispy, back bacon is cooked to taste in often a way that, at first, appears under-cooked to those used to belly bacon.

Cuts of Bacon

The names of rashers or slices differ depending on where they are cut from:

- **Streaky bacon** comes from the belly of a pig. It is very fatty with long veins of fat running parallel to the rind. This is the most common form of bacon. Pancetta is Italian streaky bacon, smoked or aqua (un-smoked), with a strong flavour. It is generally rolled up into cylinders after curing.
- **Back bacon** comes from the loin in the middle of the back of the pig. It is a lean meaty cut of bacon, with relatively less fat compared to other cuts and has a ham-like texture and flavour.
- **Middle bacon** is much like back bacon but is cheaper and somewhat fattier, with a richer flavour.
- **Cottage bacon** is thinly sliced lean pork meat from a shoulder cut that is typically oval shaped and meaty. It is cured and then sliced into round pieces for baking or frying.
- **Jowl bacon** is cured and smoked cheeks of pork

Bacon joints include the following:

- **Collar bacon** is taken from the back of a pig near the head.
- **Hock**, from the hog ankle joint between the ham and the foot.
- **Gammon**, from the hind leg, traditionally "Wiltshire cured".
- **Picnic bacon** is from the picnic cut, which includes the shoulder beneath the blade. It is fairly lean, but tougher than most pork cuts.

HAM

Ham is prepare from the hinder leg of the pork

A ham taken from a hog's upper hind leg.. Fresh hams aren't cured at all and need to be cooked. Ham is relatively low in fat, but even low-salt hams are high in sodium.

Types of Ham

1. **Fresh ham** are cuts from the hind leg that are not cured or smoked. Fresh hams are cooked using the same methods used for other fresh pork cuts and have a similar flavour to pork roast.
2. **Dry-Cured Hams:** they are cured without the injection of water. A curing compound consisting of salt and other ingredients, which may include sugar, sodium nitrate, nitrates, phosphates, and other seasonings, is rubbed on the surface of the ham. The ham is then hung to dry, allowing it to age anywhere from a few weeks to over a year, depending on the variety of ham. Dry-cured hams may also be smoked. Ham that is dry cured is saltier and drier than the typical ham you find in normal food stores.
3. **Wet (or Brine) Cured Hams:** they are cured by soaking or injecting with water and brining ingredients. The curing solution consists of water and brining ingredients, such as salt, sugar, sodium nitrite, sodium nitrate, honey, spices, seasoning, and artificial flavoring. The ham may also be cooked or smoked during this process. Wet cured city hams are mass-produced and generally ready for market in one to seven days. Their flavour is less intense than a dry-cured ham. They are normal form of ham available in market.

BRINES

Brine is used to soak food in a liquid solution made of water, salt and sugar that is used as a preservative, a meat tenderizer or a food flavoring. Foods are placed in brines as a means to cure or pickle in order to extend the shelf life of the products, such as meat, fish and vegetables. As the food soaks, the brine adds moisture, salt and any seasonings placed in the brine to enhance the quality of the product being brined.

Cure

Curing refers to various preservation and flavoring processes, especially of meat or fish, by the addition of a combination of salt, sugar and either nitrate or nitrite. Many curing processes also involve smoking.

Curing with salt and sugar may be called salting, salt-curing, sugar-curing or honey-curing. The application of pellets of salt, called "corns", is often called corning. Curing in a water solution or brine is called wet-curing or pickling or brining. The curing of fish is sometimes called kippering.

A curing may be "wet" or "dry".

- **Wet curing**, also known as brine curing, is the soaking or injecting of food with a solution that is used to pickle or preserve the food product. The solution typically includes salt and water in simple brine or a brine with salt, water, sodium nitrite, other nitrites, and flavorings such as honey or sugar.

- **Dry curing** involves the rubbing of food with a mixture that is used to preserve foods. Meat and poultry are often dry cured when it is covered with dry preservatives and spices. The dry ingredients cure the meat from the outside in. After curing, the meat is rinsed and is then ready to be served or smoked, which adds another step to the curing and flavoring process.

Marinade

A seasoned liquid in which foods such as meat, fish and vegetables are soaked (marinated) in order to absorb flavour and, in some instances, to be tenderized. Marinades contain an acid (lemon juice, vinegar or wine) and herbs or spices. The acid ingredient is especially important for tough cuts of meat because it serves as a tenderizer. Because most marinades contain acid ingredients, the marinating should be done in a glass, ceramic or stainless-steel container-never in aluminum.

Three important functions of marinating food are :

to flavour,

to moisturize and

to tenderize.

Each ingredient in a marinade serves a specific purpose, and it is necessary to understand what goes in what.

Meat or Vegetables Marinating Time in Refrigerator

Chicken (boneless)	1-2 hours
Chicken (bone-in) mutton	1 -05 hour 3-6 hour
Beef	4 hours to overnight
Fish	30 minutes
Vegetables	30-60 minutes

Marinating Food

- Marinades contain oil, an acid such as vinegar, lemon juice or tomato juice, and seasonings. For flavoring herbs, spice and alcohol can be added. Marinate covered food in the refrigerator for a period of time to add extra flavour. Success of food also depend upon marination of the food. In Indian marinating curd, spices, salt and ginger garlic paste is often used (for fish lemon juice is must). Use glass, stainless steel, plastic or disposable aluminum bowls or pans to marinate foods. Do not use aluminum or brass pans, as they react to the acid in the marinade.

  Marinades are generally made up of three types of ingredients:

- **Acid base like** include red or white wine, all types of vinegars, tomato or citrus juice, and buttermilk or yogurt Acids help the marinade food in tenderizing particularly tough cuts of meat.
- **Oil :** Oils are used to moisten the base and to add flavour (in high fat content food oil is not required)
- **Flavorings and seasoning** include the fresh or dried herbs and spices. Wine is widely used for flavouring. Indian food may carry garlic and ginger paste, chili peppers, shallots, and mustard. Salt can be used to both flavour and tenderize the meat in all kind of food, . Sweeteners such as molasses or honey are also used and the sugar can give meats a brown colour when they are cooked. Chinese use soy sauce, oyster, and fish sauce are common as well.

PÂTÉ

The term refers to force meat baked in a crust usually in a rectangular mould similar to a Loaf tin. In French it is called Pate en croute. Simply Pate is a paste of finely chopped or pounded or pureed seasoned meat which generally is liver.

A wide range of ingredients are used in making a Pate like Truffle, Herbs, Spices and variety of Meats and not to forget Liver. The livers are generally soaked in Milk for 24 hrs before they can be used. They have to be cleaned thoroughly for any Blood clots, Sinews and Veins. The mixture is supposed to be light, which makes the final product very soft and light.

PÂTÉ DE FOIE GRAS

Pate de Foie gras (French for "goose fat liver paste") is the enlarge liver of an over feed duck or goose. The very first pâté de foie gras is said to have been created in Strasbourg in 1765 by a Norman chef named Jean-Joseph Close. (Although the technique for producing "foie gras" is recorded in the ancient Egyptians) foie gras is considered one of the greatest delicacies served with. It is very rich and buttery, with a delicate flavour unlike regular duck or goose liver. Live is marinated with port wine, salt, pepper, spice, and little brandy. Then it is baked in terrine on a below 90°C. Foie gras may be flavored with truffles or liquors. It is usually accompanied by crusty bread or toast.

Mousse, Soufflé and Mousseline

A Mousse is a rich, airy preparation that can be cold or hot, sweet or savory. The word Mousse is French and translates as "froth" or "foam." There are three key constituents to a Mousse.

First is the base such as the chocolate in a chocolate mousse or orange juice, the fish or poultry.

The binder, like gelatin. Gelatin is available in powdered and sheet form. The powdered is easy to use. Both types must be soaked in a cool liquid first to soften and swell the gelatin.

Finally an aerator such as beaten egg whites or whipped cream to lighten the mousse. This produces the airy texture. Mix it in gently to prevent it from deflating.

Cold dessert mousses are often poured into decorative glasses and garnished with fruit, sweet sauces, or whipped cream. Savory mousses can be made from fish, shellfish, meat, foie gras, etc.

SOUFFLE

The Soufflé is again like mousse but there is a small difference i.e.

1. Mousse is bind by gelatin while in Soufflé it is egg white only
2. Mousse is usually sweet while Soufflé may be sweet or savory
3. Mousse are finished with cream but Soufflé may not
4. Mousse is usually uncooked but Soufflé is cooked.

The Soufflé has two things

1. Base that can be puree or sauce
2. Stiffly beaten egg white.

Base can be cooked with egg yolk for lightness and care fully mixed with egg white. Then baked.

Mousseline - a type of force meat prepared with egg white and cream. Usually dedicated and sieved through.

A sauce made airy with the addition of whipped cream or beaten egg whites. Like hollandaise sauce with whipped cream or egg whites added.

Galantines - By classical definition, Galantines is a de-boned Poultry, Game including rabbit which is stuffed with Force Meat. It is cylindrical in shape and contains flavorful forcemeat with abstract or concentric patterned fruits, nuts and even truffles at times. It has a natural casing of the skin of the meat that has been used. They are usually served Cold and with a coating of Chaud Froid and Aspic to make it more presentable after slicing. The correct cooking method used is Poaching.

Ballotine - The term Ballotine and Galantine are often confused. However Ballotine is prepared from the boneless leg of Poultry and it is stuffed with the force meat and made in to a Ballot or a Bundle, hence its name. Unlike Galantine, Ballotine is baked or Braised with their skin and are served hot as entrees. They can also be coated with Chaud Froid and Aspic and served as an Appetizer.

bindi

Chaud Froid

Literally, hot-cold. Comes from the French words "Chaux" and "Froi" which means "Hot" and "Cold". It refers to a sauce which is made and applied hot but served cold. It is a high gelatin content sauce. Cooked meat or poultry is cooled, coated with brown sauce or white sauce, decorated with pieces of truffle, carrot, mushrooms, etc. then brushed all over with clear aspic, which is allowed to set before serving. Decorative vegetable cut-outs are often set into the aspic for a colorful garnish. Possibly created in 1759 at Montmorency and named for the Marshal of Luxembourg.

Types of Chaud Froid

- Chaud Froid Cream
- Chaud Froid Red
- Chaud Froid White
- Chaud Froid Pink
- Chaud Froid Green
- Chaud Froid Brown

Uses of Chaud Froid

- Protects for any kind of pollution
- Keeps the moistness intact for the meat
- Prevents the bugs and Insects from the meat
- Acts as a back drop or even a platter center piece
- Adds Flavour to the complete dish
- Enhances the eye appeal for presentation

Precautions while making Chaud Froid

- Should not be stirred continuously to prevent bubbles
- Should be Fat free and scummed regularly.
- It should be cooked to the desired thickness.
- Stored at room temperature to avoid setting of the sauce.
- Should be made fresh as the shelf life is less.
- Should be warm and cooked before the application

Precautions while Application of Chaud Froid

- The item should be grease free from the surface.

- The item should be at room temperature or even chilled as it facilitates the setting of the sauce
- The surface of the food item should be dry to avoid drain out of the sauce.
- Try to have the surface even and smooth for better results.
- Apply to the sides first and then to the top to avoid any wastages.
- Apply generously 2-3 coating for good results.

Aspic Jelly

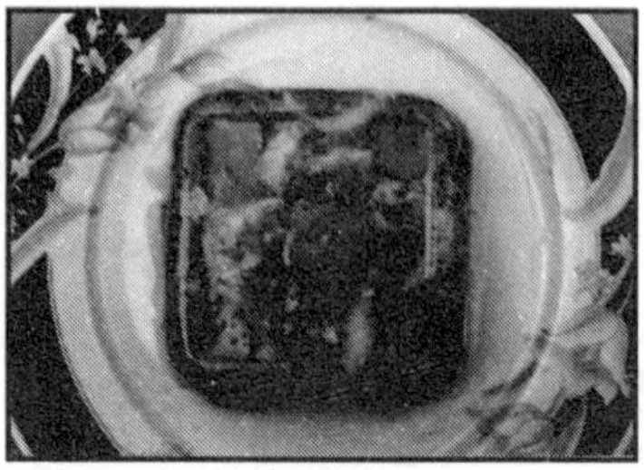

Aspic is a dish in which ingredients are set into a gelatine, jelly-like substance made from a meat stock or consommé.

When cooled, stock congeals because of the natural gelatin found in the meat. The stock can be clarified with egg whites, and then filled and flavoured just before the aspic sets. Almost any type of food can be set into aspics. Most common are meat pieces, fruits, or vegetables. Aspics are usually served on cold plates so that the gel will not melt before being eaten. A meat jelly that includes cream is called a *chaud-froid*.

Nearly any type of meat can be used to make the gelatin: beef, veal, chicken, or even fish. The aspic may need additional gelatin in order to set properly. Veal stock provides a great deal of gelatin, the meat that makes the stock is often cooked with veal for that reason. Fish consommés usually have too little natural gelatine, so the fish stock may be double-cooked or supplemented. Since fish gelatin melts at a lower temperature than gelatins of other meats, fish aspic will be more delicate and will melt more readily in the mouth.

QUENELLE, PARFAIT, ROULADES

Quenelle

A light, delicate dumpling made of seasoned, minced or ground fish, meat or vegetables bound with eggs or panada. This mixture is formed into small ovals and gently poached in stock. Quenelles are usually served with a rich sauce and can be used as a first course, main course or garnish

Parfait [pahr-fay]

1. This dessert consists of ice-cream layered with flavoured syrup or fruit and whipped cream. It's often topped with whipped cream, nuts and sometimes a maraschino cherry.

2. A french parfait is a frozen custard dessert made with egg yolks, sugar, whipped cream and a flavoring such as fruit puree. In french, *parfait* means "perfect", which is how many view this dessert. Both American and french parfaits are served in tall, narrow, footed "parfait glasses".

Roulade [roo-lahd]

1. The French term for a thin slice of meat rolled around a filling such as vegetables, bread crumbs, cheese or a mixture of vegetables and cheese or meat. The rolled package is usually secured with string or a wooden pick. A roulade is browned before being baked or braised in wine or stock.

Non-edible Display

- **Ice carving**- moldings ice block through carving tools in different shapes like swan, duck, welcome sign etc.
- **Tallow sculpture**

Sculpture is the art of producing in three dimensions representations of natural or imagined forms. It includes sculpture in the round, which can be viewed from any direction, as well as incised

Display Sculpture can be of three types:

1. **Butter base**: Butter models are usually smaller than margarine models and are intended to be decorative pieces that can also be consumed. They never have any sort of frame or base and are usually formed in a mould rather than being sculpted or made with the hands. Butter is only suitable for small models. They are made to simple patterns requiring a minimum of handling, which must, for hygienic reasons, be kept to a minimum.
2. **Margarine base**: Margarine is now among the most popular mediums from which sculptures are created for food decoration. The harder and more plastic margarine is, the better it is for Modeling. Margarine is relatively inexpensive, readily available, needs no special preparation, is an easy substance to learn to master, and has an exceptionally good shelf life. The industrial cooking margarine used for modelling has a higher melting point and is much more elastic and pliable at room temperature than butter

The Advantages of Margarine

Margarine is an ideal medium for sculpture. It advantages like:

1. Margarine can be removed and remodeled as it doesn't dry until a satisfactory result is achieved.
2. Unlike ice, margarine will not melt if kept at normal temperatures, so that a model will last for months, not hours.

3. The texture of margarine does not change like pulled sugar, so no special display cabinet or drying-out facilities are required.
4. Margarine does not set like chocolate, so the chef can work slowly on a model, setting it aside at busy times of the day.

Problems with Margarine

The only real problem from which margarine suffers as a medium is dust. It shows every speck of dust, and it will (it seems) even attract dirt. The problem can be overcome by following two simple rules:

1. Always work in a spotlessly clean area, and on the cleanest possible surface.
2. Cover it with a fine, clean cloth When not working on a model, or when storing or transporting it,
3. **TALLOW** is a Solid fat extracted from the tissues and fatty deposits of animals, especially from suet (the fat of cattle and sheep). Pure tallow is white, odorless and tasteless; Tallow is used to make soap and candles. It was formerly in common use as a lubricant. Can be stored longer

Used for carving, engraving, moulding, modelling and casting because it is sensitive to pressure and a good material for fine detail work:

- Fruit and vegetable display
- Salt dough

Pastillage

Pastillage is rolled Fondant without any of the softening ingredients (glycerin corn starch or shortening). It is used mainly for decorative ribbons, three dimensional shapes and appliqués because it dries bone-dry and crusts more quickly than Fondant.

To make pastillage-

- One tablespoon gelatin
- Scant 1/3 cup cold water (optional: replace two tablespoons water with rose-water, orange flower water or freshly squeezed lemon juice)
- Four cups powdered sugar (lightly spooned into measuring cup)
- ½ cup cornstarch
- Pinch of Cream of Tartar (optional).

1. Sprinkle gelatin over the water in a 2-cup heatproof glass measure and let stand for 5 minutes. Set into a small pan of simmering water and stir until the gelatin is dissolved. (This can be done in a microwave on high for a few seconds).
2. Combine the sugar, cornstarch and optional cream of tartar in a large bowl and make a well in the center. Add the gelatin mixture and stir with a lightly

greased wooden spoon until blended. Mix lightly with greased hand and knead vigorously in the bowl until most of the sugar is incorporated. Turn onto a smooth, lightly greased surface such as Formica or marble and knead until smooth and satiny. If the Pastillage seems dry, add several drops of water and knead well. If it seems too sticky, knead in more powdered sugar. The Pastillage will resemble a smooth, well-shaped stone. When dropped, it should not spread.

3. Rolled Pastillage may be used at once but seems to work more easily when allowed to rest for several hours. It is important to keep Pastillage covered to prevent it from drying. Wrap tightly in plastic wrap and place in an airtight container. It will firm slightly upon standing.
4. When ready to roll out, spray the work surface and rolling pin with nonstick vegetable spray.

- **Jelly logo**-molding jelly for making of logo in any shape and form. Colour can be added to make them attractive.
- **Thermacol work**-thermacol sheets are cut in different shapes. Can be colored with oil paint .

Noodles, tapioca, spaghetti or macaroni cut in fancy shapes or quenelles make simple and attractive garnishes for soup.

Cooked vegetables cut in thin strips or in Julienne style or in fancy shapes or slices, are often used to add colour and flavour and nutritive value to a soup.

Soups may be garnished also with cubes of bread or puff paste buttered and browned in the oven or friod in deep fat

Sandwich

The **sandwich** is a food consisting of two slices of bread between which are laid one or more layers of meat, cheese, or other filling, together with optional condiments, sauces, and other accompaniments. The bread is often lightly buttered or covered in a flavoured oil when it is baked, or added in the sandwich to enhance flavour

The dish was named after John Montagu, 4th Earl of Sandwich, an English aristocrat, in the 18th century. Sandwich was fond of this form of food because it allowed him to continue gambling while eating

Components of Sandwich

- ❖ Breads
- ❖ Spreads
- ❖ Fillings & Garnish

Breads

Pullman loaves: baked in special pans
Supermarket loaves
Rolls
French or Italian bread, split horizontally
Whole wheat
Rye and pumpernickel

Spreads

Help protect bread from the filling
Add flavour
Add moisture or mouthfeel

Butter

Should be soft enough to spread without tearing the bread

Mayonnaise

Might be more preferable to butter, but does not protect the bread as well as butter
Sanitation/safety issues of using from-scratch mayo

Fillings

The heart of the sandwich
Beef: roast beef (hot or cold), hamburger
Pork: roast, ham, bacon, Canadian bacon, barbecue, loin
Poultry: turkey, chicken, duck breast
Sausage: salami, hot dogs, bologna, liverwurst, lunch meats

Fillings & Garnish

Cheese: cheddar, Swiss, provolone, cream, processed, spreads
Fish and shellfish: tuna, sardines, smoked salmon, shrimp, anchovies, fried fish
Mayonnaise-based salads: tuna, egg, ham, chicken,
Mayonnaise-based salads: tuna, egg, ham, chicken, turkey, lobster

Fillings

Vegetables: lettuce and other greens, tomato, onion

Miscellaneous: peanut butter, jelly, hard-cooked egg, fresh or dried fruits and nuts

Types of Sandwiches

Hot

Simple: usually a hot filling between two slices of bread; may also contain items that are not hot

Open-faced: buttered or un-buttered bread topped with hot filling or meat and a sauce, gravy, cheese, etc.

Hot

Grilled: buttered on the outside and browned on a griddle or in a hot oven

Deep-fried: dipped in egg batter (and maybe bread crumbs) and then fried. May also be cooked on a griddle or in an oven, as frying can make them greasy

Cold

Simple: two slices of bread or two halves of a roll; does not mean that they are simple in construction

Multi-decker: more than two slices of bread; club sandwich is one example

Open-faced: similar to a large canapé

Cold

Tea: small and fancy; lighter ingredients and trimmed or shaped breads

Wraps: fillings are wrapped (burrito-style) in a tortilla or flatbread

GARNISHES

The word garnish comes from French and means "to grace or to provide". In kitchen operations we use the word garnish to refer to the decoration of food by the addition of other items.

Garnishes come in a variety of shapes and sizes, depending on the meal being served and the level of service required. A common yet effective garnish used in many restaurants is a sprig of parsley (or other herb) on the side of a plate, or a wedge of lemon to be served with fish.

There is no rule in cooking that says every meal must be garnished but if a garnish is used it should be fresh, colourful, edible and should be suited to the meal.

Some of the Garnishes

1. Lemon wedges are served with fish and seafood. The wedges should be freshly cut prior to service.
2. Parsley is a very common garnish suited to a wide range of dishes.
3. Rosemary is an aromatic herb often served with lamb dishes.
4. Croutons are small cubes (10 mm x 10 mm) of fried bread. They are used to garnish soups and salads.
5. Basil has a sweet fragrance and a sharp taste. It is a common garnish for many Italian dishes.
6. Fines herbs are a mixture of chopped chervil, parsley, tarragon and chives. This can be sprinkled over a meal before serving.
7. Chiffonnade lettuce is a popular garnish used with prawn cocktails.
8. Vegetables may be served julienne as a colorful garnish for meat and fish dishes.

Soup Garnishes

- Toasted and garnished bread
- Fried bread cubes and pieces for puree soup.
- Nuts like almond with broccoli soup
- Fried onion with French onion soup
- Chopped herbs and spices with most of the soups
- Yogurt with sweet soup
- Cream with cream soup
- Sour cream with many soup
- Fried garlic with french soups
- Cheese with Italian soup

Characteristics of Garnish

1. Garnish can be complimentary or contrast to main food for example for sweet dish garnish can be sweet or sour like orange. Colour may be as per the dish or differ etc.
2. Garnish depends upon skill and innovative ideas.
3. Sometimes food itself is garnish.
4. There are standard garnishes of some dishes which can't be altered.
5. Garnish should be used on minimal base.

bindi

Accompaniments

Accompaniments are complementary additions to the main ingredient of a meal. Accompaniments are typically things like vegetables and side salads but they also include sauces and relishes. Sometimes the accompaniment also comes with a garnish of its own

Like garnishes, there are no set rules for accompaniments but there are some dishes that are well suited to particular accompaniments.

If the meal is to be plated with an accompaniment, such as vegetables or a salad, then these need to be placed on the plate so as to enhance their natural colour and shape, yet not distract from the main dish. If serving vegetables as an accompaniment make sure there is sufficient variety of colour in the vegetables chosen. Do not use all green vegetables and avoid placing vegetables of the same colour next to each other on the plate.

Food Items Accompaniments

Fish

Crumb fried fish tatare sauce, lemon slices

Fish orly tomato sauce

Fish meuniere noisette butter

Meat and Chicken

Roast lamb mint sauce, roast gravy

Roast pork apple sauce, roast gravy

Roast chicken bread sauce, roast gravy

Roast duck with orange sauce

Turkey, Sage and onion stuffing

Cold meats mustards, pickles.

QUESTIONS

1. Define garde manger and explain the role of garde manger department in food production area.
2. Classify salads and mention different types of salads.
3. What are sausages and how they are prepared?
4. Mentioned any five types of sausages.
5. What are the different types of sandwiches can be prepared?
6. Explain the role of garnish and accompaniments in modern cuisine.

7. Why the larder is assumed to be a HEART of the food production department?
8. Plan a salad bar menu in A grade restaurant ?salad bar should be able to attract all kind of guest.
9. What are the display items ? Explain any three of them?
10. What are the standard accompaniments of following:
    1. Roast beef
    2. Fried fish
    3. Roast lamb
    4. Roast chicken.
11. Explain following terms:

    Hors d'oeuvres,

    Parfait,

    Marinade,

    Dressing,

    Force meat,

    Casein,

    Pastillage,

    Tallow,

    Ice carving,

    Brine cure,

    Aspic,

    Souffle,

    Mousse,

    Garnish.

10. Differentiate following:
    a. Ham, Bacon and Sausages
    b. Hot Hors doeuvres and Cold Hors doeuvres
    c. Simple salad and Compound salad
    d. Black pudding and Frankfurt sausages
    e. Cure and Marinade
    f. Mousse and Mousseline
    g. Tallow and Pastillage.

14

International Cuisine

OBJECTIVES

After studying this chapter student should know:

1. Process cuisine and types
2. Different types of international cuisine
3. Fast food cuisine
4. Emphasis is given on French cuisine. Italian cuisine, middle east cuisine, Thai cuisine, Chinese cuisine, Mexican cuisine etc.

CHINESE FOOD

Chinese food is most of the popular food which enjoys a high reputation in the world for its unique exciting and delicious taste that's why one can find Chinese's food all over the world. Due to the diversity of the climate, products and customs. Different food styles and tastes in local regions are available.

Easy preparation, using of fresh and healthy ingredients, colourfulness, and versatile mixed taste are few of the characteristics of China's varied cuisines.

Following are characteristic of Chinese cuisine:

1. Aroma is provided by using scallion, fresh ginger (galangal), fresh coriander, root garlic or special chili and pepper.
2. Art of using different methods of cooking like stir frying, steaming, roasting etc.
3. Food is consisting of many colours provided by regional vegetables, tomatoes, Soya sauce and sauce.

4. Thickening of sauce and soup is done by corn flour.
5. Most of the food will have combined taste like chilies, plain and sweet and sour.
6. Variety of snacks like steam Dim sum, noodles, pancake, are used.
7. Usually stir fried and fast methods of cooking are used in the preparation of dishes.
8. Soya is used in many ways like beans, tofu, Soya sauce, etc.
9. Different kind of utensils and tools are used in the preparation of dishes.
10. Garlic and MSG (Banned in certain countries) is widely used in flavoring the dishes.
11. Stock plays an important role in making of sauce and soup.

Regional Cuisine

China covers a large territory and has many nationalities; hence there is a wide variety of Chinese foods, each with quite different but fantastic and mouth-watering flavors. Because China's local dishes have their own typical characteristics, Chinese food can be divided into eight regional cuisines, the distinction of which is now widely accepted. Certainly, there are many other local cuisines that are famous, such as Beijing Cuisine and Shanghai Cuisine.

Shandong Cuisine

Shandong cuisine, clean, pure and less oily, is characterized by its emphasis on aroma, freshness, crispness and tenderness. Shallots and garlic are frequently used as seasonings so Shandong dishes taste pungent. Soups are given much emphasis in Shandong cuisine. Thin soups are clear and fresh while creamy soups are thick and taste strong. For cooking deep-frying, grilling, pan-frying and stir-frying methods are adopted

Typical menu items: Bird's Nest Soup; Yellow River Carp in Sweet and Sour sauce.

Sichuan/Schzwan Cuisine

Sichuan Cuisine or Szechwan Cuisine is known by its spicy and pungent flavours, is one of the most famous Chinese cuisines in the world. Sichuan cuisine, with a unique tastes of chili. Pepper, producing the typical exciting tastes. Garlic, ginger and fermented soyabean are also used in the cooking process. Wild vegetables and meats are often used. Food is also pickled and braised. Smoke duck a speciality, is an art which is acquired by long experiences.

Typical menu items: chicken in schuan sauce; Smoked Duck; Kung Pao Chicken; Twice Cooked Pork; Mapo Dofu.

Cantonese Cuisine

Famous for its clean, light, crisp and fresh food,. The basic cooking techniques include roasting, stir-frying, sautéing, deep-frying, braising, stewing and steaming. Steaming and stir-frying are most frequently used to preserve the ingredients' natural flavours. Artistic presentation of their dishes is another featured of this region.

Typical menu items: Shark Fin Soup; Steamed Sea Bass; Roasted Piglet.

Fujian Cuisine

Fujian cuisine is renowned for its variety of beautiful combination in food, colour and enriched tastes of sweet, sour, salt and savory seafood,.

Typical menu items: Buddha jumping over the Wall; Snow Chicken; Prawn with Dragon's Body and Phoenix's tail.

Jiangsu Cuisine

Jiangsu cuisine, popular in the lower reaches of the River Yangtze. They are popular for their carving technique on different food items such as vegetables, fruit etc. variety and abundance of ingredients in food is given by using fish and crustaceans as the main ingredients. Cooking techniques consist of stewing, braising, roasting, and simmering. The flavour of cuisine is light, fresh and sweet and its presentation is delicately elegant.

Typical menu items: Stewed Crab with Clear Soup, Long-boiled and Dry-shredded Meat, Duck Triplet, Crystal Meat, Squirrel with Mandarin Fish.

Zhejiang Cuisine

Zhejiang cuisine is non-greasy. Food is smoked or steamed. That's why food is a sign of good health, freshness, tenderness, softness, and smoothness. Food is now catching popularity due to health consciousness and mellow texture.

Typical menu items: Sour West Lake Fish, Shelled Shrimp, Beggar's Chicken.

Hunan Cuisine

Hunan cuisine is characterised by thick and pungent flavours. Chili, pepper and shallot are usually necessities in this variation. Food is very hot and spicy.

Typical menu items: Dongan Chicken; Peppery and Hot Chicken.

Anhui Cuisine

Anhui cuisine focused on the temperature in cooking and are good at braising and stewing. Pork is famous here. Even often ham is added to improve taste.

Typical menu items: Stewed Snapper; Huangshan Braised Pigeon.

Eating Style

Chinese food seems to taste better if eaten with their traditional tools chop-sticks. Food is accompanied by Chinese sauce and cruets. Soup is taken along with main meal and rice or noodles are served with sauce.

THAI CUISINE

Thai food is gaining popularity now-a-days and has many influences from the outside world. The taste and ingredients used resembles the Indian food and spices.

Thai chef will be remembered for their contribution to world for their skill of making artistic carving. In the early days, cooking techniques were limited at the initial stage of Thai cuisine. However, the Thai ancestors were so creative that even without complicated utensils; they could make several delicious dishes that still present until today.

The art of cooking Thai food has been developing over the years in accordance with the outside influences, especially from the west. With the advent of modern kitchen-ware, new ideas and techniques have been further enhanced. Today, a good Thai food cook can be more and more creative than in the early years.

Most of the old classic dishes are still present today in spite many dishes has been newly introduced or improved. Thailand is abundant in the supply of natural wood that can be applied to set the fire and cook food so the grilling of food is very popular. Local Thai people normally grill meats and fresh seafood and eat them with dips a type of fish sauce (locally called as '*Nam Phrik*') which have sweet-and-sour flavours so that they become tastier.

Thai salad is consist of local vegetables and seasoned with fish sauce, lemon juice, chili, and sometimes, garlic and shallot. Therefore, some can find a dish of 'yam' very delightful while its herb and spice ingredients are good for health as well.

Another style of food is curry. Curries were also developed in the olden days as well but the present-day curries are much different from they were previously because ancient Thais did not use coconut milk in those spicy soups.

Two types of curry are based:

(i) Green curry and

(ii) Red curry.

Chinese style of cooking has a great influence on Thai cooking as one can find large choice of stir-frying dishes in Thai menu. The art of Thai cooking evolved according to the cultural influences from other countries, mainly China and Western Europe. Another influence from the mainland reflects in an extensive use of noodles in Thai recipes. While the Chinese deep-fry noodle and create savory sauces to mix. Thais apply it in many characteristically Thai styles. Thai noodles taste sweet, sour and sometimes spicy.

Ingredients like coconut milk, rice flour, kaffir lime, galangal, lemon grass, coriander leaves, red chilly paste, fish sauce, peanuts, sun dry prawn paste is mainly used. Desserts are made of egg, coconut cream, honey and rice. In red curry there is more space to chilies while in green curry colour comes from coriander leaves.

Thai food is lighter. Moreover, the herbs and spices used as common ingredients have medicinal properties. Some of them are good for digestion while some have benefits to drive away your fever and clear your throat. Best of all, Thai cuisine can easily beat gourmets from all over the world because of their amazing taste.

The most important thing to remember about Thai food is to appreciate its lightness, its heat and its passionate smell long before it arrives at your dining table. Herbs used in our food have a dissimilar scent from western ones. They are much more aromatic and yield different flavours in each Thai dish.

JAPANESE CUISINE

- Japanese cuisine resembles their culture, religion and living style. That is simple cooking strong effect. Japanese people distinguish traditional Japanese style dishes as "Washoku" (*Wa* means Japanese style and *shoku* means food) as opposed to Western foods, which are generally called "Yo-shoku" (Yo means western-style). Washoku includes *sushi*, *sashimi* (raw fish), *tempura*, *udon* or *soba* noodles, and more. Washoku meals usually include rice. Since Japan is surrounded by oceans thus seafood is highly used in Japanese cuisine. Seaweed, fish, and other seafood are main ingredients in Japanese cuisine as soup stocks in Japanese-style meals is made from *katsuobushi* (dried bonito flakes) or *konbu* (kelp). Raw fish is used extensively. Steam rice is served with all the meals.

Regions

- *Kyoto* : the food of Kyoto is lighter reflecting perhaps the taste of old Kyoto courts.
- *Tokyo* : the food is stronger in taste as compared to Kyoto; and is famous for the flavour of its seafood.

Nagasaki: The southern island has strong influence of Chinese food.

Traditional Japanese food uses ingredients available during the season.

Breakfast might consist of *miso* soup, *gohan* (rice), *nori* (dried seaweed), pickles, and green tea.

STAPLE FOOD OF JAPAN

- Fish, rice, sea weed, noodles and vegetables as well as soy sauce predominate

Lunch is usually simple and consists of noodles (udon or soba). Two popular noodles

in Japan are soba and udon. They can be eaten hot or cold. Soba noodles are made of buckwheat and thought to have originated in China. Udon noodles are made by mixing flour with salt water, then kneading, stretching, and cutting the dough into strips.

Dinner might consist of rice, a main dish of fish or meat, a side dish of vegetables, miso soup, and pickled vegetables.

Japanese usually use chop-sticks to eat.

Sashimi and sushi are most famous food. These two dishes are often thought to be one and the same. Sashimi consists of thin slices of raw fish or other seafood served with spicy Japanese horseradish (**wasabi**) and shoyu while sushi consists of the same, served on vinegared rice, but also includes cooked seafood, vegetables and egg. The two main types of sushi are nigiri-zushi and norimaki. The nigiri type has slices of raw or cooked fish on sushi rice. Norimaki has pieces of fish and/or vegetables rolled with rice in nori (dried seaweed).

The Japanese presentation of meals is foremost visual and highly thoughtful. Japanese dishes are chosen to highlight, enhance and harmonize the presentation of food. Food is chosen for its colour, texture and season and artistically arranged to create a visual display of edible cuisine.

Few famous dishes of Japan:

- *Yakitori and Teppanyaki* : grilled poultry or meat
- *O-cha*: a type of (green tea) is must with food
- *Shioyaki*. grilled fish
- *Sashmi*: marinated raw fish served with soy sauce, very hot horseradish relish and vegetables.
- *Shabushabu*: dip paper-thin slices of beef in a pot of boiling water and stock for a few seconds and then dip the cooked beef in sesame sauce (**goma dare**) before eating. Later, vegetables such as enoki mushrooms and Chinese cabbage, tofu and shirataki are added

- *Sushi* : vinegared rice served cold with raw fish, shrimps, prawns, vegetables, etc.
- *Sukiyaki*: this is a savoury stew of vegetables and beef (lean sirloin or rump steak) cooked and dipped in a bowl of beaten raw egg.
- *Tsukemono*: a pickle of various vegetables like aubergine, cucumber, turnip etc.
- *Tempura*: deep frying of items in batter. Seafood or vegetables dipped in batter and deep-fried, tempura is served with a dipping sauce.
- *Teriyaki*: cooked pieces of marinated fish, meat and poultry on charcoal grills or fried in little oil served with rice (gohan).

Food is eaten by sitting around a low table on straw mats. Traditional Japanese meals are often eaten on a tatami

MEXICAN CUISINE

Mexican food has a strong influence on the cuisine of Central American countries, also is popular throughout the world for its tacos with guacamole, quesadillas, enchiladas and carnitas. With it's variety of indigenous civilizations, each region in México is marked by a distinct aroma, taste and texture. México is known in the world to new culinary horizons with its universal contribution of vanilla, avocado, corn, tomato and chocolate, among others.

Staple diet of Mexico is corn, beans and chilies.

In México one can find a blend of Aztec (the civilization which cultivate the maize, red beans and rice) and Spanish influence of cooking. Typical is the centuries old "mole poblano", a thick, dark sauce made with dried chilies, nuts, seeds, spices, cocoa and other ingredients. Dish by the name of "mole poblano de guajolote" made with poultry, cocoa and spices is a delicacy from Guatemala. México, with its more than 100 variety of chillies ranged from red to brown colour is used in variety of dishes and is famous for its savory herbed stews and sauces. Tortillas are used in various ways and are made of cornmeal. Enchiladas are folded tortillas stuffed with sauce; beans etc. tacos are fried or baked can be stuffed with variety of veg, chicken etc.

Seafood, garnished with tomatoes and herbs followed by rich coffee is the basic meal along the Pacific Coast. And in the Yucatán Península, dinner is likely to be a Mayan delicacy like "pork pibil" cooked in banana leaves with the famed "achiote" sauce.

In food, as in everything else, the Mexican people have found a way to raise the everyday basics to an art form.

Special ingredients: flor de calabaza (squash blossoms) are used in everything from soups to sauces. Huitlacoche is a small, dark fungus, which grows on a corn stalk and is surprisingly creamy and delicious. **Crepas de huitlacoche** (huitlacoche crepes bathed in a dreamy cheese sauce) are a singularly Mexican treat. **Romeritos** and **epazote** are two pungent herbs which add a special zest to fish, beef and chicken dishes. **Pepitas** (pumpkin seeds) are used in sauces, most commonly in pipian, which is used to top many chicken dishes.

Followings are the famous Mexican dishes:

Tortillas: Tortillas made of flour or maize. Often served alongside a meal as bread would be, tortillas are also used in many typical dishes - rolled and baked for enchiladas, fried for tacos or grilled for quesadillas

Salsa: A blend of the red or green mix of tomatoes, onion, chili and cilantro (coriander) served on as a relish or a dip.

Frijoles (type of beans): Commonly boiled and then fried. They can be a main ingredient in a meal or served almost as a garnish.

Guacamole: Mashed Avocado with tomatoes, chilies and cilantro (coriander). Served as a dip or as a garnish.

Ceviche: Raw fish marinated in lime juice, often used in salad.

Chillie corn carne: Red beans coked in mince beef with tomatoes

Enchiladas: Tortillas coated in a tomato and chili sauce, stuffed with vegetables or chicken or pork then folded/ rolled and baked

Huachinango: Red Snapper fish, a common feature on the menus at coastal resorts. Often available. cooked in various style.

Quesadillas Tortillas stuffed with cheese, folded and grilled. A simple dish often served with beans or a little salad and suitable for those avoiding anything spicy.

Mole sauce: A wonderful rich sauce made with the unlikely combination of chocolate, chilies and many spices. It can be red or green depending on the ingredients The sauce is often served over chicken, though turkey is more traditional.

Poc Chuc: Pork fillet is cooked with tomatoes, onions and spices.

Pollo Pibil: Traditionally consists of chicken marinated in orange and spices then barbecued in banana leaves.

Tacos: Tortillas fried until they are crispy and served with various fillings like souyr cream, salad etc.

Tamales: Cornmeal paste wrapped in corn or banana husks and often stuffed with chicken, pork or turkey and/or vegetables, then steamed.

Tortas: Mexican sandwiches, often large rolls with generous fillings.

Tostadas: Thin and crisp tortillas served loaded with guacamole, sour cream, chilies, chicken etc.

SPANISH FOOD

Located in southwestern Europe, it controls the crossroads between two seas - the Mediterranean and the Atlantic. Spain is known in food for unique ingredient like olives, olive oil, parsley, almonds, garlic, and saffron.

The communities of Spain each have their own, unique tastes. South is known for rice and pork while north is rich in beef and potatoes. Spaniards of the central regions enjoy roasted meats mainly because this is where they raise a lot of lamb and pork, and feed the animals lots of wild herbs, which gives the meats a distinctive flavour. Smoked hams are one of the major specialties of Spanish cuisine. *Lamb* is of much more importance. Lamb (*cordero*) is prepared in Spanish cuisine certainly with *garlic*, and lamb chops (*chuletas de cordero*) often with tomato sauce, *a la Navarra* (as the region of Navarra grows the most tomatoes in Spain)

Tapas, are the appetizer served in a little plates of food which reflect the most creative Spanish cooking available. Anything from shrimps cooked in garlic, to croquettes with a béchamel sauce, to clams marinara, to "boquerones" (fried sardines) can be enjoyed as a snack. Every Spaniard has his favourite *tasca*, as the tapas bars are often called.

The Spanish consume more rice than any other European people, and that does make Spanish cuisine more easily adopted by Asians. A very well known Spanish rice dish is *paella*. It is internationally popular and Basically it consists of spiced, saffron rice, garnished with shrimp, crab, Spanish sausage, and pieces of fried pork, beef, chicken, and lamb etc.

Garlic is extensively used as condiments due to its medical advantages in Spanish cooking. A dish like *gambas al ajillo*, shrimp with garlic fried in oil or butter, champignon *al ajillo* (mushrooms sauteed in garlic), *sopa Juliana* (vegetable soup, prepared the Spanish way with garlic).

Using of Wine is another character of Spanish cooking. *Sherry* and Madera is generally added in Spanish dishes. Spanish cuisine has a few standard procedures to prepare meats. Meats may be marinated for a short time before being fried in a sauce of vinegar, oil, garlic, and onions (*adobado*). Games are used in deluxe menu and Spanish cheese like cabrales, manchego etc. usually accompany the food.

Olive oil - one of the best cooking oil is Another general feature of Spanish cuisine which is widely use in all kind of culinary style. It can be use in innards or uncommon cuts of meat like tongue or feet. In Spanish cuisine a number of innards and uncommon cuts are prepared in an elaborate manner, and they then are not considered a poor man's dish of minor quality but a delicacy.

Lots of sea food is consumed in Spain. Another gift to world is famous gazpacho soup which is serve cold consist of pureed tomatoes, cucumber and pepper. Beef is used throughout Spain, and is made into savory stews. One of the regional dishes is a "cocido" or stewed beef. This is invariably made with chickpeas, and stewed for a long time, to tenderize that tough old bull. Other vegetables in this "cocido" vary from region to region, and upon availability.

As far as sweets and desserts are concerned, Spain is still under Moorish influence with the majority of cakes usually sickly sweet with marzipan and candied fruit as the main ingredients. The national desert is flan, which is nothing more than boiled custard covered with syrup made of burnt sugar. The other popular offering is a churro, which is just a fried piece of dough covered with sugar. Glimpse of Spanish food can be seen in many parts of world that is due to extensive traveling of Spanish traveler.

AMERICAN (U.S.A.) FOOD

America is the land of dream and is build by the migrants came from all over the world. Also they brought their cuisine to this country. Cooking in the USA is not just fast food like hamburgers, pizza and burgers!. But also consist of the traditional dishes. As the melting pot of many different cultures, the US has also become the mixing pot for many different cuisines. Most were introduced by the early European immigrants but modified to take advantage of the locally available ingredients and to conform to local tastes. Fried chicken, meatloaf, baked potato, corn, baked beans and apple pie would be considered traditional American dishes.

Regional Cooking is highly influenced by the types of ingredients locally available and varies from area to area. Southern cooking has definite African influences. Cajun cooking, from the New Orleans area, is a spicy mixture of Spanish, French and African styles. California cooking is known for the use of fresh fruits and vegetables in interesting combinations with Asian, Mexican and Spanish flavorings.

There are the regional specialties of the South, addictive green chiles in the Southwest, solid German and Scandinavian "real-food" of the Midwest, and corn bread and sweet baked beans from New England. As Americans became more exposed to and comfortable with the European tradition of cooking as an art. Inspired by the traditions of more ancient cooking cultures, while working in kitchens free from the restrictions of those cultures, chefs let their imaginations run. The diversity of regional cuisines and the plethora of local ingredients have become the genius of American cooking. American haute cuisine has become an exuberant hybrid, fishing all the best tied bits out of the melting pot and re-creating them in ever-changing ways.

FRENCH CUISINE

Indisputably, one of most rich and experimental cuisine in the world is the French cuisine. The French cuisine is the first professional and organized cuisine of the world and has an ongoing respect toward with food. Their reverence for time spent eating is evident in any culinary establishment nationwide. French food has a credit to provide intensive knowledge in culinary art that is due to extensive research and experiment.

France has a great climate variation and this thing add variety in the food of different region. Despite France's history of centralization (Paris), each region has its own distinctive specialities: In the south the heat of Mediterranean add aroma to food through olive oil, garlic and herbs.

In the north finest of fish and seafood cooked with butter and cream add flavour to the different menu. In the east chestnut, mushroom, cabbage, cheese, sausages, beer and sauerkraut. Wine etc. are widely used. Bread is an important part of the French diet and is Made of the barley, wheat and other grain.

What is perhaps less widely recognized is that France's reputation for fine food is not so much based on long-held traditions but on constant change. Not only do basic cooking techniques require great skill, but they also demand a deep understanding of the ingredients themselves. Although not very old French culinary has gain popularity in very short period. French cuisine is characterised by its extreme diversity. Producing of the best wine in the world is another feature and plus point into the french cooking as the wine is extensively used in the french food as an ingredient and accompaniment both. The French have a custom to take wine with all the courses that match with food. Wine is drunk with the meal, but rarely without food.

This close relationship between food and wine may, in part, closely parallel the evolution of great cooking and great wine making. That's why some of the best dishes were born in France.

A French meal begins with a hors d'oeuvre (appetizer) followed by soup, main course, roast, cheese, and many more with dessert. Each course has its own custom of consuming, service, accompaniment and portion. That's why all royal banquets function in the French style.

French cuisine can broadly be divided into three categories:

"Cuisine bourgeoise", also called "haute cuisine" which includes all the classic French dishes which is heavy, require long preparations and are complex in preparing. These are not (or no longer) specifically regional, but which have been adapted over the years to suit the taste of the elite classes. This type of cooking includes the rich, cream-based sauces and somewhat unique cooking techniques that many people associate with French cuisine. French cooking is considered by many to be the standard against which all other cuisines are measured. This standard was introduced into the French courts by

Catherine de Medici in the 1500s, and later perfected by Auguste Escoffier (1846-1935), who is considered the Father of French Cooking. At the outset of this category a highly experimental and refined approach to food preparation and kitchen management is applied. **"Cuisine du terroir"**, which covers regional specialities with a strong focus on quality local produce and peasant tradition.

"Cuisine nouvelle" or "nouvelle cuisine", which developed in the 1972 in opposite to traditional cuisine, under the influence of chefs such as Michel Guérard. This type of cooking is characterized by shorter cooking times, much lighter sauces and dressings, and smaller portions presented in a refined, decorative manner. Its modern, inventive approach sometimes includes new techniques and combinations. the concept change the basic principles of food presentation. The basic purpose of this cuisine was to retain the freshness, lightness and nutrients of the ingredient by using simple and quick cooking method. Garnishes and accompaniments are simple and suite the main dish.

Food fashions and trends in France tend to alternate between these three types of cuisine;. The "fusion" cuisine popular in the English-speaking world is not widespread in France, though some restaurants in the capital have a "fusion" theme, and many modern French chefs are influenced by a variety of international cooking styles.

For French people, cooking is part of culture, and they consider cooking to be a way of life.

MIDDLE-EAST CUISINE

Middle Eastern cuisine includes Egypt, Syria, Iran, Iraq, Lebanon, Jordan, Saudi Arabia, Israel, along with the nations of Afghanistan, Kuwait, Yemen, Armenia and others.

Overlapping in part with the Eastern Mediterranean, the Middle East has formed the cradle of Islamic civilization since the 8th century, and its cuisine reflects the different cultures that have influenced this civilization. Food in these countries are partially effected by the European culture but it has successfully retains the ancestral heritage of its peoples. Traditional food is yet in used in the cultures, and the foods they eat are the same what it used to be in ancient period.

The cuisine of particular region depends on its abundance of fruits, grains, legumes, vegetables, nuts, olive oil, roasted flavours and spices to provide great variety and healthy life. Some countries in this region have similar cuisines, but at many place the name is changed by converting the some ingredients.

The region of the Middle East was the site of great ancient civilizations, Mesopotamia and Egypt, as well as the birthplace of Judaism, Christianity, and Islam.

LEBANESE CUISINE

The food of most Middle Eastern cuisines is similar in someway. Many of the dishes carry the same names from region to region, though they may be prepared or seasoned somewhat differently. Because of this, the cuisines of the Middle East are often sadly lumped into one homogenous category, when in truth they can be differ in style of cooking.

Situated between the east and the west, Lebanon is a culinary and cultural crossroads. Lebanon is located on the eastern most shore of the Mediterranean in the Fertile Crescent, where western civilization is said to have begun. The cuisine of this ancient land is diverse and steeped in history; both the eastern and western influences in its cookery are apparent. Though its mainstream popularity is relatively new, the cuisine is not; the cuisine of Lebanon has been in the making since pre-biblical times. The influence that Lebanon has had on the world is totally out of proportion to its size; culinary contributions from this tiny country have had the greatest impact on modern Middle Eastern cuisine. Roughly encompassing an area of land the size of Connecticut, the people and cuisine of Lebanon are known throughout the world-Lebanese cuisine is a true reflection of its welcoming culture.

The cuisine of Lebanon is the epitome of the Mediterranean diet. It includes an abundance of starches, fruits, vegetables, fresh fish and seafood; animal fats are consumed sparingly. Poultry is eaten more often than red meat, and when red meat is eaten it is usually lamb. It also includes large amounts of garlic and olive oil.

Most often foods are either grilled, baked or sautéed in olive oil; butter or cream is rarely used other than in a few desserts. Vegetables are often eaten raw or pickled as well as cooked.

The national dish of Lebanon is kibbeh. It looks like a pate "an emulsified paste of the freshest lamb and bulgur wheat". Kibbeh is popular dish for festivals holidays, or Sunday dinner.

Lebanon is also rich in grapes varieties thus it is also a producer of good wine. Arak. Arak is the national drink of Lebanon. Which is an anise-flavoured liqueur?

In Lebanon One of the more healthy and entertaining aspects of Lebanese cuisine is the manner or custom in which their food is often served, it's referred to as mezze. Similar to the tapas of Spain and antipasto of Italy, mezze is an array of small dishes placed before the guests creating an awe-inspiring array of colours, flavours, textures and aromas. This style of serving food is less a part of family life than it is of entertaining and cafés. Mezze may be as simple as pickled vegetables, hummus and bread, or it may become an entire meal consisting of grilled marinated seafood, skewered meats, a variety of cooked and raw salads and an arrangement of desserts. They can be stuffed in pastry and rolled in triangle form. Can be baked and serve with hummus.

Although simple fresh fruits are often served towards the end of a Lebanese meal, there is also dessert and coffee. Baklava is most popular Lebanese dessert. Baklava required high level of skill and It is a layered dessert stuffed with clarified butter mix with dry nuts and then baked. It has many variety and the layers can go up to 18 to 20. The main difference between the Lebanese variety and its Greek cousin, is Lebanese baklava often contains pistachio nuts and is drizzled with a rose-water syrup, the Greek variety usually contains walnuts and honey.

Famous dishes of Lebanon:

Tabouleh (Bulgur Wheat, Parsley, and Mint Salad)

Fattoush (Toasted Bread Salad)

Hummus bil Tahina: a chickpeas base dish

Roast Red Pepper Hummus

Baba Ghanouj - (Roast Eggplant Puree)

Green Beans with Onions, Tomatoes and Mint

Lebanese Chicken and Rice: chicken breast stuffed with mincemeat and cooked with rice

Kibbeh.

PROCESSED FOOD

Man's efforts have been directed toward gathering and storing food ever since he gave up his roaming habits and the onset of technical age happened. Today storing the processed food has become a way of life as it provides a mean of making invaluable quick and convenient cuisine at hundred of store all around us. From time consuming classical preparation to quick preparation the need of processed food has gone up which combines the aspect of hygiene, cost efficiency and customer satisfaction. Food processing has been ever evolving from pickling vegetable meat and fish to the modern day's vacuumed packed

1. *Pasteurization*: Destroying of micro-organism by applying high temperature in short time/low temperature in long time.

2. *Canning:* Application of thermal sterilization with initially blanching the cuisine and removing the air from the container and sealing it, than sterilizing with high-pressure steam.
3. *Freezing:* With quick freezing technique like multiplate freezing, tunnel freezing, immersion freezing and cryovac processing.
4. *Drying:* which will reduce the moisture content required for deterioration e.g. are spray drying, accelerated free drying.
5. *Vacuum packaging:* which eliminates the available oxygen and lengthen the shelf life of food. By using of special pumps available oxygen is sucked out. Dry fruits, nuts and chocolate products are usually packed by this method.

Some times addition of additives (material, acids, salt like etc.) is done to improve shelf life. Thus cuisine industry adopts the different best option available for the process food. An increased number of researches are being made to improve the current scenario of process food.

In India a new "National food processing policy "has been design by union cuisine processing ministry to provide grants for development of food processing industry.

FAST FOOD

From pizza to burgers, fast food is one of the world's fastest growing types of food. It now accounts for roughly half of all restaurant revenues in the India and continues to expand here and in many other industrial countries. But some of the most rapid growth is occurring in the developing world, where it's radically changing the way people eat.

People buy fast food because it's cheap, quick, and heavily promoted. But its benefits can be deceptive. Meals devoured in the car or at our desks are replacing home-cooked fare enjoyed with family and friends. Around the world, traditional diets and recipes are yielding to sodas, burgers, and other highly processed and standardized items that are high in fat, sugar, and salt - fuelling a global epidemic of obesity, diabetes, and other chronic illnesses. Meanwhile, fast food producers require farmers to raise uniform fields of crops and herds of livestock for easy processing, eliminating agricultural diversity.

Those in less of a hurry are finding alternatives. Fresh organic foods are increasingly popular in Europe, Japan, and the United States. And a "slow food" movement founded in Italy in 1986 to promote appreciation of food and the cultural experience of shared meals now claims 100,000 members in 80 countries worldwide.

India's fast-food industry is growing by 40 per cent a year and is expected to generate over a billion dollars in sales by next year. Meanwhile, a quarter of India's population remains under-nourished - a number virtually unchanged over the past decade.

QUESTIONS

1. What is process food? Define its use and types?

2. Write a note on different cuisine like French cuisine. Italian cuisine, middle east cuisine, Thai cuisine, Chinese cuisine, Mexican cuisine etc.
3. Chinese cuisine is a wonderful blend of spicy, healthy and variety type of food. Explain the statement by describing the food and specialties of Chinese cuisine.
4. Explain the French cuisine and how it converts the concept of food worldwide?
5. Compare the cuisine of Mexico with Italian cuisine.
6. In today's world fast food is taking over the authentic food globally. Explain the concept of fast food in details.
7. Thai cuisine is not very old cuisine but still it has gain the popularity in very short period. What is the concept behind Thai food. Give detail.
8. Explain followings:
    1. Anti Pasta,
    2. Schzewan Cuisine,
    3. Use of Wine in Cooking,
    4. Washoku and Yoshoku,
    5. Sushi,
    6. Guacamole,
    7. Enchiladas,
    8. Tacos,
    9. Tapas,
    10. Haute Cuisine,
    11. Nouvelle Cuisine,
    12. Kibbeh,
    13. Process food.

15

KITCHEN MANAGEMENT Layout, Production Planning and Work Flow

The prime objective of kitchen management is to lead, organize and control the means of production and service of food, to run the business profitability.

The catering establishment's policy should be interpreted to the best of advantage, whether they are concerned by being an establishment of repute or to earn a good profit.

To manage the kitchen, the kitchen manager/ Executive Chef should have a sound practical knowledge and have the ability to organize labour, delegate the responsibility to appropriate staff who communicate well. Proper controlling of labour needs great tact and ability, their comfort, skill, work and welfare has to be seen. A strict disciplinarian is respected by many, provided he/she has a good judgment in dealing with matters and understands superiors and subordinates.

A good management indicates that food cost is controlled and the people working in the kitchen are content in their jobs and the work given is comparable with their ability. Staff should be trained on the job and if the performance is good, incentives, increments or promotions should be given, if need be.

- Certain factors such as budgetary control, portion control, and cost control, proper purchasing, control of production and service, control of waste etc., play an important part in managing the kitchen.
- Proper design and layout of work areas in kitchen, contribute to a successful catering establishment which will not only satisfy customers but also the staff will be contented.

- Cramped and improper use of spaces provided , delay food preparations and service, certain points have to be kept in view before planning, such as the type of meals to be served, number of persons to be served, forecast of peak period, ventilation, proper drainage, etc.
- It is always advisable that the kitchen should be closed to the restaurant to facilitate efficient service.
- **A work plan** identifies the precise steps for the task—type of food to be prepared and served, number and size of portions, time taken for food service and presentation, location for food service.

FOOD PREPARATION PREMISES

All food preparation premises must be operated as per the guidelines of public health standards. A perfect planned kitchen is one, where raw and cooked materials need the minimum of movement and require only covering the same route once. Attention must be given to lighting, wiring, ventilation, planning, hot and cold water service and appropriate specialist should be consulted. A well planned layout is largely depends upon the following factors.

1. Cooking of different types of food
2. Preparation - Mise-en-place
3. Placing machinery and equipments
4. Receiving supplies— (checking quality and weight)
5. Scullery (crockery, cutlery, wash up)
6. Scullery (pan wash)
7. Selection of equipments
8. Storing of food properly
9. Utilization of every corner

KITCHEN PLANNING

Along with the restaurant, the kitchen determines the number of customer to be dealt with during service period. The area may be 40% of the restaurant area, kitchen space estimates have been as low as 2.5 to 4 sq.ft. Per catering unit for a kitchen catering for 1000 to as much as 9 to 10 sq.ft. per head per meal served in small establishments, now a days even 3 sq.ft. per head is adequate.

Kitchen areas vary according to the type and number of meals provided and if allowance is to be made for special functions. As the number of customers increases, the areas of the kitchen relative to the seating capacity tend to be reduced. Knowledge of peak load is essential for intelligent forecasting.

PRODUCTION PLANNING

Food preparation is is a complex process. A proper planning is needed for smooth production of food items. Meal production follows a flow pattern which commences with the purchasing and selection of materials, their handling and processing and the ultimate presentation of the dishes to the customer where food service takes over. It is therefore obvious that we should start at the beginning and see that the purchasing of food is done properly. Depending upon the requirements of customers the production planning also changes.

The budget committee is formed for the purpose of preparation, coordination, review and revision of budgets. The various departmental budgets and master budget represent a coordinated effort. The budget is made period wise or annually. The seasonal character of the business is taken into consideration. The first step in preparation is giving management objectives for the forthcoming year and giving a Performa to be used in preparation of budgets. The account session prepares their budget in duplicate and sends one copy to the head of the unit, who is responsible for the budget of the catering establishment and the budget committee reviews it.

STORES MANAGEMENT- TYPES, PRINCIPLES, LAYOUT AND CONTROL

Store Management

The term store, storehouse, or warehouse refers to a building or room or place where materials are kept. The storage is just an overhead- a cost with no return and hence the importance of economic operations, while keeping efficiency at a desired level. An organization can have various or specific type of stores,

- Raw materials store,
- Processed or semi- finished materials store,
- Finished goods store, yard store and so on

Such stores range from ordinary one with shelves and bins to cold or the humidified storage system, huge silos for storage of food grain or bonded stores for keeping goods on which customs and excise duties have not been paid. Storage is an essential part of the economic cycle and store management is today a specialized function which can contribute significantly to the overall efficiency and cost effectiveness of the materials function. The task of store management relates to safe custody and preservation of the material stocked and to their receipt, issue and accounting. The objective is to efficiently and economically provide the right material at the time when it is required and in the condition in which it is required.

The **capital cost** components consist of the expenditure on land, buildings and roads, stock yards, storage and material handling equipment. **Machinery** and other facilities provided. The revenue expenditure consists of salaries and wages, insurance, maintenance cost, stationary, communication expenses and the cost of maintaining the inventory. Efficiency require planning in the store. That has to be forecast with the considerable degree of accuracy.

One of the indicators of efficiency in the store is the number of times the stock have turned over. Money is a scarce resource and once it is converted into material, it is useful only when the material have been reconverted back into money. This is the significance of stock turnover. This is also called inventory turnover.

There are many variety of materials stored - **Chemicals, metals, liquids, gases, spare parts, equipment or finished goods, ranging from engineering components to drugs and pharmaceuticals.** Each of these items will require a specific type of storage and their handling and preservation methods will vary accordingly. There is a high degree of specialization requires to store and handle these product and in many cases special storage license is to be obtained from the government.

OBJECTIVE AND RESPONSIBILITIES OF THE STORES FUNCTION

The basic objective is to provide a service to an operating functions and this aspect of service must be fully appreciated. All the other activities, although they have their own importance, are subordinate to this main responsibility of service.

The service rendered by the stores can be categorized into four broad divisions.

1. To make available a balanced flow of raw materials, components, tools, equipment and any other materials necessary to meet operational requirements.
2. To provide maintenance materials, spare parts and general store as required.
3. To receive and dispatch finished products
4. To accept and store scrap and other discarded material as they arise and also arrange for their disposal.

Responsibilities

The major responsibilities of the stores are listed below.

1. Dispatch of finished goods
2. Identification of all materials stored.
3. Inspection of all receipt from vendors and sub contractors.
4. Inventory control
5. Issue of materials to users within the organization
6. Maintenance of stock records
7. Material handling
8. Packing
9. Processing of customer orders
10. Receipt of incoming materials

11. Stock taking
12. Storage and preservation
13. Store accounting
14. Submission of management information reports

These are described in brief

1. **Identification:** Identification is the process of systematically defining and describing all items of materials in stock. It includes the giving of the code number to all materials and preparation of stores code or store vocabulary, the adoption of materials specification of a degree of standardization. In certain cases a part of it may be done by the design, engineering, or some time the purchase department.
2. **Receipt**: Receipt is the process of checking and accepting, from all sources (vendor, sub- contractors, production units, repair units etc.), All materials and parts which are used in the organization. These include supplies for manufacturing or operating process, plant maintenance, and office and capital installations.
3. **Inspection**: Inspection involves the examination of incoming consignments for quality. Very often there is a separate quality control or inspection department which undertakes this work for most materials. Otherwise, goods are inspected by the stores personnel. Whatever may be the system of inspection in force, it is the duty of the store to ensures that the inspection procedures laid down are carried out before material are accepted into stock.
4. **Storage and preservation**: Materials are stored in pallets, in bins, on racks and shelves and sometimes in the yard. The location is usually indicated in the stock – card. The storage period may vary between one day and one year or more, depending upon decampment procedures, safety stock required, etc. storage is the physical act of storing the materials.
5. **Preservation** involves the maintenance of materials to retain their quality. Quite often, temperature, humidity, dust and other factors cause deterioration of materials. The store is expected to issue materials to the user in factory fresh condition, i.e., the same condition in which they were received. Preservation of material has, therefore assumed considerable importance in store management.
6. **Material handling**: Materials handling involves movement and handling. This can be manual or mechanical or may be automatic. Heavy items, dangerous or inflammable goods and delicate merchandise have all to be handled differently.
7. **Packing: material** dispatched to the customers from the finished goods store or from one store to another at different locations required to be packed. Material requires packing according to their nature and this may vary from heavy wooden crates to ordinary paper cartons.
8. **Issue:** This is the process of receiving demands, selecting the items required from storage and handling them over to users.

9. **Processing of customers orders:** The finished goods store or depots of the distribution network of the company are responsible for this work. The goods asked for are picked from the shelves and an invoice is prepared.
10. **Dispatch of goods**: This may be to a customer or a depot or a stockiest of the company or to a sub- contractor, for processing the material to sent.
11. **Stock records**: These are the documents which record, from day to day, full particular of individual receipts, issue and balance of material in stock. Increasingly, computers are being used for this purpose.
12. **Stores accounting**: Stores accounting is the process of recording details of the stock movements and balances in terms of financial value. It is sometimes undertaken by the accounts department, but there is much to be said for it being handled by the store itself. In practice it is often found that such an agreement saves a good deal of work and duplication. It has the added advantage of making the store's personnel responsible for providing their own financial information which they require for the purpose of inventory control. Computerization simplifies this work.
13. **Inventory control**: It is the operation of continuously arranging for receipt and issue in such a way as to ensure that the stock balances in quantity. Instructions are given for the placing of an order to control corresponds with future estimated requirements.
14. **Stock taking**: Is the process of physical verification of the quantity and condition of goods in the store.
15. **Submission of management information reports:** This is an important task. There are many reports of varying periodicity to be submitted. The accuracy and timeliness of such reports are most important.

Relationship Betwee Stores and other Departments

Stores have maximum interaction with purchase which feeds the store, and production which are store feeds in turn. But store has to deal with all the departments in the hotel.

1. **Store and purchase**: These two functions of material management are complementary to each other. Apart from the close relationship that exists on the day to day basis in the purchase of various materials, there are other important activities which can best be done by a close coordination between stores and purchase. These are material identification (coding of materials) and store vocabulary (The coded catalogue), standardization and variety reduction, inventory control, value analysis, salvaging operations and disposal of surplus and obsolete items and scarp.

   The store sends the indent to purchase for replenishment of stocks based on inventory levels desired. While indenting it is important to write the correct specification, code number, unit etc. The stores should also promptly inform purchase of changing production trends, slow or non moving stocks, obsolete or surplus stock, scrap etc.

2. **Stores and production**: The production department is usually the chief customer of the stores. At production meetings, if the store is represented, coordination can be excellent. Any change in a production schedule needs to be communicated to the stores to enable prompt corrective action to make materials available on time.
3. **Stores and sales**: In a marketing organization, the sales department is the chief customer of the finished goods store. The sales department wants to ensure stock at all time and this might be a costly philosophy in terms of inventory holdings. Close cooperation and an integrated approach can aid management objective to increase profitability by closely monitoring inventory levels.
4. **Stores and accounts**: Usually the accounts department does all the store accounting, ensuring a day to day working relationship.
5. **Stores and personnel**: selection of the right person for stores work and giving him adequate training in storage, preservation and accounting techniques are vital.

TYPES OF STORES

The stores are mainly divided into two categories.

a. **Functional**: depending on the use to which the material is put, e.g. Chemical store, tool store, raw material store, etc.

b. **Physical:** depending on its size and location, e.g. Central store, sub- store, transit stores, site stores, etc.

Functional store: Some typical kinds are discussed below:

1. **Raw material stores:** This is where raw material used in the factory are stored, usually this the largest kind and the location should be such that it is situated alongside a railway line, canal or river, if supplies are received other than by road, where the deliveries are by road, there must be an adequate space for trucks to move, turn and park. If sufficient provision is not made for quick and easy loading or unloading, heavy demurrage or detention charges can result. An ideal location fr such store would be adjacent to the production facilities. This will reduce handling.
2. **Production stores**: Besides raw materials, production also requires a large number of materials, generally called "consumables" like eye- shields, cutting oils, abrasives, gloves, aprons, jigs, small tools, etc. A store stocking such item is usually called a production store.
3. **General Stores**: various kinds of miscellaneous items like paints, brushes, cleaning material, wood and spirit are kept here. In some cases where there is no production store, the material mentioned in Production store is kept here.

4. **Tools store:** All kinds of tools like files measuring instruments, saws, small tools like hammers, pliers, etc. or special tools required in the factory are kept here.
5. **Refrigerated stores**: This type of store is used for storage of perishable items. Like fruit, meat, vegetables, etc. It could be from -20°C to 10°C.
6. **Dry store**: Place where all the groceries can be stored and it is protected from the moisture.
7. **Vegetable store**: All the vegetables and fruits are stored and issued from this store only.
8. **Sundries store:** for non food items like paper goods, cleaning

Standard Recipe Formulation

Standard recipes are required for achieving the desired results. It also acts as a tool for cost control. Standards are made to treat each customer with same food without any difference in shape , color, structure and taste. Once the recipe is made, the team involved in standardization, practices the same recipe and records the result. Wherever needed the adjustment are done. As recipes are made for customers so the taste for customers are considered as focal point in recipe formulations. New recipes should be started with few customers and their feedbacks are necessary. As per the need and wants adjustments should be done accordingly. It is a written schedule for producing a particular menu item. A standard recipe card should be prepared for each menu item.

New Product Development

The needs and desire of customers increases day by day. They always look for new ingredients, new taste, new cuisine, new fusions and presentation. In order to meet the guest expectations chefs and cooks should always go for research and developments. While doing so we must follow the basic rules for safety and sanitations and related public health regulations. As a Product Development Chef we should work with the team to develop innovative new dishes and continuously improve long time favorites with ensuring that all products are developed to the specific customer brief & within target costs as allocated within the budgeted targets.

Special instruction and guidelines must be properly illustrated must be understandable by all users. At the same time there has to proper theoretical training and practical session for new developed recipes. The development team must have experienced people in concerned field and should be supervised regularly. If needed, they can be exposed to concern areas.

RECIPE CONVERSION AND ADJUSTMENTS

Modifying Recipes for Indenting for a Large Scale Catering

Recipes must be modified for a large scale catering to avoid the barrier of cost factor

Change the ingredient: Some time it requires for the chef to change the ingredients in the recipe to get red of the hike in the cost or to make big margin of profit. The most expensive item may be removed from the recipe by keeping some alternative of it .

Eg. If the recipe contains Green and Red capsicum, you may omit the Red capsicum and substitute with Red Kashmiri chili instead.

Replacing the Ingredients

The Chef feels that some of the ingredients are very expensive in the market, which are used in the recipe, which makes him modify the recipe, replace those items which are expensive and increase those which are cheaper to maintain the food cost and the quality. By doing these kind of exercises chef helps the organization to make a big margin of profit and he should be smart enough to give the best of the quality with the change also.

Practical Difficulties While Indenting For Volume Feeding

Most of the time the chef faces a big problem while indenting for mass. The reason could be various:

1. Which kind of people are attending the function
2. The ratio of veg and non veg guest in the function
3. Some time the guest emphasizes only on one item or two only
4. The kids become the problem if in advance he is not told about them.
5. The host may not be able to predict about the number of guest
6. If the host is of different cast and invitees are of different cast and from different place.
7. If the guest is fussy and start allowing the take away from the function
8. The price of the menu
9. when guest brings their own eatables without pre informing

When guest comes very late to attend the function

Bin Management

Bin Card is also called as **Cardex**, Tag Card etc. The detailed information about the materials is contained in the Bin Card. Normally Bin Card Consists of the information like Qty Received, Qty Issued, Minimum Stock Level, Maximum Stock Level, Reorder Level, Re Order Quantity, Closing Stock, Opening Stock etc. Maintenance of Bin Card System is part of perpetual inventory accounting system.

BIN CARD

Abc Hotels Ltd
Bin Card

Commodity :.......	Supplier..........
Minimum Stock........	Reorder No.......
Maximum Stock.......	Bin No..............

Date	Reference	Received	Issued	Balance
	Balance brought forward			
	....			
	....			

What is Bin Card

Bin card is a record of receipt and issue of materials Quantity of store received is entered with receipt column and the quantity of store issued is recorded in the issue column of Bin Card. Balance of quantity of stores is ascertained after every receipt or issue. It shows the balance of the stock at any moment of time. Bin Card is maintained by the store-keeper. He is answerable for any difference between physical store and the balance shown by the Bin Card. Thus Bin Card does not only records the receipt an issue of the stores but also assist the store keeper for control of the stock. For each item of stores minimum level maximum level, and ordering level are shown in the part of the Bin Card. By seeing the Bin Card the store keeper sends the material requisition for the purchase of materials from time to time.

A bin card is also known as bin tag or stock card and is usually hung up or placed in shelf, rack or bin where the material has been kept. Bin cards can also be in the form of loose sheets which can be maintained in a ledger kept in the stores.

Understanding Bin Card in a more Lucid Way

A Bin Card makes a record of the receipt and issue of material and is kept for each item of stores carried. Quantity of stores received is entered in the receipt column and the quantity of stores issued is recorded in the issue column of the bin card and a balance of the quantity of stores is taken after every receipt or issue, so that the balance at any time can be readily seen. These cards are maintained by the storekeeper and the storekeeper is answerable for any difference between the physical stock and the balance shown in the bin card. These cards are used not only for recording receipts and issues of stores; minimum quantity, maximum quantity and ordering quantity are stated on the bin card. By seeing the bin card, the storekeeper can send the material requisition for the purchase of material in time.

Are Bin cards necessary at all?

Some persons argue that where a store ledger is maintained, the bin card is a duplicate record and as such should not be maintained. This is wrong and is against the basic principles of stores accounting on account of the following reasons:

The storekeeper is responsible for the maintenance of stores and as such he should have a stock record under him.

The storekeeper is held responsible for the difference in the physical stock and the stock record. The responsibility for difference in stock will get divided if the stock records are not kept by the storekeeper.

The store ledger is not kept up-to-date because posting of transactions is done periodically and as such the maintenance of bin cards is desired to have up-to-date balance of stock. In bin cards, posting is done before the transaction takes place.

Keeping in view the above reasons it is said that storekeeper should himself keep the stores ledger. This is also wrong because a stores ledger is a record of both quantity and value and figures for calculation of the cost of production are taken from this record. The calculation of cost is the responsibility of the cost accountant; so the store ledger should not be outside the control of the cost accountant. Further, it is not fair to burden the storekeeper with the responsibility of the valuation of the receipts, issues and balances; his recording should be restricted to quantity alone. It is, therefore, necessary that both stock records should be kept.

The two records act as a cross check on each other because balance of stock disclosed by bin cards should agree with the balance shown by the stores ledger. Thus, the accuracy of both records is established.

PURCHASING AND RECEIVING

Purchasing

Buying quality and freshness of supplies and portion control are of the utmost important for the operation of a successful business.

Large establishment will often employ a purchase manager as he can concentrate and get the best supplies. Requisition for supplies are placed with the stores/ kitchen stewarding department at a specified time in advance by the chef de cuisine for highly perishable supplies. The storekeeper will forward his requisition for dry stores and cleaning materials in the same manner. Supplier should be changed time to time.

Knowledge of buying is quite essential. The buyer should have a reasonable technical knowledge in catering, as he will be able to follow the requisition properly & understand the importance of delivery times, size, quality and specifications etc. The purchaser should assimilate information, new ideas and techniques, gathered from trade journals, visit to exhibitions and food processing plants. The comparison of competitive price list from suppliers must be done occasionally.

While selecting suppliers following points should be considered.

- The prices are competitive for the goods specified in relation to quality
- The goods offered should meet the specifications by look and other related factors. Samples should be taken for checking.
- Financial terms offered relating to credit facilities and discount for settlement.

Selection will then be made of at least two suppliers for each group of supplies required in certain groups which include many commodities such as groceries, three or even more suppliers may be selected. Where supplies are obtained by contract, this will not apply.

Ordering Of Supplies

Orders for supplies generally fall in three categories:

1. Daily order (for perishable, meat, poultry, game, fish, fruits, veg, milk and cream)
2. Weekly order (dry store- i.e groceries etc.)
3. Standing orders. (Milk, egg, bacon, etc.)

Quality Control

Quality control depends upon organization to organization. Generally the establishment with smaller business volume follow the simple control procedure while the larger one practices the complex one. Quality control follow the following procedures:

- Establishment of standard specification:
- Checking the quantity and quality for commodities.
- Testing the finished food products.
- Feedback to management for reviewing.

Yield Management

Yield management, also known as revenue management, is the process of understanding, anticipating and influencing consumer behavior in order to maximize revenue or profits from a fixed, perishable resource. Yield management is the practice of pricing to maximize the amount of revenue received per unit sold. It is the process of allocating the right type of capacity to the right kind of consumer at the right price as to maximize revenue or yield.

Yield testing: Yield is the usable/edible part remaining after processing as the purchased quantity of food items.

Yield test: It is an indispensable preliminary for purchasing of food-stuffs and for choosing the most appropriate cooking methods. A panel will create for example, each soup base regards to taste, and test is under taken to establish the most economical method of preparation

A.P. = As purchased

E.P. = Edible portion

Yield factor: it can be defined as the ratio as usable quantity to purchased quantity.

Yield factor = Usable quantity
Purchased quantity

It is always less than 100 %

When it comes for yield amount it is always varies from product to product.

Yield test must be conducted several times in order to give a final result.

Raw yield test: when all trim is a waste.

1. A. P. – trimmed produced = **trim loss**

2. A.P. – trim loss = **total yield weight**
3. A.P.________ = **yield factor**
   Trimmed yield

Food cost can be defined as food used in fabricating a menu.

Food cost % = (food cost / Sale) *100

Standard Yield

It is the usable part of a particular food product after its initial preparation and cooking. In large food establishment as large quantity of food purchased therefore standard yield available for each item. In smaller establishment, standard yields determined for most expensive items.

- A standard for the quantity and number of proportion obtainable from specific item of food.
- Comparison with orating result and measuring the efficiency of production department.
- Evaluating standard purchase specification.
- A standard cost factor for the item of food.
- Menu costing and pricing.
- In converting forecast requirement into raw material requirement

HACCP AS CONTROL TOOL

HACP is a universal science based, documented system for identifying and assessing hazards and risk of food production and the implementation of coat effective controls and monitoring procedures for food safety.

SAFE FOOD- is the food from all types of contaminants which will cause no harm, injury or illness to the customers.

WHO has also emphasized the use of HACCP principles in all food establishments, food production industries and service restaurant.

Haccp Principles

Conduct of hazards analysis, prepare a flow diagram of the steps in the process. Identify and list the hazards and specify the control measures.

- o By using the discussion making identify the CCP'S (critical control points).
- o Establish targets levels and tolerance that must be met to ensure that each CCP is under control.
- o Establish a monitoring system to ensure the control of each CCP by schedule testing and observations.

- o Establish a corrective action to be taken when monitoring indicates that a particular CCP is moving out of control.
- o Establish documentation concerning all procedures and records appropriate to these principles and their applications.
- o Establish verification procedures that includes appropriate supplementary test, together with the review, which confirms that HACCP system is working effectively.

Important Critical Control Points Put Down Under (Haccp)

Food Restrictions: Raw or un-pasteurized food such as raw eggs, un-pasteurized milk, raw shellfish, etc. which are known to carry pathogenic bacteria.

Food supplies: Unsafe food supplies.

Food Thawing: Proper thawing under controlled temperature for acceptable time (below 8°C, 24 hrs). In emergency, thawing should be done in cold running water and surface temperature below 15°C for 30 min. maximum.

Food preparations: Proper washing, cleaning and processing of food stuff.

Personal Hygiene: Of the staff to avoid contamination during cooking or storage.

Equipment cleaning and disinfection: To avoid contamination during cooking or and further processing.

Food cooking: Cooking to required temperature to kill pathogens (Case temperature 75°C minimum).

Food Chilling: reduction of temperature from 60°C to 5°C within 4 hrs.

Food storage: Storage below 5°C.

Re- heating 75°C

Hot holdings: Above 60°C, maximum 2 hrs.

FOOD COSTING AND FORECASTING

Food costing

Food cost can be defined as cost of raw material, used for production. The total cost of a catering business can be broken down into three main areas

Total cost = food cost + labor cost + overhead expenses

Thus the price charged for a meal must be sufficient to cover both the cost of the food used and also a share of other costs.

Accurate food cost is help by carrying out the yield test of major commodities such as meat, fish, poultry, game and vegetables. Yield test tells us about amount lost during trimming. the percentage left for the intended dish and the real cost of the commodities.

Selling price = [{food cost/(100-required gross profit)} * 100]

Cost Control

The main aim of the kitchen management is to keep the low or the set cost of the menu so that the required margin of the sale of the food can be obtained. This completely depends upon the effective purchasing system and minimum wastage with required quantity of food cooked. Standardized recipe also plays a very vital role in controlling the food cost as with the help of these recipes chef is in a position to indent the complete menu exactly.

For effective purchasing, order should be placed in a systematic manner. Good purchasing saves time, eliminates errors, and gives right food at correct time.

The cost of meal falls naturally in to three distinct sections, the first being the cost of the food, and second the cost of the overheads, which include fuel, light, heat, water, staff uniforms and laundry, social security payments, superannuation contribution, printing and stationary, cleaning materials, advertising, telephones and postage, postage etc. Licenses, maintenance, contracts, replacement of crockery and cutlery, linen, utensils, repairs in general, insurance and finally rent, rates and investments on capital outlay. The third section is labour, the salaries and wages. The relationship between these classes of cost is always a matter of interest, which varies considerably from one type of catering establishment to another, the overheads etc. usually being greater than the bare cost of food.

The problem of any management is to make sure that a predetermined food and wage cost percentage has been decided. This figure will take in all aspect of expenses. The final trading results will show that a correct return has been made. To obtain this the following information should be studied

1. A record of cost for each section(wine, cigars, flowers, meals, rooms) must be made and recorded. These must be compared.
2. A weekly summary of all the relevant details must be prepared.
3. All purchase must be controlled.
4. An efficient system of cash control.
5. Any overproduction of food must be checked and of course reused in a best and most economical way.
6. Check for sales with direct number catered for.
7. Details of all merchandise received must be recorded, as and when issued.
8. Production – ingredients and amounts.
9. Sales of any kind checked with cash receipts.
10. The trading profit and loss account should be prepared.
11. Total daily wages costs must be recorded.

Material Costing

There are three basic methods of cost control.

1. Control on quantity
2. Control on selling price
3. Control on cost price

An effective system will disclose short falls in receipt which may be due to more of the following.

- o Faulty buying
- o Inefficient storing
- o Bad and wasteful cooking
- o Petty theft and leakage

Indenting and Costing

Indenting is similar to a requisition which is an interdepartmental document sent for, lets say, requirements of food, requires to cook food. It is a document stating requirements of goods in a terms of description of goods, the quality, the satisfaction, the units and the quantity required and sent to the stores who in turn will procure them on the day specified and dispatched to the department concerned. When one indents for a smaller quantities for one recipe, it seems simple, as it requires only what is needed. When quantities are more for more people, then one has to look into several factors, such as:

1. Ala carte, banquet or buffet
2. Choice provided on the menu
3. Number of Desserts
4. Number of items on the menu
5. Number of people to dine
6. Number of persons to feed, if number of people are large, then quantity is less.
7. Number of vegetarians and non- vegetarians
8. selling price of the menu
9. Silver plated or buffet service

In terms of food production, we have to be well versed and try to maintain the food cost of items as against their selling price depending on the policy of the restaurant. To maintain the food cost the actual consumption on that day will be termed as the food cost of the day.

All the factors must be considered and then one has to work out exactly the cost per portion of each dish. This should be updated yearly in terms of increase in prices and the selling price will give an accurate indenting and costing procedure.

Quantity Control

The control of a quantity consumed ensures that everything consumed has been announced for. It does not ensure profitability, but provides a useful supplementary check and is simple to operate. For simple dishes, this method is good but not for complex dishes. For small establishments when one storekeeper is responsible and issue one egg and two bacon rashers for breakfast, it controls consumption.

Selling Price Control

This method is also most suitable for establishment with a limited range of item on the menu, specially when each item contains a small number of standardized ingredients. It can be used in conjunction with quantity control. When a comprehensive range of dishes is served and the composition in each is not rigidly standardized, It becomes necessary to adopt a different method based on cost.

Cost Price

This system is most practical and best understood. It allows for certain elasticity and provides the chief with a margin for elastic development. The kitchen percentage entails the application for the following simple formula.

Gross profit*100 / takings = Rate % of gross profit

e.g.	Takings	Rs. 197.50
	Purchase	Rs. 82.25
	Gross profit	Rs. 115.25

Therefore, kitchen % (gross profit) to second decimal place is: 82.25 * 100 divided by 197.50= 41.64%

When stock checking is done, there may be minor discrepancies in the percentage, but this has to be taken into account.

When kitchen percentage drops below the normal figure, It should be presumed that some thing is wrong. The decline could have been caused by the following factors.

1. Faulty purchasing
2. Incorrect billing
3. Inefficiency and waste in the kitchen
4. Portion too large
5. Dishonest practices

Each dish is tagged and priced to show the desired percentage. At the cost of the day's business, the overall percentage is worked out and should agree with the figure budgeted for, in the pricing. Some fixed priced menus may be more profitable than others. What is important is the final results.

Net Profit

All expenditure can be classified as material cost, labour cost and overheads. It follows that the difference between total revenue and the cost is the net profit before tax.

Total Income

In a business solely concerned with the sale of food, the gross profit would be the difference between total income and cost of materials and would therefore be equal to labour cost + overheads + net profit

Portion Control

"Portion Control" means the amount of size of a portion of food to be served to a customer as per the policy of establishment. Food costing and portion control are complimentary and the need for this form of control comes from both sides of the business- from the caterer and his customers. There is a natural tendency for clients to eye on one another's portion when they are served and if one is thought to be slightly larger than the others, there is apt to be resentment and a reaction detrimental (harmful) to the good name of the not something that can be introduced at the service point, It must start when orders are placed for supplies.

Monitoring portion control could be done by direct supervision by sales analysis and by comparing the requisitions of each department with issues.

Purpose of Portion Control

1. To ensure fair portions for each customer.
2. To see that each department utilizes purchased raw materials maximum to the full.
3. To control waste.
4. To ensure that standard costing is as accurate as possible.

Methods Of Monitoring Portion Control

1. Ordering the right quantity, quality and supervising when receiving it.
2. Even preparing the food in the production area, under direct supervision.
3. By proper checking of the service of the food.
4. Comparing the requisitions of each department with issues
5. By sales analysis.

The standard food cost is determined on the basis of size of the portion served to a customer and the ingredients that go into the preparation of a particular item.

For determining the standard food cost following factors is considered:-

- ❖ Establishment of standards and standard procedure
- ❖ Pre-calculation of standard portion cost and ongoing development of number of portion sold in the past i.e. sales history and forecasting.

The percentage of total restaurant sales spent on food product, should stay around 28-30%, a steakhouse will have a higher food cost of around 35%, this number must be accurately tracked to figure out total profits for restaurant

Portion Size of Various Items for Different Types of Volume Feeding

Hypothetical Assumptions

A wise chef should know the following while indenting for any function.

1. 1 kg mutton cut serves 4-5 portion (a la carte) 9-10 portion (Volume)
2. 1 kg mutton mince serves 4-5 portion (a la carte) 9-10 portion (Volume)
3. 1kg Chicken cut serves 5 portion (a la carte) 9-10 portion (Volume)
4. 1 kg Chicken mince serves 4-5 portion (a la carte) 9-10 portion (Volume)
5. 1 kg paneer serves 5 portion (a la carte) 9-10 portion (Volume)

- 1 kg well dressed chicken serves approx. 400gms of B/L flesh.
- Average weight of rice served for a la carte is approx. 110-150 gms.
- Average weight of rice served for buffet is approx. 70-90 gms.
- 3 kg of dal makhni serves 60 portions in a la carte and 100 portions in buffet.
- Average weight tawa roti peda is 30 gms and tandoori roti is 50 gms.
- An average weight of Naan/ Parantha is 110gms.
- 1 kg of B/L chicken flesh serves approx.40 pcs.

Modifying Recipes for Indenting for a Large Scale Catering

Recipes must be modified for a large scale catering to avoid the barrier of cost factor

Change the ingredient: Some time it requires for the chef to change the ingredients in the recipe to get red of the hike in the cost or to make big margin of profit. The most expensive item may be removed from the recipe by keeping some alternative of it .

Eg. If the recipe contains green and red capsicum, you may omit the red capsicum and put red kashmiri chili instead.

Reducing the ingredients:- It stands for if chef feels that some of the ingredients are very expensive in the market which will go in the recipe he must modify the recipe and try reducing those items which are most expensive and increasing those which are least expensive. By doing these kind of exercises chef helps the organization to make a big margin of profit and he should be smart enough to give the best of the quality with the change also.

Practical Difficulties while Indenting for Volume Feeding

Most of the time the chef faces ~~a big problem while~~ indenting for mass. The reason could be various

1. If the guest is fussy and start allowing the take away from the function
2. If the host is of different cast and invitees are of different cast and from different place.
3. Some time the guest emphasizes only on one item or two only
4. The host may not be able to predict about the number of guest
5. The kids become the problem if in advance he is not told about them.
6. The price of the menu
7. The ratio of vegetarian and non vegetarian guest in the function
8. when guest brings their own eatables without pre informing
9. When guest comes very late to attend the function.
10. Which kind of people are attending the function

FORMS AND FORMATS

Portion control

Portion control is to understand how much a serving size is and how many calories a serving contains. Portion control is important for weight management as the weight is defined by the total calorie intake. Healthy eating, using Aristotle's philosophy, is the desirable middle between two extremes of excess and the other of deficiency (over eating and not eating enough), the "golden mean." Portion control is eating a healthy balance of amount and types, of varied foods. Food guide pyramids are used as a visual aid to help people eat a varied diet and control portions.

The failure to control portions is often caused by emotional factors such as a depressed mood or boredom. To avoid overeating triggered by emotions, planning meals ahead and using smaller dishes may be helpful. Portion sizes can be estimated by using objects as a point of reference. One way of determining portion size is to compare hand size. For example a healthy serving of protein should not be larger than a palm size piece of meat. Carbohydrate servings such as pasta can be measured by fistfuls. A healthy serving of pasta should be one fistful.

Meat Tag
Item No......
Cuts Total weight Total value Cost/kg Supplier Date received Date issued
Food store copy Send to food control on day of issue to kitchen

16

PURCHASING

"Purchase can be defined as a function and process which is concerned with search, selection, purchase, receipt, stooge and final use of a commodity in accordance with catering policy of the establishment".

In current scenario purchasing is a much broader concept and includes a wide range of related activities such as market research, source development, vendor rating, import substitution, follow up, evolving proper system, standardization, selective control negotiation, surplus disposal, inventory management, transportation and coordination with the departments and so on. A successful operation of any business depends upon, to a large extent, on the availability of goods or raw materials: the right quantity, at the right time, from the right source and the right price.

The purchase manager is responsible for the entire purchase of the unit. Therefore he must have a good knowledge of merchandise, the source of supplies and availability, description of the items and price, both whole sale and retail.

Aims and Objectives of Purchase Policy

Purchase Policy

The primary objective in the purchasing of food is to obtain the best quality of merchandise, based on the specifications established for each hotel, at the lowest possible price. Below are given some fundamentals for effective purchasing.

1. A qualified and honest purchasing agent.
2. A sound set of standard purchase specifications.
3. Effective buying methods and procedures.
4. Centralized purchasing- Only one person buys all food, beverage and supplies of any kind.

5. The executive chef should be consulted in all purchase pertaining to his department.
6. All major purchase – such as direct importation – has to be authorized by management.
7. Perpetual record of purchase unit prices will be instituted.
8. The purchasing agent will develop and establish a record of standard purchase specifications.
9. The purchasing agent / should use "daily price quotation" sheet in order to maintain competitive buying.

Aims and Objectives

1. Correct storage and optimum stock level for smooth operation.
2. Determine the choice of item available to customer.
3. Estimate the quantity to be purchased.
4. Feedback of information to management aiming to improve more and more.
5. Inspect for quantity and quality of food items.
6. Measurement of performance of all outlets involved in production.
7. Proper preparation of items purchased.
8. Provision of satisfactory products at the cost selling price/cost.
9. Select suppliers and ensuring the continuous supply.
10. To determine, what market segment is aimed at.

Purchase Procedure: There are different procedures for the various categories of provisions.

Perishable Purchases: are generally done by inviting tenders for an annual rates contract. This not only helps in a regular supply at a fixed rate throughout the year, but also enables the management to forecast and calculate the actual food cost on a rational basis for budget purposes. The purchase manager invites vendor and obtains offer sufficiently in advance of the commencement of the financial year. The offers are analyzed with particular reference to the ability and dependability of the vendor, the quoted price, comparison with the other vendor, etc. The quotations of the short-listed vendors are then negotiated by the food committee consisting of the purchase manager, food and beverage manager, Executive chef, food and beverage controller and chief accountant before the contract is awarded for the duration of the year. Perishable provisions which are required on a continuous basis are requisitioned by the Executive Chef.

Non Perishable Purchase: Like canned and bottled provisions, spices pulses etc. are non contracted item. Once the order has been placed with the purchase department by the stores, the purchase manager sends the enquiries in this respect to all well established manufacturers / agents/ dealers. The samples are obtained and sent to the Executive chef or food and beverage manager for his or their approval. A final comparative statement of quotations indicating items, brand names, purchase rates, quantity to be purchased, cost and the names of the suppliers are prepared. The price and quality are the two factors which decide the choice of the vendor. Non perishable provisions are requisitioned by the store in-charge.

Central Purchasing

Centralized purchasing system is very popular in chain operations. Food and beverage commodities are purchased in bulk and later send to concerned department for processing. According to this system the requirements of each individual unit are relayed to a central office. The central office or the purchase department determines the total requirements of all units and then makes total purchases either for delivery to the individual units by the dealer or for centralized delivery.

Advantage

1) All purchasing are made as per specification.
2) Easy to check and control over all units of purchase.
3) Helps in maintaining large inventories.
4) It provides the opportunity to obtain desired quality.
5) Volume purchasing leads to low pricing and reduces food cost.

Disadvantage

a) Everybody has to accept the standard item in the stock/store.
b) Little freedom to purchase own item.
c) The establishment or the concerned unit cannot take advantage of local reduced prices.
d) Very little freedom to change the menu due to menu standardized.

Identifying Regular Suppliers

Finding vendors that will supply the items needed to operate efficiently is an important task for food service managers. The key factors behind successful relations between vendors and food service managers are product quality, available quantity, and dependable service. A survey of vendors in the surrounding area is a good way for a food service operation to begin searching for vendors that fits its needs. Record of past performance, if available, are the most reliable source to consult when choosing vendors. When a manager is just starting out, however, it is helpful to have opinions and recommendations from personal contacts. Salespeople are another good source of information for vendor selection. Telephone directory can also be useful to locate vendors. After all possible vendors have been explored management must narrow down the group by comparing vendors on product quality and quantity, dependability and price.

There are some suppliers who are able to offer full supply services of all commodities. A food and beverage establishment may agree for such suppliers This system has the advantage of only having to negotiate with one supplier, a reduce volume of paper work and fewer deliveries.

Under proper purchasing procedure it is necessary to secure for each item at-least two or three quotations from two or three dealers before placing an order. It is obvious that without specifying the size of the flank and other consideration like quality, age etc. the highest quotation might be the cheapest because so much depends upon the size of the flank. The same consideration must be given to the cuts of meat where a substitution of cheaper cuts for the higher valued cuts might bring forth a lower quotation to the detriment (loss) of the hotel. In case of a new supplier is to be selected, a great deal of exercise and detailed inquiries be made as regard to:

1. A visit to a new firm.
2. Delivery procedure of the supplier.
3. Details about other customers who are using the products of concern supplier.
4. Details about the firm/ reputation
5. Feedback/Information of other customers of their product
6. Minimum order level which can be easily handled by supplier.
7. Other procedures and formalities needed by the supplier
8. Capable of handling part deliveries or standing orders.
9. Recent price list of food items.
10. Sample of products for listing purposes / quality of the product.
11. Trade terms and conditions such as cash discount, trade discount, group or company discount etc.

On selection, the suppliers are put on an approved "suppliers list". Periodically the evaluation of their performance could be done using a rating system based on: Price Performance, Quality Performance and Delivery Performance.

Job Description of Purchase Manager

Purchasing managers, buyers, and purchasing agents take several steps to reach these goals, they research sales records and inventory levels of current stock, find foreign and domestic suppliers, and stay current on any changes in either the supply of or demand for needed products and materials.Companies hire purchasing managers, buyers, and purchasing agents to find the best merchandise at the lowest possible purchase cost. Purchasers typically buy goods and services for their company or organization to use, while buyers ordinarily buy items in order to resale them for profit. Purchasers and buyers find the best goods or services, choose suppliers, negotiate prices, and grant contracts that ensure that the right amount of the product or service is received when it is needed. Manage and facilitate all facets of supply management activities between division business units and their suppliers.

1. To create and maintain mutually beneficial long-term partnerships with suppliers for faster feedback and continuous improvement.
2. Develop cross-functional teams to understand company-wide needs and evaluate suppliers.
3. Developing strategies for assigned procurement area to include spend analysis, market and geographic considerations, strategic importance, etc.
4. Drive continuous improvement in all aspects of the procurement process.
5. Implement appropriate sourcing strategies to control the company's purchased material costs and to assure an adequate source of supply.
6. Implement sourcing strategies to support corporate and divisional objectives, providing the company competitive advantage in the areas of materials, supplies, and services.
7. Locate, analyze, and develop a consolidated supplier base to meet current and future commodity needs.
8. Maintains and promotes sound relationships with suppliers and the business community
9. Manage suppliers, cost, quality, and delivery performance.
10. Managing and optimizing supplier performance, including continuous improvement, innovations, obsolescence and reduction in total cost of ownership.
11. Keep an eye on all Negotiation and manage all contracts and agreements for assigned commodities
12. Understand, track, and forecast the key cost drivers and market factors for assigned commodities.

Methods Employed in Purchasing

While purchasing any food and beverage items it is always necessary to do a comparative study of the actual cost and printed price list from supplier. Depending upon the location and availability of merchandise various buying methods can be seen in market, however some of the methods practices in most of the food and beverage establishments are described below

1. **Contract Purchasing**: A contract is a legal document and the condition of the contract should be carefully prepared, if needed revised preferably by the solicitors of the firm. There are two common types of contracts:
   a) **The Specific Period Contract:** The aims of specific period contract is to determining the source of supply and the price of goods for a stated period says three or six months. Such contract is suitable for items which have stable prices such as bread, butter, milk, cream etc.
   b) **The Quantity Contract:** The aims of the Quantity Contract is to ensure the continuous supply of a given quantity of an essential item at an predetermined

agreed price over a particular trading period. Such type of contract is most suitable for fruits, frozen vegetables etc.

2. **Periodical Purchasing:** Depending upon the estimated average consumption of food and beverage product within a span of week/ month or fortnight, a master quotation list ids prepared A master quotation list is prepared so that stock is maintained at regular basis. This form of buying is mostly used for groceries type commodities.
3. **Daily Market List Purchasing:** Most of the time Daily Market List Purchasing is used for perishable products and it is always made with two or more supplier. As per the requirement of the food and beverage preparation the senior members of kitchen make the daily market list for purchasing.
4. **Cash and carry method**: Cash and carry method is mostly used for for small and medium sized establishments. It provides the complete freedom for purchasing from the market at competitive price and the buyer can personally check the quantity and the taste of the item. If the warehouse is situated nearby kitchen it makes the purchasing process faster and reduces any undo running.
5. **"Paid reserve" method**: "Paid reserve" method is used when it is necessary to ensure the quantity of supply of an item for the menu which is of particular importance for a specialty restaurant / establishment or any other related catering outlets. For all purchasing the payments are done well in advance so the there should be a continuous supply. The products mostly includes are lobster, shrimps, steaks, mushroom etc.

- **Cost plus method: Cost plus method** is very popular and suitable for welfare catering institutions such as hospitals, boarding house etc. The approved supplier is paid exactly the same price that he paid for the commodities plus an agreed percentage to meet the other expenses.
- **Total supply method:** There are some suppliers who are able to offer a full supply service of all commodities. A food and beverage establishment may agree for such supplier. This system has the advantage of only having to negotiate with one supplier, a reduced volume of paper work and fewer (smaller amount) deliveries.

Types of Purchases

The primary purpose of establishing control over purchasing is to ensure a counting supply of sufficient quantities of the necessary foods, each of the quality appropriate to its intended use purchase at the most favorable price. Therefore we must establish the essential standard and standard procedures for effective purchase. Standard must be developed for the:

1. Quality of food purchase
2. Quantity of food purchased
3. Prices at which food is purchased.

Perishables (Meat, Poultry, Dairy products, Fruits and Vegetables)

Are those items, typically fresh foods that have a comparatively short useful life after they have been received. Various kinds of lettuce and fresh fish, for example, begin to lose their quality very quickly. Some meats and cheeses will retain their quality for somewhat longer periods, but the quality of these perishable will begin to deteriorate much sooner than will the quality of non perishable, - Cans of tomato puree, for example. Perishables then should be purchased for immediate use in order to take advantage of the quality desired at the time of purchase. If a steward is always careful to purchase the best quality available for intended use, then it would be wasteful and costly not to make use of that carefully selected quality.

Non-Perishable

Are those food items that have longer shelf life, often referred to as groceries or staples, they may be stored in the packages or containers in which they are received, often on shelves and at room temperature, for weeks or even months. They do not deteriorate quickly as long as they are unopened or and kept at reasonable temperature. They are typically purchased and stored in jars, bottles, cans, bags and boxes; the storage area in which they are kept, usually called a storeroom, would resemble the shelves of a super market to the lay man. Because these foods do not deteriorate quickly, it is possible to keep reasonable supply of each on hand, for use as needed. For example, the restaurant that used an average of four no. 10 cans of whole, peeled tomatoes daily, could keep a supply of eight cases on hand without running any risk of spoilage. Foods that typically fall into this category of non perishable include salt, sugar, canned fruits and spices.

Chemicals and Cleaning Supplies

Although there are a number of regulations that may affect the use and disposal of specific chemicals, two particular sets of rules should be kept in mind for all chemicals:

- Most chemicals used in the workplace are covered by OSHA's **Hazard Communications Standard (HazCom)**. It establishes uniform requirements to make sure that the hazards of each of these chemicals are evaluated, and that this hazard information is transmitted to employers who deal with the chemicals and to employees who might be exposed to them. Hazcom also covers chemical hazards labeling.
- Used or discarded chemicals may be regulated under EPA's **Resource Conservation and Recovery Act (RCRA)** hazardous waste regulations .Among other rules, RCRA requires small and large quantity generators to take steps to reduce their waste.

Cleaning chemicals in common use at healthcare facilities fall into several product categories including:

- Air fresheners
- Bathroom and tile cleaners
- Dusting aids
- Fabric protestants
- Floor polishes/waxes
- Furniture maintenance products (aerosols)
- General purpose cleaners
- Glass cleaners

Waste reduction of cleaning chemicals can be achieved by purchasing less toxic chemicals in the first place and by improving the use of materials so that less chemical is used. While purchasing cleaning chemicals, look for products that are certified to meet certain environmental and health and safety criteria. There are several accrediting bodies that make determinations about whether cleaning chemicals have met environmental criteria.

To improve use and handling of cleaning chemicals, consider the following:

- Ensure that employees:
  - o Use supplies only for their intended purpose
  - o Use only the amount necessary
- Provide transfer methods which prevent spills and quality problems:
  - o Gravity spigot or pump to dispense bulk liquid materials
  - o A spout and funnel for transferring liquids to different containers
- Control access to hazardous raw materials:
  - o Designate central personnel to distribute materials
  - o Limit access to employees trained in hazardous materials handling and who understand the importance of first-in first-out policy
- Keep records of when and why larger spills occurred in order to identify spill prevention opportunities and document related costs

Engineering Items (spares) & Capital Supplies

Purchase of capital supplies depends upon the organization structure of the establishment. The concern departments the experts explain the need of the particular equipments and the information is send to top management for final approval. The equipments purchased must be cost effective for purchaser and user. At the same time it must follow the safety guidelines as well as NOC from environment department.

Petty Purchases

Petty purchase accounts are those accounts which deals with the recording for all minor purchasing made for smooth operation. Most of the time it includes the local purchasing and related travel expenses in exchange for bills and cash payments. In accounts department we used to have special staff that take care of all recording and payments in petty purchasing. There are certain credit limits which depends upon organization to organization.

17

PURCHASE ORDER GENERATION

PREPARING AND FORWARDING REQUISITIONS

Procedure of an establishment of organization always reflects the kind of business and place in the market. While preparing the requisition we should check all kinds of previous stocks. It includes dry stores, cold rooms, processed items in hand and most important thing is the coming functions. Following procedure must be followed while making requisition.

- Check previous stocks and future requirements
- Requisition from an authorized member of kitchen.
- Select the sources of supplies for concerned commodities.
- Entering into contract with related supplier
- Acceptance of food and beverage goods and commodities in terms of quantity and quality.

Purchase Order Generation

This is another important document to be issued for all items ordered. This should be prepared listing all items ordered, delivery time, terms of payments, the agreed price and another conditions. It includes the following process.

1) Requisition from an authorized person from kitchen (For food related commodities).
2) Check for purchase specification of all food items
3) Check the previous records of all concerned items from purchase office.
4) Select the sources of supplies.
5) Details from supplier about commodities.

6) Selection of a supplier from pool of approved suppliers.
7) Negotiations on pricing and delivery specification.
8) Preparation of purchase order for selected supplier.
9) Place the purchase order

Purchase Order

A complete record of all order made would help the receiving department to take necessary action for any food stuff late in arriving. All purchase should be made strictly as per the purchase indent or standard list. The purchase order is made for all items except standing rates contract items.

It is usually made in six duplicate:-

- o Original (white) Supplier
- o Duplicate (yellow) Accounts
- o Triplicate (Pink) purchase
- o Quadruplicate (blue) Master copy
- o Quintuplicate (Green) Receiving
- o Six duplicate (Orange) Indenting Department

Telephone Transmittal Slip

In the eventuality of the purchase order not being made in time, telephonic information must be sent to receiving department followed by their copy. The order on phone must be placed by the purchase manager, which is recorded on the Telephone Transmittal slip (TTS) and purchase order.

First copy of TTS goes to Accounts Department, Second copy to Receiving Firm, where it goes to accounts department along with the bill.

Forms and Formats

Formats involved in Purchase Order Generation

1. Steward List/Daily Meats/Perishable Order

ABC Hotels Ltd.

Order Place on........... Required By...............

Item	Unit	Par Stock	Stock on Hand	Quantity Requested

Executive Chef Store Keeper

XYZ Hotels Ltd.

PURCHASE ORDER

No.______ For stores________

Department________________________

To_________ Date______ Requisition No. ______

(Concern Suppliers)

Please enter your order for;

Quantity	Description	Price	Total

All Goods delivered to

____

____

The acceptance of this order is an acceptance of all conditions herein

(Signature)

XYZ Hotels Ltd.

TELEPHONE TRANSMITTAL SLIP

Vendors No.........

Name Ref. no.....

Address Date......

S.O.No.....

S.NO	Items	Quantity

Date of Delivery Signature

2. Daily Market List

ABC Hotels Ltd.

Date.......

Item	Stock on Hand	Requisition	Supplier			Item	Stock on Hand	Requisition	Supplier		
			A	B	C				A	B	C

Executive Chef Store Keeper

Purchase Indent

All purchase indents should be marked "Urgent", or "Routine" depending upon the urgencies of the requirement. For Non-Perishable items there identification number is needed to prepare the purchase indent. Any goods which is an non-storeroom inventory must need the approval of General Manager of concern organization or establishment.

ABC Hotels Ltd.

From: _______
Purchasing Dept.
Please Supply

Indent No_____
Date: ________

S.No.	Description/ Specification	Quantity Required	Unit	Delivery required by	Delivery Schedule Consumption	Average monthly	Stock in Hand	Due	Expected	Remarks

Attention:

1. Only one category of item should be indented.
2. Reasonable lead time must be allowed.
3. Proper description with complete description.
4. All indents are to be through stores.

Signature

18

RECEIVING

All goods and commodities received in an establishment always have a monetary value and hence must be taken care seriously. Receiving is not just accepting of and signing for goods brought to the hotel. It includes verification of quality and specifications. The receiving department therefore requires a strong and vigilant staff with a professional background of food and purchasing.

All goods handling at the receiving platform should be accompanied by an invoice. An invoice is a document listing the items sent to a buyer, stating a price, quality and other specifications. Each item on the invoice should be checked – weighed and / counted – against the purchase order. Any unsatisfactory items should be returned to the supplier immediately and the purchase department should be intimated accordingly. The invoice should then be signed, dated and stamped as received by the receiving clerk.

A record should be maintained of the items received and, at the end of the day, a daily report is prepared. This report will show the name of the supplier, item and quantity. It helps in maintaining control of all items and provides a basis for subsequent verification and Accounting.

Most of the time meats and fishes are usually not received in the exact amount ordered unless portion controlled or specially packed. But it is always advisable to make the proper specification for receiving. It is necessary that the receiving clerk write the correct weight on the invoice and initial it. It is also advisable to receive meats, fish and poultry in the presence of the butcher chef. Once approved by him, the supply should be weighed and dispatched to the stores, deep freezers/ walk- in or the butcher's shop.

All food items should be dated and special instruction for using and storing must be mentioned along with food items or commodities. This system establishes the FIFO method. For all meats received, the meat tag must be used. The tag has a printed number, space for the date, supplier's name, the cut, the weight and the price. This aids in issuing as well. Tagging also helps in discovering the shrinkage, if any, at the time of issuing. The vendor can then immediately be identified and penalized.

Aims of Receiving Department

- **Quality inspection of food items**: it has been saying as if you want to make the best product, always start with best ingredients. It can happen only when we will receive the food items with proper check for the quality. Photographs can be displayed in receiving areas for checking the quality. Of receiving goods. A copy of the purchase specification manual should be handy for this purpose.
- **Quantity inspection of food items**: As per specification and requisition the receiving clerk checks the delivery of the goods against the delivery notes and against the purchase order. Items are counted, weighed and checked against the delivery notes.
- **The invoice:** It is a document which has detailed information about the food deliveries. It is presented to the receiving clerk in duplicate by the person making the delivery, who expects the receiving clerk to sign and return the second copy, thus acknowledging to the supplier that the hotel has received the commodities listed.
- **Time tabling of deliveries**: Since hotel personnel are busy in their routine activities, irregular movements of suppliers with their food items forcing for receiving may creates confusions among the kitchen personnel. The usual practice in many hotels is to take deliveries of perishable items early in the morning and groceries items are delivered in the afternoon. For purpose of convenience and saving of time, it is advisable to time- table deliveries with the cooperation of suppliers.

Jobs Description of Receiving Manager

1. All requisitions are collected in time so the it can be dispatched to purchase and order can be given in time.
2. Check the amount mention by the supplier that should tally with the agreement notes.
3. Coordination between all the departments that receiving has to deal with.
4. Goods should be accepted by the specifications.
5. Information to the stores the moment delivery comes.
6. Make sure that the deliveries come to the hotel in time.
7. Make sure that the items weighed are correct and there is no pilferage by the supplier or the employees.

8. Make sure that there is no discrepancy in the purchase order and the supplies brought by the supplier.
9. Minimize the purchasing errors by involving the employees who are involve in the purchase of the items.
10. To depute a responsible personnel to receive incoming deliveries.

Equipment Required for Receiving

- o Commercial weighing scale
- o Toed boxes (lexons)
- o Trolley
- o Racks
- o Cage
- o Fork lifter

Receiving Procedure

Receiving department must be ready with all documents and receiving equipments. If required proper briefing should be done well in advance. The duties and responsibility need to be properly delegated so that there should not be any type of confusion among receiving employees. As soon we receive the food items, they must be proper check for quantity and quality as per Receiving specification. Once all records are maintained the perishables must be transferred to concern stores. Following points should be taken care for better receiving.

- Efficient receiving requires adequate receiving space in the receiving area as well as necessary equipment, qualified receiving personnel, and appropriate storage space for food and supplies.
- Scales being properly adjusted for accurate weighing.
- Incoming orders are unloaded in the receiving area, which also serves as an entrance for salespeople and food service personnel.
- Storage space located near the receiving area also prevents delivery personnel and sales people from passing through the production area of the kitchen.
- The manager's office should be located near the receiving area, and it should have a clear view of the entrance so that the manager can monitor deliveries, salespeople and personnel.
- Time and money are saved if the receiving area is designed to promote prompt storage.

DOCUMENTS REQUIRED WHILE RECEIVING (FROM HOTEL AND FROM SUPPLIER)

Blind Receiving

In blind receiving it generally seen that there is no invoice accompanying along with delivery of food and beverage products. The supplier always makes a regular invoice and sends them to hotel accounts via mail or fax. In this method the job of receiving employee becomes more prominent. The concern employee record all received items manually and the report are send to account office for comparison with the earlier mailed/ fax send by the supplier to hotel account

FOOD STORE BLIND RECEIVING REPORT

No __________ Date ______________

BEVERAGES / CIGARETTES

Stock No.	Quantity	Description	Unit	Remarks

Store keeper In-charge Store

Delivery Note

The receiving clerk compares all the receiving good with purchase order, for quantity and quality. When there is any short supplies or any kind of return due to unacceptable quality are recorded in delivery note. For any kind of short receiving usually in most of the hotel a printed slip "requested for credit" is completed and signature of the delivery man's signature are obtained thereon. Delivery Note always made in duplicate. The original copy is kept in store department and duplicate goes to supplier with authorizes signature from receiving department.

Meat Tag

Most of the time the tagging is done for the most expensive items such as processed meats such as ham, smoke salmon, poultry and seafood, etc. which gives an idea about cut, weight, costing, self life, supplier details, date of receiving and date of issuing.

This serves many purposes such as:

1. Assist in controlling the stock level of these items.
2. Helps in calculating food cost percentage more accurately.
3. It helps in control of expensive food
4. Receiving department weighs and records each item against the specific weight range.
5. With clearly marked date on the tag, it helps in efficient rotation of stock.

DELIVERY NOTE

Customer's Copy

To__________

No __________

Date ________

Order No.	Quantity	Description	Unit value	Remarks

Delivered by

Received by

Signature

Signature

MEAT TAG

ITEM	No......................
Cut	....
Total Weight	....
Total Value	....
Cost/ Kg	....
Supplier	....
Date Received	....
Date Issued	....

Goods Receiving Report

Daily Receiving Report

DATE ______

P.O. NO	Qnty	Purveyor Description	Unit	Unit Price	Total of Invoice	Meat	Perishable	Groceries	Dairy	Misc.	S.tax

Receiving Manager

Use of Standards and Specifications while Receiving

Standards and specifications always results uniformity in production of goods and services. Whenever we make recipes or any checklist it is always advisable to get raw materials as per the requirements and instructions. There are so many advantages of receiving goods as per specifications and standards.

- It provides standards products for preparation of recipes.
- Suppliers get requisitions in written so it helps in proper receiving as stated earlier in requisition.
- Written information helps in further processing of concern items.
- With the help of specification anyone from concern department can take part in receiving with the help of written documents in form of purchase specifications.
- It also gives guidelines for proper storage, self life and usage.
- These standards and specifications are useful in proper training and developments for receiving.
- The written documents provide the base for proper controlling on the receiving and further requisition.

19

STORES - RECIEPTS/ ISSUE CONTROL

The term store, Storehouse, or Warehouse refers to a building or room or place where raw materials are kept in an organized manner for further processing. The art of store management is largely that of optimizing the use of resources to meet actual needs in an efficient manner.

Storage is an essential part of the economic cycle and store management is today a specialized function which can contribute significantly to the overall efficiency and cost effectiveness of the materials function.

An organization can have various or specific type of stores, like a raw materials store, processed or semi- finished materials store, finished goods store, yard store and so on. Such stores range from ordinary one with shelves and bins to cold or the humidified storage system, huge silos for storage of food grain or bonded stores for keeping goods on which customs and excise duties have not been paid.

The task of store management relates to safe custody and preservation of the material stocked and to their receipt, issue and accounting. The objective is to efficiently and economically provide the right material at the time when it is required and in the condition in which it is required.

The storage is just an overhead- a cost with no return and hence the importance of economic operations, while keeping efficiency at a desired level. The capital cost components consist of the expenditure on land, buildings and roads, stock yards, storage and material handling equipment.

Machinery and other facilities provided. The revenue expenditure consists of salaries and wages, insurance, maintenance cost, stationary, communication expenses and the cost of maintaining the inventory. Efficiency requires planning in the store. That has to be forecast with the considerable degree of accuracy.

One of the indicators of efficiency in the store is the number of times the stock has turned over. Money is a scarce resource and once it is converted into material, it is useful only when the material have been reconverted back into money. This is the significance of stock turnover. This is also called inventory turnover.

There are many variety of materials stored - Chemicals, metals, liquids, gases, spare parts, equipment or finished goods, ranging from engineering components to drugs and pharmaceuticals. Each of these items will require a specific type of storage and their handling and preservation methods will vary accordingly. There is a high degree of specialization requires to store and handle these product and in many cases special storage license is to be obtained from the government.

AIMS OF STORE CONTROL

The main objective of store control is to provide service to the operating functions and this aspect of service must be fully appreciated. All the other activities, although they have their own importance, are subordinate to this main responsibility of service.

The service rendered by the stores can be categorized into four broad divisions.

1. Available maintain the balanced flow of raw materials, components, tools, equipment and any other materials necessary to meet operational requirements.
2. Maintenance materials, spare parts and general store as required regularly.
3. To accept and store scrap and other discarded material as they arise and also arrange for their disposal.
4. To manage the received and dispatch finished products

Job description of the Store Manager

The major responsibilities of the Store Manager are listed below:

1. Adequate Storage and preservation
2. Formulation of Stock taking
3. Identification of all materials held in stores.
4. Issue of materials to users within the organization
5. Management and maintenance of stock records
6. Management Inventory control process and action against any discrepancies
7. Management of store accounting
8. Material handling
9. Packing and dispatch of finished goods
10. Processing of customer orders
11. Receiving and management of incoming materials
12. Regular Inspection of all receipt from vendors and sub contractors.
13. Responsible for dispatch of finished goods

14. Submission of management information reports for further improvement and policy making.

1. **Packing and dispatch of finished goods:** This may be to a customer or a depot or a stockiest of the company or to a sub- contractor, for processing the material to send.
2. **Identification of all materials held in stores:** Identification is the process of systematically defining and describing all items of materials in stock
3. **Inspection:** Inspection involves the examination of incoming consignments for quality. Very often there is a separate quality control or inspection department which undertakes this work for most materials
4. **Inventory control:** It is the operation of continuously arranging for receipt and issue in such a way as to ensure that the stock balances in quantity. Instructions are given for the placing of an order to control corresponds with future estimated requirements.
5. **Issue:** This is the process of receiving demands, selecting the items required from storage and handling them over to users.
6. **Management of store accounting:** Stores accounting is the process of recording details of the stock movements and balances in terms of financial value. It is sometimes undertaken by the accounts department, but there is much to be said for it being handled by the store itself. In practice it is often found that such an agreement saves a good deal of work and duplication. It has the added advantage of making the store's personnel responsible for providing their own financial information which they require for the purpose of inventory control. Computerization simplifies this work.
7. **Material handling:** Materials handling involves movement and handling. This can be manual or mechanical or may be automatic. Heavy items, dangerous or inflammable goods and delicate merchandise have all to be handled differently.
8. **Packing:** material dispatched to the customers from the finished goods store or from one store to another at different locations required to be packed. Material requires packing according to their nature and this may vary from heavy wooden crates to ordinary paper cartons.
9. **Preservation** involves the maintenance of materials to retain their quality. Quite often, temperature, humidity, dust and other factors cause deterioration of materials. Processing of customers orders: The finished goods store or depots of the distribution network of the company are responsible for this work. The goods asked for are picked from the shelves and an invoice is prepared.
10. **Receiving and management of incoming materials:** Receipt is the process of checking and accepting, from all sources (vendor, sub- contractors, production units, repair units etc.),
11. **Stock records:** These are the documents which record, from day to day, full particular of individual receipts, issue and balance of material in stock. Increasingly, computers are being used for this purpose.

12. **Stock taking:** Is the process of physical verification of the quantity and condition of goods in the store.
13. **Storage:** Materials are stored in pallets, in bins, on racks and shelves and sometimes in the yard. The location is usually indicated in the stock – card. The storage period may vary between one day and one year or more, depending upon decampment procedures, safety stock required, etc. storage is the physical act of storing the materials.
14. **Submission of management information reports for further improvement and policy making.**This is an important task. There are many reports of varying periodicity to be submitted. The accuracy and timeliness of such reports are most important.

Issuing

Issuing is a process of removal of the products from the storage area to be moved to main production area for the processing with prior authorization from senior member. It involves transfer of goods which have a particular value to the department which is going to apply certain processes and create new items with added values to get revenue. This calls for special procedures for issuing the products from the storeroom.

The Issuing Procedure

The most common procedure for issuing is use of requisition forms. These requisition forms are to be filled in by consuming department to seek the materials required. As per control techniques, these requisition forms should be only made and signed by authorized persons. The time of issuing can be regulated so that the store department does not have to issue the items all the time, but there will be a fixed time to issue the goods so that the store can keep the stocks up to date. The consuming department should also be required to forecast and plan for the required materials beforehand..

There should be a strict order that issues will be made only against authorized requisition forms and at specified times. The issue form should be well designed so that it gives information about the sr. no. of requisition slip, along with quantities of issued materials, any exceptional item which is not available in the stores must be made available with in prescribed time so that operation does not suffer. There should be a system to value the issue slips so that this information can be effectively used to ascertain the costs for the day viz a viz sales and control the same.

Special Measures for the Issue of Beverages

While issuing beverages there are certain points which must be considered. Whenever beverages are issued, the bottles are marked as the house property so that the same bottle will be consumed and not any other bottle, which can be brought by the service staff with intention to sale the beverage at the menu prices and pocket the sales. Issuing can form an important function and link in control techniques because it is a major link between the goods stored and the goods ready for processing. There should be a tight control over the authorization of products to be indented and issued to avoid fraud and waste.

FORMAT OF REQUISITION FORM

Hotel XYZ

Requisition Slip

No.____ Date _____ From _________ To _________

Sr.	Ingredient	Qty Req.	Qty Issued	Rate	Amount
1					
2					
3					
4					
5					

Prepared By Authorised By Issued By Received By

Copies

1. For stores Dept
2. For Consuming Dept
3. For Accounts/ Control Dept.
4. Book Copy

Receiving Personnel

Must be trained in following areas for proper and sound receiving.

1. Understand and recognize product quality
2. Understand proper receiving procedures
3. Know how to complete internal receiving control documents
4. Know how to use equipment properly
5. Correctly respond when problems or errors occur
6. Must practice good hygiene and follow strict sanitation procedures
7. Must cooperate with other departments in the operation

Receiving Procedures

1. Check incoming products against ***purchase orders*** or ***purchase records***
2. Check incoming products against the standard written ***purchase specifications***

3. Check incoming products against delivery ***invoices***
4. Accept incoming products
5. Move accepted products into the proper storage area immediately or directly into production
6. Complete the necessary receiving documents
   - o **Daily Receiving Report**
     - § Separates Beverage costs from food costs
     - § Calculate the value of the "directs" (i.e., the products that went directly to production)
     - § Transfers control from Receiving to Storeroom
   - o **Request for Credit Memo**
     - § Should be used whenever a delivery invoice is modified
       - · Wrong quantity delivered
       - · Quality problems
       - · Incorrect pricing or price extensions
     - § This document should include the following...
       - · Note specific problems with the invoice
       - · Have the signature of the delivery person
       - · A copy should be given to the delivery person to take back to the supplier
       - · A copy should be attached to the invoice
       - · Problem invoices should be stored in a separate file until they are resolved
       - · Call supplier to notify them of the error on the original invoice
7. Mark and tag items before they go to the storage area
8. Put date and price information product

Security Concerns in Receiving

a) Supplier delivers lower quality product

b) Short weight or short count

c) Thawed products represented as fresh

d) Meat may have ice ground in, fillers, or excessive fat to increase its weight

e) Weight of packaging material may be included in product's weight

f) "Slacked out" seafood (frozen seafood, thawed and then packed on ice) may be sold as fresh

g) Expensive steaks and cheaper meat may be packed together, an empty bottle is included in a case

To Guard Against Theft in Receiving F&B Operators Should...

1. Separate the purchasing and receiving functions
2. Train employees to receive properly
3. Try to schedule deliveries at slow times
4. Have deliveries made to a specific location in the facility
5. After receipt, move product immediately to storage or into production
6. Do not let salespersons or delivery personnel have access to the storage areas
7. Keep the receiving door locked
8. It has been saying:
   § if the product is weighable, weigh it
   § if the product is measurable, measure it
   § if the product is countable, count it

TYPES OF STORES IN HOTEL (FOOD, DRY, ENGINEERING, CHEMICAL AND CLEANING, BEVERAGE, DEEP FREEZER)

Types Of Stores

The stores are mainly divided into two categories.

a. Functional: depending on the use to which the material is put, e.g. Chemical store, tool store, raw material store, etc.
b. Physical: depending on its size and location, e.g. Central store, sub- store, transit stores, site stores, etc.

Functional store: Some typical kinds are discussed below:

1. **Dry store:** Place where all the groceries can be stored and it is protected from the moisture.
2. **General Stores:** Various kinds of miscellaneous items like paints, brushes, cleaning material, wood and spirit are kept here. In some cases where there is no production store, the materials mentioned in Production stores are kept here.
3. **Production stores:** Besides raw materials, production also requires a large number of materials, generally called "consumables" like eye- shields, cutting oils, abrasives, gloves, aprons, jigs, small tools, etc. A store stocking such item is usually called a production store.
4. **Raw material stores**: This is where raw material used in the factory are stored, usually this the largest kind and the location should be such that it is situated alongside a railway line, canal or river, if supplies are received other than by road, where the deliveries are by road, there must be an adequate space for trucks to move, turn and park. If sufficient provision is not made for quick and easy loading or unloading, heavy demurrage or detention charges can result.

An ideal location fr such store would be adjacent to the production facilities. This will reduce handling.

5. **Refrigerated stores:** This type of store is used for storage of perishable items. Like fruit, meat, vegetables, etc. It could be from 20° C to 10° C.
6. **Sundries store:** for non food items like paper goods, cleaning supplies.
7. **Tools store**: All kinds of tools like files measuring instruments, saws, small tools like hammers, pliers, etc. or special tools required in the factory are kept here.
8. **Vegetable store:** All the vegetables and fruits are stored and issued from this store only.

Storing Food

Different kinds of food are stored in hotels due to variable patterns in the volume of business and consumption of food ingredients. Storing food can be categorised broadly into:

- Storage of dry food
- Storage of food in refrigerators
- Storage of food in deep freezers

REFRIGERATORS/ COLD STORAGE/ REACH-INS/ WALK-INS

Usually used for storing perishables and cooked meals.

- Different food items should be stored separately.
- Raw materials and processed foods are stored in separate areas/ in different racks.
- The stored goods are wrapped/ covered to reduce drying and it prevents them from absorbing and emitting odours.
- By separating the different groups of raw materials, the probability of cross-contamination is reduced.

Recommended Temperature in Storage

Vegetables	Between 5°C and 8°C
Meat, poultry, fish and shellfish	Between 2°C and 5°C. Fresh fish is stored in special refrigerators called fish files.
Prepared meals	Between 2°C and 5°C
Dairy products	Normally stored in separate refrigerator at temperature between 2°C and 5°C.

Dry Stores

Features	Essentials	Considerations
A well planned store should include the following: • It should be cool, dry, well lit and well ventilated. • Convenient for receiving and storing. • High standard of hygiene. • Easy to clean metal shelves. • Any food items should be sealed or kept in airtight containers.	• Follow first in first out procedure. • Commodities with strong odors should be stored separately. • Tinned goods should be checked for their date of expiry.	• Severely dented and blown tins (bulged tins) must be thrown away as the contents may cause food poisoning. • Check for best before/expiry dates. • Cleaning materials and chemicals are always stored in different store.

DEEP-FREEZE

- Deep-freezers are used for storing frozen food items, e.g. meat and poultry.
- The temperature should be kept between - 16°C and - 18°C.
- The food items stored in deep-freeze should be vacuum packed, wrapped in polythene bags tagged for identification.

Inter Departmental Relationship with Stores

Store has maximum interaction with purchase which feeds the store, and production which are store feeds in turn. But store has to deal with all the departments in the hotel.

1. **Store and purchase:** These two functions of material management are complementary to each other. Apart from the close relationship that exists on a day to day basis in the purchase of various materials, there are other important activities which can best be done by a close coordination between stores and purchase. These are material identification (coding of materials) and store vocabulary (The coded catalogue), standardization and variety reduction, inventory control, value analysis, salvaging operations and disposal of surplus and obsolete items and scarp.

   The store sends the indent to purchase for replenishment of stocks based on inventory levels desired. While indenting it is important to write the correct specification, code number, unit etc. The stores should also promptly inform purchase of changing production trends, slow or non moving stocks, obsolete or surplus stock, scrap etc.
2. **Stores and production:** The Production Department is usually the chief customer of the stores. At production meetings, if the store is represented, coordination can be excellent. Any change in a production schedule needs to be communicated to the stores to enable prompt corrective action to make materials available on time.
3. **Stores and sales:** In a marketing organization, the sales department is the Chief Customer of the finished goods store. The sales department wants to ensure stock at all time and this might be a costly philosophy in terms of inventory holdings. Close cooperation and an integrated approach can aid management objective to increase profitability by closely monitoring inventory levels.
4. **Stores and accounts:** Usually the accounts department does all the store accounting, ensuring a day to day working relationship.
5. **Stores and personnel:** selection of the right person for stores work and giving him adequate training in storage, preservation and accounting techniques are vital.

Cardex

All kind of groceries and canned items which are maintained in Food and Beverage office is recorded in Cardex. It must be arranged in same as per inventory books and store merchandise. It should contain the following information

1. Name of merchandise
2. Date of purchase
3. Number of units purchased
4. Units of merchandise issued
5. Balance in hand

Security Aspects

The food is the basic need of human being. The food service areas are most affected areas where theft and pilferage usually happens. In stores we keep all commodities which are used on daily basis or as per requirement. There are certain measures which should be taken in account for smoothes flow in proper storing.

- The storage area must be secured with locks and security guards.
- Staff member from other department should not be allowed for access if it is really not required.
- Different kinds of commodities must have different time of issue.
- In case of emergency requisition all procedure to be followed and recording of data must be completed in presence of a supervisor and must be informed to store keeper the very next day.

20

INDENTING

In food and beverage industry, a quite big experience is required in purchasing the required amount of ingredients for a function, and for purchasing it has to be great expertise in enlisting the required items for final preparation. **The material and the item that required for final preparation is called indent, and the process of enlisting those items on paper is called indenting**.

So a manager who is responsible for indenting material must be very much expertise and upon whom the responsibility lies for a smooth running of an establishment. In F&B production the process of indenting is done by the F&B Manager, Ex- Chef or the Kitchen In-charge.

Indenting may be done for

a) **Short Time Period Indenting**- Where the material intended are used up within a couple of days. This type of indenting is done mostly to perishable items, which tends to spoil quickly if not used in time.

b) **Long Term Indenting**- is done for the items which are non perishable like butter, flour, oil, rice, pulses, canned or bottled products etc.

Principles Of Indenting for Volume Feeding

As indenting procedure requires **lots of skills and experience**, so an expert manager is always appointed for this purpose. There are certain points to remember while indenting materials for F&B operations.

1. Type of establishment
2. Type of customer whom the establishment is to cater. Their religion, eating habit etc.
3. Paying capacity of the customer

4. Type of food service
5. Type of function
6. Availability of raw material
7. Seasonal availability
8. Use of leftovers
9. Equipment and space and capability of the cooking staff
10. Time required for purchasing
11. Fuel saving and pilferage
12. Price quoted on the article
13. style of operation-type of service
14. Carefully reading the paste records
15. Type of menu
16. Stock in hand
17. knowledge of standard yield.
18. Knowledge of portioning.
19. Should be within the budget.
20. Policy of the establishment.

Portion Size of Various Items for Different Types of Volume Feeding

Hypothetical assumptions

1. A wise Chef should know the following while indenting for any function.
2. 1 kg Mutton Cut (Volume) — 4-5 portion (a la carte) — 9-10 portion
3. 1 kg Mutton Mince (Volume) — 4-5 portion (a la carte) — 9-10 portion
4. 1kg Chicken Cut (Volumc) — 5 portion (a la carte) — 9-10 portion
5. 1 kg Chicken mince (Volume) — 4-5 portion (a la carte) — 9-10 portion
6. 1 kg Paneer (Volume) — 5 portion (a la carte) — 9-10 portion
7. 1 kg well dressed chicken serves roughly 400gms of B/L flesh.
8. Average weight of rice served for a la carte is roughly 110-150 gms.
9. Average weight of rice served for buffet is approximately 70-90 gms.
10. 3 kg of dal makhni serves 60 portions in a la carte and 100 portions in buffet.
11. Average weight tawa roti peda is 30 gms and tandoori roti is 50 gms.
12. An average weight of Naan/ Parantha is 110gms.
13. 1 kg of B/L chicken flesh serves approx.40 pcs.

Portion Control understands how much a serving size is and how many calorie serving contains. Portion control is important for weight management as the weight is defined by the total calorie intake. Healthy eating, using Aristotle's philosophy, is the desirable middle between two extremes of excess and the other of deficiency (over eating and not eating enough), the "golden mean." Portion control is eating a healthy balance of amount and types, of varied foods.

Portion Sizes can be estimated by using objects as a point of reference. One way of determining portion size is to compare hand size. For example a healthy serving of protein should not be larger than a palm size piece of meat. Carbohydrate servings such as pasta can be measured by fistfuls. A healthy serving of pasta should be one fistful.

Standard Portion Size

A standard portion size represents the amount of each food item which is sold to the guest of a stated price and should be establish for all items.

Name of Dish	Portion Size	State of Preparation	Other Data
			Signature of Supervisor

Standard Recipes

It is a written schedule for producing a particular menu item. A standard recipe card should be prepared for each menu item. All food stuff used must be listed and from this information cost of portion is

<table>
<tr><td colspan="7">ABC Hotels
Unit
Portion Size:
Yield:</td></tr>
<tr><td rowspan="2">S.No.</td><td rowspan="2">Ingredients</td><td rowspan="2">Quantity</td><td rowspan="2">Unit</td><td rowspan="2">% of loss</td><td colspan="2">Rate</td></tr>
<tr><td>Useable Weight In Season</td><td>Off Season Average</td></tr>
<tr><td></td><td></td><td></td><td></td><td></td><td></td><td></td></tr>
</table>

Cost for Projection and Impressions:
Preparation and Service of the Dish:
Method of Preparation:
Procedure:
Temperature:

Cost Price:
Total Cost:
Sale Price Per Portion:
Cost Percentage:

PURCHASE REQUISITION

ABC Hotel
Purchase Requisition

Date:

Serial No.______

Department: ____________________

S.No.	Article and Description	Quantity	Unit	Budget code	Remarks, required by

Department Head

Authorized for Purchase

FOOD STORE ROOM REQUISITION

ABC Hotel
Perishable and Diary

Date: Serial No.______

Department: ____________________

Stock No.	Item	Unit	Quantity requested	Quantity issued	Unit Cost	Total Cost

____________________ Requested by

____________________ Delivered by

____________________ Received by

____________________ Cost Controller

ABC Hotel
Perishable and Diary

Kitchen No.: Date:

Sl. No.	Item	Unit	Quantity	Unit Cost	Total Cost

Requested by | Delivered by | Received by | Cost Controller

ABC Hotel

Please deliver and charge to________________ Department ____________

Date of Requisition ________________ Date of Using ____________

Stock No.	Description of goods	Unit	Quantity required	Quantity issued	Unit Cost	Extension

Requested by   Delivered by   Received by   F&B Controller

Weekly Issue Book

ABC Hotel

Weekly Issue Book

S.No.	Description	Unit	Unit Cost	S	M	T	W	Th	F	S	Total Rs.

Kitchen Transfer Food/Beverage

ABC Hotel Ltd.

From: No.: Date:

To________________

Reg. No.	Items	Size	Quantity Transferred	Unit Cost	Total Cost

Requested by Delivered by Received by Cost Controller

MEAT TAG	
ITEM	No......................
Cut	....
Total Weight	....
Total Value	....
Cost/ Kg	....
Supplier	....
Date Received	....
Date Issued	....
Food store copy Send to food control on day of issue to kitchen.	

Modifying Recipes For Indenting For A Large Scale Catering

Recipes must be modified for a large scale catering to avoid the barrier of cost factor

- **Change the Ingredient:** Some time it requires for the chef to change the ingredients in the recipe to get red of the hike in the cost or to make big margin of profit. The most expensive item may be removed from the recipe by keeping some alternative of it. Eg. If the recipe contains Green and Red Capsicum, you may omit the Red Capsicum and put Red Kashmiri Chili instead.
- **Reducing the ingredients:** If chef feels that some of the ingredients are very expensive in the market which will go in the recipe he must modify the recipe and try reducing those items which are most expensive and increasing those which are least expensive. By doing these kind of exercises chef helps the organization to make a big margin of profit and he should be smart enough to give the best of the quality with the change also.

Practical Difficulties While Indenting For Volume Feeding

Most of the time the chef faces a big problem while indenting for mass. The reason could be various:

1. Which kind of people are attending the function
2. The ratio of veg and non veg guest in the function
3. Some time the guest emphasizes only on one item or two only
4. The kids become the problem if in advance he is not told about them.

5. The host may not be able to predict about the number of guest
6. If the host is of different cast and invitees are of different cast and from different place.
7. If the guest is fussy and start allowing the take away from the function
8. The price of the menu
9. When guest brings their own eatables without pre informing
10. When guest comes very late to attend the function.

Inventory

Inventory management: It is a process through which the stocks held in an organization are carefully and precisely balanced with expected sales, resulting in an asset commitment level that can be considered optimal. It help in proper flow of goods and services as per the policies and guidelines of the establishment.

- Holding inventory for smooth production and service of meals and to meet the on the spot demand to exceed customer expectation.
- Inventory helps in meeting unexpected situation, like hungry customers, disturbance in regular supply, sudden staff absenteeism.
- Aim of profit making the organization can stock more commodity/items as per projected profit.

Inventory Assessing Methods

Following are the methods of holding inventory which is operated universally.

ABC Analysis Method

In this method all commodities are grouped as per priorities and consumption which is important for production and service. As per the priorities the total annual consumption are calculated.

- The list of item is made along with their annual consumption unit.
- Annual Monetary value is computed as per the rate of the commodity.
- Depending upon the priorities manager can take decision as per menu requirements.

Par Stock Method

The most common approach to inventory calculations still much in favour to day, because of its simplicity is the par stock method. To begin with the buyer accepts the supplies delivery schedule or negotiates a more suitable one. The buyer consults the user, then determines the par-stock i.e. the level of inventory items that must be on hand to maintain a continued supply of goods from one order period to the next.

Par-stock levels changes from time to time depending upon the level of sales for a particular product. This is particularly evident where Banquets are conducted. Assessing par-stock levels in this instance can be difficult. Usually the problem of varying demand is dealt with by adding to the known par stock on extra amount of each item, which is termed as safety stock.

- Assess the right time to bring the stock level up to par, depending on the storage space available and self-life of the item.
- Set par stock for foods, beverages and other items at levels, which will ensure a continued supply between re-ordering periods.
- When ordering, subtract what is on hand from the par stock, and add additional amount to cover extras (safety stock)
- Periodically re-evaluate par stock levels and adjust as needeu.

Minimum-Maximum Method

This is an inventory management method or practice or process for non-perishable goods. This system works by determining:

- The minimum quantity below, which the level of each item of inventory should not fall.
- The maximum quality above, which the level of each inventory item should not raise.
- In both instances the quantity to be obtained by reducing the quantity needed by the quantity in hand.

Quantity needed - Quantity available = Quantity to be Purchased

Establishing the Minimum Level

The minimum (safety) level is the point below that the inventory items level must not decrease. This is set by considering the following:

- The lead-time for re-ordering, as the frequency of deliveries decreases, the lead-time increases. If delivery periods are unpredictable the minimum inventory level must be increased.
- Usage rate of the product must be known along with the portion size. As these increases, so should the minimum level. The objective is to prevent stock outs. If usage rate is unpredictable, minimum inventory level must be increased.

Advantages

- Provisions for safety stocks reduce the stock outs.
- System easy to maintain.

- Excessive inventory level can be prevented, thus minimizing storage costs and preventing spoilage.

Theoretical Method

The right order size is influenced by the storage cost and ordering cost or administrative cost.

Storage cost: This is the sum total of all the costs associated with handling inventory such as maintenance of storage facilities, insurance, breakage spoilage etc. But the biggest storage cost is that of the money tied up in the stock. This is called Capital cost. This is referred to as an opportunity cost. If your money is invested in cans and bottles, you loose the opportunity to invest this money in some other way that would pay interest.

Ordering cost includes cost such as office costs such as telephone, fan, postage, stationary, as well as wages paid to staff in purchasing, receiving and storage.

Economic Order Quantity Method

An inventory-related equation that determines the optimum order quantity, which a company should hold in its inventory, gives a set cost of production, demand rate and other variables. Economic order quantity is the level of inventory that minimizes the total inventory holding costs and ordering costs. This is done to minimize variable inventory costs. The full equation is as follows:

$$EOQ = \sqrt{\frac{2SD}{PI}}$$

Where:

S = Setup costs D = Demand rate

P = Production cost I = Interest rate (considered an opportunity cost)

Types Of Inventory

There are two systems of assessing stock in hand:

- By means of record (Perpetual inventory)
- By actually counting the goods (Physical inventory)

Perpetual Inventory

A Perpetual Inventory record is a card or sheet on which employees note the receipt, withdrawal, amount and cost of items in cold and dry storage areas. At any given time, a manager or buyer can glance at the perpetual inventory record to determine the quantity and the value of all inventoried items. A perpetual inventory record form should contain space for an items description, and specifications, size, unit, quantity and unit cost as well as adjacent columns for noting when and in what amounts items are received and withdrawn. This system of inventory control relies on careful record keeping and it requires two documents:

Bin Card

ABC Hotel Ltd.

Commodit:________________ Supplier:________________

Minimum Stock: ________________ Reorder No.:________________

Maximum Stock: ________________ Bin No.: ________________

Date	Reference	Received	Issued	Balance
	Balance brought forward			

ABC Hotel Ltd.

PERPETUAL INVENTORY RECORD

Items: Unit/Size: Quantity:

Unit/Cost: ____________

Description & Specification:

Vendor: ____________________

Date	Amount Received	Amount Withdrawn	Employee Withdrawing	Unit on Hand	Cost per Unit	Total Cost

Bin Card

It is a perpetual inventory keeping for displaying next to each inventory item, a card achieve self –stable goods with the running balance of stocks on hand. This Bin card records deliveries, issues, returns and balances of each item. The balance shown on the Bin card must correspond to the actual balance of the stock left on the self.

Par Stock

The par stock is often used in conjunction with the Bin card. Par stock requires us to determine a level of stock according to the average daily usage rate and replace stock each day to bring it up to that level. The perpetual inventory system although costly and time consuming, it offers tight control of inventory if it is operated correctly. It makes possible to constantly monitor inventory levels, inventory costs and usage rate.

Physical Inventory

A physical inventory record is a monthly or quarterly report on all the items physically in a facility's storage areas. The employees responsible for this record should inventory items systematically and, if needed, arrange items as changes occur. A physical inventory record form may be designed to reflect the order in which items are stored. The form should include the date and Rs. Amount recorded during the last inventory, item descriptions and sizes, actual counts of cans and cases on hand, unit cost, the total cost of all items, the date, and the signature of the employee taking the inventory. It is counting the stores and recording stock levels within the stores and in production is a time-honored practice and is still indispensable. The physical inventory process is called "Comparing the Theoretical to the actual stock level" because the inventory items are actually sighted, physically counted, recorded and valued.

21

Bakery

After studying this chapter students should know:

1. Basics of bakery and patisserie.
2. Definition of bakery and patisserie.
3. Types of ingredients used in bakery and their role.
4. Types of cake.
5. Types of pastry.
6. Types of icing.
7. Types of cookies.
8. Chocolate, role and types.

BASICS OF BAKERY AND PATISSERIE

Baking is the method of cooking food in an oven by using dry heat applied evenly throughout the oven. Bakery coexist from the ancient time egypetians were the first to use the baking method to make their breads. Breads, desserts, and many other products like rolls, pudding etc. are often baked, and baking is the primary cooking technique used to produce cakes and pastry-based goods such as pies, tarts, and quiches. Such items are sometimes referred to as "baked goods", and are sold at a bakery. Bakery is the very important section of culinary art and this section require a different kind of skill and training. Although somehow this section is related with other sections of culinary arts but in certain cases this section is very unique on its own. Few unique features to learn the art of bakery is:

1. Bakery requires a special skill and training to learn the art of baking.
2. Measurement of ingredients, temperature control and timings are essential to deal with otherwise product will not be of right quality.

3. Quality of ingredients has to be superior otherwise final product will be substandard.
4. Right kind of equipments and accessories to be used for right product.
5. Product glace is must as product finishing must be attractive.
6. Right type of accompaniments with right product is essential.
7. Product should have Uniformity.
8. Knowledge of principles and basics is essential.

INGREDIENTS MOSTLY USED IN BAKERY

Flour

Use of flour depends upon the ratio of its gluten content in bakery. The protein content of flour i.e. gluten, affects the strength of dough and thus product. Recipes sometimes use all-purpose flour, which has a moderate gluten or protein content. For lower gluten content with a more tender outcome, one should use whole wheat pastry flour or cake flour. High-gluten flours, such as bread and regular whole wheat, as well as a moderate one, all-purpose, are typically used in yeast breads where a strong framework is desirable. But, in cakes, quick breads and pastries, high protein flour makes a tough baked good.

Toughness of gluten is also depends upon other factors like:

1. If the flour and moisture are over mixed or handled, more the gluten strands strengthen and toughen. That's why in some recipes one should not over mix them.
2. Fat plays an important role in coating the proteins in flour, minimizing their contact with moisture, and shortening the gluten's development.
3. flour handling also play an important role

Fat

Butter margarine and solid fats are used in bakery. Oils are rarely used in bakery. For better products butter can be used but it is very expenses so margarine can be best substitute.

Sweetener

In sweetener sugar is the main substance which can be used in many ways like caramel, fondant etc.

Following are the roles of sugar in bakery-

1. Sugar speeds the effectiveness of yeast by providing an immediate, fast cooking course of nourishment for its growth- thus hastening the leavening process.

2. A small amount of sugar is added to aid in the baking process. Sugar helps in fermentation process by feeding the yeast.
3. Crystallization ability of sugar gives a delightful variety in bakery and dessert.
4. Sugar gives puddings, breads, buns and bread rolls a unique flavour (caramel), the characteristic golden brown colour, tender and even texture.
5. Sugar act as a preservative. And can be stored for a long time without getting spoilt.
6. Helps in Whipping Aid as in foam-type cakes, such as angel and sponge, sugar enables the creation of light foam that serves as the basic structure of the cake.
7. Bodying/Bulking Agent: Sugar imparts satisfying texture, body, mouth feel and bulk to many processed foods, such as ice cream, baked goods, icings, beverages and candy.
8. Browning (Maillard reactions): when sugars and proteins interact in complex ways it gives a Color in cooking. This is known as the browning (Maillard) reaction, important in candy making, baking and other processes.
9. Solubility: Sugar is readily soluble in water. The ability to produce solutions of varying degrees of sweetness is important in many food applications, particularly beverages and confectionery.

LEAVENING AGENTS

Leavening agents that are used to increase and raise the volume of baked product such as breads, cakes and cookies. Baking powder, baking soda and yeast are the most common leaveners used today. When mixed with a liquid they form carbon dioxide gas bubbles, which cause a batter or dough to rise during (and sometimes before) the baking process

Yeast + sugar = CO_2 + alcohol

PASTRY

There are basically six types of pastry:

- Short crust
- Hot-water crust
- Flaky
- Puff
- Choux
- Filo (or strudel)

The basic difference between them is the method of introducing the fat. In the short pastries it is rubbed into the flour. In the puff and flaky types the fat is rolled into the dough. In hot-water crust and choux pastry the fat is melted in hot liquid before being added to the flour. There is also a short crust made with cooking oil and a pastry made from yeast dough.

Ingredients for Pastry-making

- **Flour** - Plain flour should be used, though in suet pastry, where a raising agent is needed, self-raising flour may be used instead of plain flour and baking powder.
- **Raising Agent** - Baking powder is generally used in suet pastry. Steam acts as the raising agent in puff and flaky pastries, in combination with the air enclosed between the layers of the paste. In choux pastry the raising agents are eggs plus steam.
- **Fat** - Butter, lard and margarine used to be the fats most commonly used, but nowadays proprietary vegetable shortenings, both blended and whipped up, and pure vegetable oils are also used. Butter gives the best flavour and should always be used for puff pastry. Lard is suitable for shortcrust and flaky pastry, used with butter or margarine, in the proportion of half butter or margarine to half lard.

General Hints for Pastry-making

1. Always sift the flour and salt together into the mixing bowl, as this helps to lighten the mixture. Additional air is incorporated by lifting the flour from the bowl with the finger-tips when rubbing in. Always rub in with a light, rather than a heavy hand.
2. Coolness is important for good results. Handle the pastry as little as possible and always use the finger-tips for rubbing in the fat. Rich pastries are improved by being made on a cold slab and placed in a refrigerator between rollings so that the pastry remains firm.
3. The liquid should be very cold and must be added carefully. An excess of liquid causes a sticky, unmanageable dough and any extra flour then added will alter the proportions of the ingredients and cause the pastry to be tough. Chill the liquid in the refrigerator before use.
4. Rolling out must be done lightly and firmly; do not roll more than necessary. Always use firm, light strikes, rolling in one direction only.
5. Pastry requires a hot oven. Too slow an oven causes pale, hard pastry.

Shortcrust Pastries

These include pastries which are of a crumbly in texture. In this type of pastry the fat percent is generally 40-80%. The fat must be chilled while rubbing the flour in it. The rubbing should be done with soft handed otherwise the gluten will be hardened.

Before rolling the dough should be rested at least for one hour. Flan pastry (also called biscuit crust) and suet crust. Short crust is the most widely used type, being used for a great variety of pies, tarts, turnovers and pasties, both sweet and savory.

Short Pastry

Flour	500 g
Butter	300 g
Icing sugar	150 g
Egg yolk	02 nos
Whole egg	01 no
Vanilla essence	02 drops

Method

1. Take 2 egg yolk and d one whole egg, icing sugar, butter and few drops of vanilla essence with flour.
2. Knead it gently and form a dough.
3. Roll the dough in 02 mm and cut it from cutter and place it in mould.
4. Prick them by help of fork.
5. Bake it for 20-25 minute at 200° C.

Hot Water Crust Pastry

This is a type of pastry made by melting lard in boiling water and pouring the mixture onto the flour. It is kneaded to dough and used for 'raised pies'. The pastry is placed in a special mould, or molded around a suitable container before being filled with veal, ham or pork filling to make a traditional hot-water crust pastry pie

Flaky Pastry

Also one of the commonest of the flaked types, it can be used in many sweet and savory dishes like pie crust, cream roll, vegetable puff etc.; are particularly popular. Good flaky pastry must have the evenness of the flakes when it is baked, and the rolling and the even distribution of the fat are two important factors in achieving this result. Fat is added in flakes for layering and in the dough also. Giving the rest to the dough is must in between is essential.

Puff Pastry

One of the richest and involved arts of all the pastries. It gives the most even rising, most flaky effect and crispest texture. It should be handled very carefully. The fat used in it should have high melting point and the dough must be mixed with chilled water. It is used for vol-au-vents and teatime pastries such as cream horns the dough should not be too loose or too tight for handling purpose.

Choux Pastry

Choux pastry is a paste prepared by beating eggs into a thick mixture of flour, fat and liquid. The eggs cause the pastry to swell in cooking. It is used chiefly for Èclairs, profiteroles, cream buns, rich fancy cakes and savoury or sweet fritters.

Filo/Strudel Pastry

This is a form of pastry which is very popular in Greece, Austria, Germany and central Europe generally and has become fashionable in Britain over recent years. It is made from a soft dough which is stretched out by hand until paper-thin, covered with a variety of fillings (e.g. apple, black cherries, nuts, poppy seeds, cheese and vegetables) and rolled like a Swiss roll.

FLAKY (PIE AND TART CRUST) AND SHORTCRUST

Shortcrust includes pastries which are of a crumbly rather than a flaky texture – shortcrust, flan pastry (also called biscuit crust) and suetcrust. Shortcrust is the most widely used for pies, tarts, turnovers and pasties, both sweet and savoury. Flan pastry is used for sweet tarts, etc., and suetcrust for sweet and savory puddings, which may be steamed, boiled or baked. Cheese pastry is another short type used for making cheese straws.

The simplest and most commonly used for pie and tart crusts is flaky pastry dough, sometimes known as medium flake. A basic recipe involves taking flour, fat, water and salt. The chilled fat is cut into cubes and rubbed or cut-into the flour and salt, previously mixed then a minimum of ice water is added until the dough barely comes together. Good flaky pastry is judged by the evenness of the flakes and their distribution.

Pie and tart crust recipes sometimes include added sugar and an egg. The result is cookie-like, crumbly and sweet. If it has little sugar and no eggs, it is called Pate brisee (meaning broken textured pastry in French). If it is sweet-ened with a large dose of sugar with an added egg, it is then called Pate sucree (sweet pastry in French), also called Pate seche (dry pastry in French). Tender pastry ingredients can also include cream cheese, baking powder, vinegar, ground nuts and other ingredients.

Puff Pastry

Puff Pastry gives the most even rising, most flaky effect and crispest texture from "rolled in butter" and is also referred to as a laminate dough. Danish are made from similar techniques, but Danish is made from a yeast dough.

Choux (Pâte à Choux)

Choux pastry is a paste prepared by beating eggs into a thick mixture of flour, fat and liquid, and cooking until smooth. The eggs provide the leavening and "puff". It is used chiefly for éclairs, profiteroles, cream buns, rich fancy cakes and savory or sweet recipes.

Phyllo (Filo) Dough and the like, such as Strudels, etc. Phyllo dough is made by flour and water only, which is kneaded and stretched so thin that it looks like tissue paper. The dough can encase a filling, and brushed with butter in between the layers, after baking it resembles puff pastry. In strudel pastry, it includes added fat and egg, plus a little vinegar.

Hot Water Crust: (Not discussed in detail here.) This is a type of pastry made by melting lard in boiling water and pouring the mixture onto the flour and is kneaded to a dough. It is used for making 'raised pies'. The pastry is molded around a suitable container before being filled with veal, ham or a pork filling.

Suetcrust

In suetcrust the main ingredient is chopped suet. It is best used with savory fillings.

Sweet Dough

Sweet Dough encompass a wide variety of pastries. This usually includes yeast-raised recipes such as Cinnamon Buns, Raised Doughnuts, sweet rolls, hot cross buns, coffee cakes, pannetone, Brioche, Danish pastry and Croissants. Sometimes the broader category of breakfast foods is used or other chemically leavened doughs like Puff Pastry, Sponge Cake, Pound Cake and cake doughnuts. Many recipes are finished with fillings and toppings, such as icings, glazes, fruit jellies, nuts, etc. with a more breadlike texture.

Sweet dough is made from wheat flour (all-purpose) with a relatively high percentage of sugar in the dough. Some potato flour or rice starch can be added for lightness. When I make my light and fluffy Cinnamon Buns, I substitute 2 tablespoons flour with ¼ cup potato flour.

Shortcrust Pastry

Flour	500 g
Butter	250 g
Sugar	50 g
Vanilla essence	02 drops

Method

1. Take, butter and few drops of vanilla essence with flour.
2. Knead it gently and form a dough.
3. Roll the dough in 02 mm and cut it from cutter and place it in mould.
4. Prick them by help of fork.
5. Bake it for 20-25 minute at 200 C.

Lemon Tart

Egg yolk	150 g
Sugar	150 g
Butter	150 g
Lemon juice	30 ml
Lemon colour and essence	02 drop

To make the tart, collect all above ingredient in a bowl and keep it on a double boiler.

Whisk and leave for another 30 minute. Fill into the tart through the help of nozzle.

For jam tart fill with fruit jam. (Jam can be cooked with butter 10:1)

Different varieties of filling can be added into the tarts like savory, fruit and cheese etc.

Puff Pastry

Flour	500 g
Fat	500 g
Salt	a pinch
Cold water	300 ml

Mrthod

1. Sieve the flour and salt together. Rub in 125 g of fat.
2. Now add water and make smooth dough.
3. Roll the dough with roller and stuff it with 375 g of fat. Fold it carefully.
4. Roll the dough by forming the layers. Repeat this process three times. So that more layers can be obtained.
5. Cut it into square shape. Make the pocket by giving triangle shape.

6. On the other hand prepare the stuffing for patties as desired.
7. Fill the stuffing in the pocket. Give the egg wash in and above the pocket. Now bake it in the oven at 200°C for 20 to 25 minute.
8. Give egg wash two to three times to escape it from getting dry.
9. Serve hot with suitable sauce.

Choux Paste

Egg	04 nos
Butter	100 g
Flour	150 g
Water	260 ml
Sugar and salt	¼ tsp

Method

1. Boil water/milk in a pan with butter and sugar.
2. Add flour and stir on low fire. When the flour starts leaving the sides of pan take it off.
3. Now cool it and add egg and stir continuously.
4. When it will achieve the piping consistency shape through piping bag and bake at 190° C for 20 minute then reduce to 150 to get it dry for 15 minute.

Chocolate Éclair

Choux paste	as above
Cream	600 ml
Chocolate melted	50 g
Icing sugar	100 g
Butter (unsalted)	50 g

Method

1. For éclair fill whipped cream in it through the nozzle. Prepare chocolate sauce using butter, chocolate and icing sugar.
2. Dip the top of each éclair case in the melted chocolate. Set aside until the topping as set.
3. Sprinkle icing sugar on top and Place the éclairs on a platter.

Fillo (Phyllo) pastry

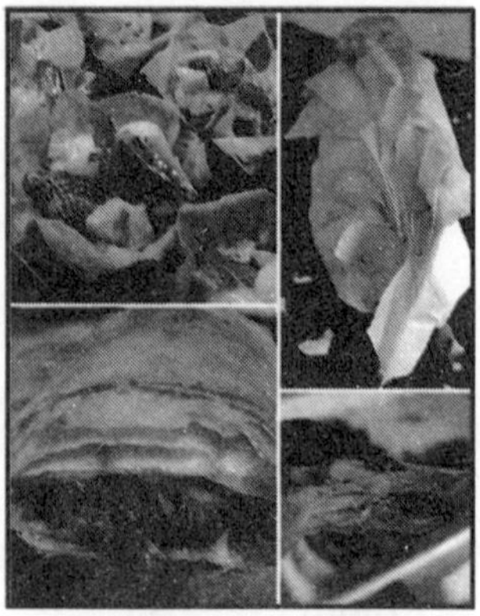

Flour	01 kg
Sugar	10 g
Salt	10 g
Egg	02 nos.

Method

1. Mix all together to form dough.
2. Freeze the dough for one hour before use.
3. Can be used for the making of baklava, almond cigar, and pistachio bunches.

Hot Water Crust Pastry

Ingredients

200 g shortening
¼ cup hot water
1 Tbsp. milk
2¼ cups all purpose flour
½ tsp. salt

Preparation

1. In a bowl place the shortening and Pour hot water and milk over the shortening. And beat quickly with the help of fork until the mixture looks like whipped cream.
2. Now add flour and salt over it and beat with the fork to form a dough.
3. Used according to the recipe.

CAKES

There are two types of raised cakes:

1. Foam Cakes and
2. Butter or Shortened Cakes.

Foam cakes have a high proportion of eggs to flour. They are leavened solely by the air beaten into whole eggs or egg whites. They contain very little, if any, fat and have a spongy texture.

The three categories of foam cakes are:

i) Those that contain **no fat** - Angel Food Cakes, Meringues, and Dacquoises.

ii) Those where the **only fat** is from **egg yolks** - Sponge Cakes, some Biscuits, Roulades

iii) Those that **contain fat** (butter, shortening) plus egg yolks - Genoises and Chiffons

Butter or **Shortened cakes** contain fat (butter, margarine, shortening) and raising is done by a chemical leavener (baking powder, baking soda) for their rise. They are flavorful, and have a good texture and volume. Other examples of butter cakes are the white and yellow cake, coffee cakes, tea-cakes, and fruitcakes. Some butter cakes are rich and flavorful enough to stand alone (fruitcakes, tea-cakes) or with a sifting of confectioners sugar or drizzled with a glaze. Others, layer or sheet butter cakes, taste even better with a layer of frosting, lemon curd, jam and preserves, nuts, or even ice cream.

Most butter cakes are prepared using one of three methods. The most popular of the three is the creaming method. This is the easiest and produces the lightest cake with the best volume. The one bowl, quick, or blending method is the quickest and easiest cake to make and produces a melt-in-your-mouth texture but it is denser with less volume than a cake made with creaming method. The combination method is similar to the creaming method but involves whipping the egg whites separately from the yolks and then adding them to the batter.

Icing (frosting)

Icing is the sweet sugary mixture used to fill and cover cakes, pastries and other confections.

Americans tend to use the word 'frosting'. Other countries tend to use the word 'icing'. The name 'icing' probably has something to do with the fact that 'confectioners' or 'powdered' sugar is also known as 'icing' sugar. Hence, combining icing sugar with other ingredients makes an 'icing'. The fact is that 'frosting' and 'icing' is the same thing and food writers used them interchangeably.

There are numerous types of frostings (icings) is available. Most important is to decide the type of icing which match the product on which it has to be applied.

Followings are the points to be considered while using icing:

- The icing should complement the flavors and texture of the dessert being frosted.
- Icing should be different from the ingredient used in making of cake.
- The frosting should have the proper consistency so it spreads easily over the product.

- Never apply the icing on a warm baked product. Otherwise the frosting will melt into the baked good or become too thin and run.
- Always apply the icing completely in cake. Incomplete application will spoil the look.

Types of Frostings (Icings) and their Uses

Icing can be based on following:

1. **Butter base-like butter cream.** Sweet, buttery flavour. Tastes the best and looks beautiful for most decorating. Can use shortening, instead of butter, to make. Butter-creams may contain powdered sugar, white granulated sugar, whole eggs, egg whites, egg yolks, unsalted butter, shortening, milk or cream, pastry cream, fondant, and various flavorings (extract, purée, chocolate, liqueur). Icing can be piped for smooth, borders, writing. Most decorations including roses, drop flowers, sweet peas and figure piping. Flowers remain soft enough to be cut with a knife. Icing can be refrigerated in an airtight container for 2 weeks or frozen. Iced cake can be stored at room temperature for 2-3 days
2. **Cream base:** Whipped Cream Frosting, Creamy, delicate sweetness. But Perishable. Can be used in all cakes but especially those decorated with fruits. Chocolate powder can be used with cream for choco-cream icing.
3. **Egg base:** Royal icing is made by beating egg white and confectioner's sugar. Very sweet flavour. Dries candy-hard so it produces delicate and long-lasting decorations. Royal Icing was traditionally used to ice Wedding and Christmas cakes and consists of powdered (icing) sugar, egg whites or meringue powder and water. This pure white icing when dry produces a perfectly flat, smooth and glossy hard surface which makes it ideal not only for frosting cakes and cookies, but also for intricate piping of decorations (flowers, borders, lettering, etc.) Icing can be **stored** under certain conditions. Air-dried decorations last for months.
4. **Chocolate base:** Ganache is both a frosting and a glaze and is widely used in the pastry kitchen it is made from chocolate, usually dark, heavy cream and sometimes butter in varying ratios depending on what you're making. Can be poured like a glaze or whipped. Dark: decadent, rich, and very-very chocolaty. Does not need refrigeration. White: Rich velvety taste - a little more complex flavour than a butter-cream
5. Sugar syrup base:
   a. **Simple and sugary**. Made from confectioner's sugar and water. Syrups turn dry cakes into moist and flavorful ones.
   b. **Fondant icing**. This thick, malleable dough is made of sugar, glucose, and glycerin. It is rolled out and then draped for a flawless matte finish. Is ideal for keeping larger cakes fresh when they become too large to refrigerate. Used for its special look on wedding cakes. Rich, sweet flavour. Covers cakes with a perfectly smooth. Seals in freshness and moisture. Can be used on firm

pound or fruit cake. Gives a perfectly smooth, satin-like surface. Can be stored two months in an airtight container. Do not refrigerate or freeze. Iced cake can be stored at room temperature for 2-3 days.

6. **Ice-cream base:** Ice-cream can be used as outer covering. Chocolate, vanilla or other flavoured ice-cream can be used. Care must be taken with temperature.
7. **Gum Paste**: Also known as candy clay or sugar paste, it is basically made by mixing icing sugar in gelatin and can be modeled into almost anything. This pliable mixture is most often used for handmade flowers because they turn out realistic looking and for other three-dimensional decorations. It dries very hard, but is susceptible to heat and humidity where it will soften. If properly stored, Gum paste decorations will last for years.
8. **Marzipan:** is ideal for keeping larger cakes fresh when they become too large to refrigerate. It is made with almond paste, confectioner's sugar, corn syrup and flavorings. It gives a smooth look and has a delicious and unique flavour. Dough-like consistency that is rolled out before applied to cake. Is stretchy. Stays semi-soft on cakes. Keep almond paste well covered and refrigerated, since it contains almonds which can go rancid.

MERINGUE

Meringue is a type of dessert, originally from France, made from whipped egg whites and caster sugar. It must be beaten into the whites a tablespoon at a time. Some meringue recipes call for adding a binding agent such as Cream of Tartar. Meringues are often flavoured with a small amount of essence, e.g., almond or coconut. They are very light and airy and extremely sweet.

Meringues is used for cookies cakes like Angel Food Cake, Pavlova, Baked Alaska, Queen of Puddings and Lemon meringue pie.

Types of Meringue

1. **Regular meringue:** It is uncooked meringue. Egg whites are beaten with sugar in a certain way: In the bowl beat the egg whites with sugar at room temperature on low speed until foamy. Then, add one at a time, the cream of tartar or lemon juice and any flavorings, such as vanilla extract. Continue whipping until the whites is strong, Baked as a topping
2. **Italian Meringue:** Italian meringue is made by slowly beating hot sugar syrup into stiffly beaten egg whites. The resulting meringue is very dense and shiny and smooth. Italian meringue is used as cake frosting.
3. **French meringue:** is baked. The French type, which this recipe uses, starts with raw egg whites and adds the sugar in stages; then the meringue is poached or baked in its form:

4. **Swiss meringues:** are cooked. In the Swiss style mixes the egg whites with sugar and cooks them over a double boiler to a temperature of 130 degrees to stabilize the meringue: Whisk egg whites and sugar while heating over simmering water. Here the sugar melts which makes the finished meringue more stable.

After heating, the meringue is whipped until cool and increased in volume.

Baked meringues should be stored in airtight, moisture free containers. They can usually keep for a week at room temperature and up to a month in the freezer. Baked until crisp in dry in a pie plate (Angel Pie) Filled with custard and fruit.

BISCUIT (COOKIES)

Biscuit (cookies) word comes from the French word 'bis' meaning twice and 'cuit' meaning cooked. The term originates from the word-pair biscuit which means bread twice cooked. Sliced bread twice-baked was the staple diet of many armies, travellers and adventurers till about two centuries ago because it was light, dry and resistant to spoilage.

Basically, biscuits are pieces of dough made from flour, water, sugar and baking powder, plus some amount of shortening. There are a variety of innovative biscuits that can be created by the hands of a creative baker which could be well used to impress many a valued guests at hotels.

Biscuits and cookies may be prepared by any one of the following methods.

One-stage Method

In this method all the ingredients are mixed at once the baker has less control over the mixing. Therefore the one stage method is not frequently used. When over-mixing is not frequently used and it is not a problem as with some chewy cookies, it can be used. Limited types of cookies can be prepared from this type of dough.

Creaming method

This is like creaming methods used for cake making. Except less liquid is used since biscuits and cookies require less liquid.

The amount of creaming affects the texture of biscuits, the leavening and the spread. Only a small amount of creaming is required when the biscuits and cookies should retain its shape.

Sponge method

This method is similar to the sugar batter method or whisking method used for cake making. Batter is then piped by piping bags and baked in trays. The procedure will vary considerably depending on the ingredients.

Types and make up methods for biscuits and cookies:

1) **Dough base** - These are made from soft dough. The dough should be soft enough to be forced through a pastry bag, but stiff enough to hold its shape.
2) **Dropped** - Similar to bagged cookies, they are also from a soft dough. But in some situations when the dough contains pieces of dry fruits, nuts or chocolate chips, it would clog the pastry tube. You can scoop or spoon the mixture onto a greased baking tray allowing space between two portions for expansion.
3) **Rolled** - Cookies rolled and cut from a stiff dough are called rolled up cookies or biscuits. They are not often made in a bake shop. A disadvantage of this method is that the scraps left over when re-rolled make inferior quality cookies. The advantage being one can prepare or attempt to get a variety of shapes.
4) **Moulded** - The dough in this case is stiff and chilled. It is then divided into equal portions, each piece is then moulded into the desired shape. It usually consists of flattening the pieces out with a rolling pin. For some traditional cookies, special moulds are used to flatten the dough. Shapes like crescents, fingers, hexagons etc. can be moulded up in this case.
5) **Ice-box** - This method is ideal for operations that wish to have freshly baked cookies on hand at all times.

   The cookies can be rolled up and kept in advance and be cut out, baked as and when required. This method is used to prepare chequer board, pin wheel cookies and biscuits.
6) **Bar** - It is a process in which the dough is baked in long narrow strips, which are then cut crosswise into bars. These should however not be confused with sheet cookies.
7) **Sheet** - The dough is rolled out on a table top, cut out, then baked or they can also be baked on a baking sheet and then be divided into portions. These are usually flat in appearance.

Faults in Biscuit and Cookie Manufacture

Crispiness

Cookies and biscuits are crisp if they are low in moisture. The following factors contribute to crispiness:

1) Low proportion of liquid in the mixture. Most crisp cookies are made from stiff dough's.
2) High sugar and high fat content.
3) Small size or thin shape so that they dry faster.
4) Proper storage. Crisp cookies can become soft if they absorb moisture.

Softness

The following factors contribute to softness:

1) High proportion of liquid in the mixture
2) Low sugar and low fat content
3) Honey, molasses etc. used in the recipes. As these sugars are hydroscopic they readily absorb moisture from the atmosphere
4) Under baking
5) Large size or thick shape
6) Improper storage.

Chewiness

Moisture is necessary for chewiness but other factors are also important. All chewy cookies are soft but not all soft cookies are chewy. The following factors contribute to chewiness:

1) High sugar, liquid content, low fat
2) High proportion of eggs.
3) Strong flour or gluten being developed during mixing.

Spread

Spread is desirable in some cookies. The following factors contribute to spread:

1) High baking powder content
2) Creaming a mixture until light
3) Low oven temperature
4) A slack dough, one with hyper liquid content in the dough
5) Strong flour decreases spread due to activation of gluten
6) Cookies spread more if baked on a heavily greased tray.

CHOCOLATE

The word "chocolate" is said to derive from the Mexico i.e. Mayan "xocoatl"; cocoa from the Aztec. "Cacahuatl". The Mexican Indian word "chocolate" comes from a combination of the terms choco ("foam") and atl ("water");

Chocolate was first noted in 1519 when Spanish explorer Hernando Cortez visited the court of Emperor Montezuma of Mexico. They drank the liquid form of cocoa.

Sources

Chocolate is solid at room temperature. Since this fat melts at mouth temperature, chocolate is an excellent flavour conductor. Cocoa powder is made by separating most of the cocoa butter out of the liquor. -

Manufacturer and Processing of Chocolate

Cocoa beans are dried and roasted, ground cocoa bean nibs (the pulp of the cacao bean) is used to makes chocolate. Thus, unsweetened chocolate is pure chocolate liquor and about 50% cocoa butter. Bittersweet chocolate blends at least 35% liquor with as much as 50% with cocoa butter, sugar and vanilla. Semisweet chocolate has the same ingredients as bittersweet with the addition of more sugar. Milk chocolate, which contains about 10% chocolate liquor, akes the process a step further by adding about 12% milk solids.

Care must be taken when melting chocolate. Chocolate should be melt at lower temperatures. Never let chocolate get above 46° C. The best method is using a double boiler. Simmer the water over low heat and stir the chocolate often. Remove from the heat as soon as the chocolate is melted and stir until smooth.

Types of Chocolate

Different types of chocolate/baker chocolate should be used for different purposes and not all are good for cooking.

Couverture chocolate

Couverture chocolate also called covering chocolate it is an original form of chocolate with a high percentage of cocoa butter giving it an excellent flavour. It is usually used for handmade chocolates and decoration. Normally it is tempered (Heated on double boiler, repeat 2-3 times) before use.

Plain Chocolate

This is the best chocolate to use in desserts, cakes, etc. but, percentage of cocoa solids which vary in plain chocolate from 30% to 70%. The higher the percentage, the better the flavour.

Milk Chocolate

They are straight away consumed and is commercially popular chocolate is quite low in cocoa solids, only containing about 20%. It is sweeter than plain chocolate. Generally, it should not be used for cooking as it become difficult to handle when in liquid form.

White Chocolate

This chocolate is made of butter and vegetable fat also gets its flavours from cocoa butter because it contains no cocoa solids. It is made from vegetable fat, milk solids, sugar and vanilla.

Drinking Chocolate

This is much sweeter than cocoa and is generally not as good to use for cooking. It makes a lovely comforting drink, though, on a cold miserable day!

Cocoa powder

This is found in powder form and is easy to use for giving a chocolate flavour to cooking. It is made after the cocoa butter has been removed.

QUESTIONS

1. Differentiate between bakery and patisserie.
2. Define the role of fat, flour, leavening agents and egg in bakery.
3. Explain the different methods of cake making.
4. Explain the different methods of icing.
5. Explain the different methods of pastry making.
6. Explain the different methods of biscuit cake making.
7. How the chocolate works effectively in the patisserie? Write a note on chocolate with its types and uses.
8. Differentiate the following:
   a) dough and batter
   b) leaveners and binder
   c) flaky and puff pastry
   d) foam and butter cake
   e) ganache and choco cream icing
   f) meringue and Italian meringue
   g) gum paste and marzipan
   h) Couverture chocolate and white chocolate

22

Quantity Production Management

After studying this chapter students should know:

1. Concept of quantity cooking.
2. Principles of quantity cooking.
3. Dealing with quantity cooking.
4. How to form a recipe.
5. Different types of recipe and their uses.
6. Conversion factors.
7. Yield test and operations.
8. Food trials and their procedures.
9. Organoleptic and sensory evaluation test.

INTRODUCTION

Quantity food production is required for each kind of catering establishment. It may be hotel, banquets, buffet, institutional, industrial, hospital or off premises catering. For a chef preparing food is not sufficient as he should know the quantity when planning a bulk food. He must know that how much food is needed to serve when there is a function or banquet. Although the art of preparing quantity food depends upon the experience and capability of the chef. There is also a unfixed formula to solve this dilemma. This involves more art than science as the formulas depends upon the habits, food and occasion.

Many factors come into mind when one make the plans including the length of party, the type of food to be served, the composition of men, women and children in group, and above all the type and richness of the food you plan to serve. The time of party is also very important. An after-dinner cocktail party requires much less food than an all-afternoon barbecue. Some of the factors which influence the menu planning

For examples:

1. Add some easy and low price items in buffet to cover the gap. For examples potatoes dishes or mix vegetables in buffets. For a sit-down dinner have variety of bread / rice to fill in any hungry spots. If hosting a cocktail party, nuts, cutlets, etc. provide a little extra security that one has enough for all but requires no extra work.
2. Plan the menu which can be easy to prepare and also does not require the complex preparation?
3. One should Keep some dishes which is most popular and than the general portion of the rest dishes. For example, chicken galantine or shellfish are always popular, so keep balance of these dishes.
4. The more choice offered in menu, individual portion decrease. Less choice means increase in individual portion.
5. Regional habits of the eating foods of people, types of customer, i.e. kids, adult etc. and occasion play a very important role.
6. Multi-cuisine menu is always a better choice as it provides variety, and taste in food. For example Chinese food, along with continental and Indian food, is easy to prepare and low in cost.
7. Always overestimate the quantity around 10%, don't ever underestimate

Here are basic guidelines for individual serving sizes of various foods. Multiply these estimates through recipe conversion formula

PORTION SIZE PER PERSON

Snacks

6 -8 pieces when followed by a meal.

It also depends upon-

1. Occasion like if served in cocktail parties number of portion will increase.
2. Duration of function -The longer the function, number of selections will increase.
3. Type's non vegetarian snacks may be more popular then vegetarian.
4. Variety in cooking methods like fried, steam etc. should be there.

The Main Meal should be consist of

Green Salad - 50-60 g per person

Poultry, meat or fish - 100-150 g per portion when you have two or more main dish, 150-200 g when you offer one main courses.

Rice, grains – if served with breads 50 g otherwise half.

Bread - 50-100 g

lentils - 30-40 g

Vegetables - 50-80 g

Note: quantity depends upon the personal choice, diet and health condition, can be changed to individual.

Desserts

1-2 no Indian dessert such as *halwa* or Bengali sweet

50 ml ice cream and one slice cake, tart or pastry

When serving two of the above, reduce each by a little less than half.

A Few other Menu Planning Tips

- Don't repeat a main ingredient. For example, don't serve a fish in appetizer and main dish.
- Consider the variety in colors of the food that will be served together and make sure there is no repetition.
- Food should be the combination of both hot and cold foods on a buffet.
- Mix textures of food such as fried, stream or roasted dish should be there.

A Guide to Estimate Quantity of Food

Food	25 Servings	50 Servings	100 Servings
Bread (with rice)	60 no	110 no	220 no
Butter (optional)	500 g	01 kg	02 kg
Rice	03 kg	05.5 kg	10 kg
Indian dessert	2.5 kg	05.0 kg	10 kg
Chicken	06 kg	10 kg	19 kg
Coffee	100 g	200 g	400 g
Fish, fillets or steaks	03 kg	05 kg	10 kg
Mix Fruit Cup	06 kg	11.5 kg	22 kg
Ice Cream	2½ kg	4 ½ kg	8.5 kg
Pickles and Preserves	300 g	½ kg	01 kg
Soft drink	12 lt	23 lt	45 lt
Salads	04 kg	08 kg	15 kg
Vegetables	05 kg	09 kg	18 kg
Meat with bone	10 kg	18 kg	36 kg

Meat boneless	12 kg	22 kg	40 kg
Rolls	03 dozen	05 dozen	09 dozen
Soup	03 lt	05 lt	09 lt

Note: Depends upon occasion, types of guest and various other factors.

Following are the basic principle of quantity food production:

1. menu planning
2. recipe formation
3. recipe costing and pricing
4. food costing
5. purchasing
6. storage

Menu planning is the task of choosing dishes for the function

Choosing of dishes depends upon

a) type of establishment
b) purpose
c) cost factor
d) availability of ingredient
e) equipment requirement
f) skill requirement
g) storage
h) cliental
i) length
j) repetition of dishes flavour wise, colour wise and taste wise

Recipe formation. There are two types of recipes

a) Standard recipe
b) Instructional recipe

Standards recipe are already developed recipe and have been tested various times before.

They are a written formula for producing a food item of a specified quality. And quantity. These recipes give specification in the following areas:

a) Quantity and quality of ingredient required.
b) Consistent Procedure of cooking and preparing the dish.
c) Equipment to be used.
d) Cooking temperatures and time
e) Portion size

f) Service details, including garnishes and accompani-ments, serving temperatures.

Instructional recipe are the recipe used only for providing instruction for preparation of the dish. Like cuts of vegetable, application of heat like slow, medium high etc. these recipe can be changed from time to time.

STANDARD RECIPE FORMAT

Sl.No.	Ingredient	Quantity	Price/ Unit	Cost 1	Cost 2	Cost 3
			Total Year			

Objectives of a standard recipe

1. The quantities and qualities of ingredients to be used – a standard purchase specification means the quality and size of ingredient to be purchased for making of particular dishes.
2. The yield obtainable from the recipe.
3. The maintaining of food cost per portion;
4. The retaining nutritional value of a particular dish.
5. Uniformity of taste and presentation in dishes.

Recipe costing and pricing. All recipes needed to be evaluated. For costing each ingredient must be valued against its market price and indirect cost like fuel, labour must be added. Costing is used to inform that how much it cost per person and also helps in deciding the selling price

CONVERSION FACTOR

The conversion factor is to adjust the recipe by using the formulas.

In this is method desired yield is divided by old yield. For example to increase a 4 portion recipe into 100 portion recipe divide 100 by 4 and the factor is 25.

Conversion factor = new yield (desire) / old yield

Recipe adjustment form

Ingredient	Original amount (g)	* factor amount	New yield

Recipe costing form

Ingredient	Amount in recipe	Unit cost	Extended cots

Developing New Recipes and Menus

Recipe is the list of required ingredient along with the instruction to make a particular dish.

Information included in the recipe formulae.

- **Name of the dish/drink** - like chicken a la king
- **Number of pax** - it should serve 4 pax only
- **Quantity of ingredients** - in gram or liter etc.
- **Type of ingredient** like chopped, round, small etc.
- **Preparation/cooking methods** - like frying or roasting etc. mere cooking word is not sufficient
- **Cooking times and temperatures** - in centigrade or Fahrenheit.

Food Trials

These are done as an experiment for introducing new dishes in the menu. They include:

1. forming standard recipe.
2. Change old recipe by altering some ingredient or cooking technique.
3. Trials for specific purpose or occasion.
4. Keeping the dishes data bank for further use.
5. Cost controlling.
6. Special training of the staff.

7. Special demand of guest.
8. Latest changes in customer choice.
9. Research and experiment.

Orgenoleptic and Sensory Evaluation Test

Sensory evaluation is based on consumer perceptions of taste and choice. Sensory evaluation test is done to know the organoleptic nature i.e. the human being's 5 senses which are: Hearing, touch, sight, taste and smell.

The test is done by a expert group of people those come into contact with a product and experience their own individual sensations. The ability to analyse, perceptions, reactions and, above all, to understand them, provides the resources to adjust the product to meet his expectations.

This is why sensory measurement techniques is done to ensure that the quality of their products is faultless, and to adapt them precisely in line with the expectations of their targeted consumers. The test determine food attribute like colour, surface. appearance, specific flavour, taste (salt, sweet, bitter, sour) and food texture.

In food industry, sensory evaluation can be done related to product development and quality testing. Conclusion obtained from a sensory evaluation depends much on preparation, panelist and tester capacity, facility and equipment used type of sensory evaluation used, and method of sensory data analysis. Therefore, knowledge and skill needed to execute Sensory evaluation must be mastered.

Food costing -it is done to evaluate the cost of food being prepared in kitchen. It is a major part of prime cost. It is done to take monetary decision and future budgeting. It acts as information for management. Higher the cost lowers the profit and *vice-versa*. So management is more interested in knowing the food cost.

Food cost can be calculated as follows:

Food cost percentage

$$\frac{\text{Total cost of raw material}}{\text{Selling price}} \times 100$$

Controlling food cost

Control the food cost is very important role of the chef. He by remains stick to the pre determines standards control the cost.

A few of the steps to be taken for controlling the food costs are:

- Purchasing of the items.
- Control portion sizes.
- Minimize waste in the kitchen. Track waste as well.
- Yield testing.

- Organize the storage room and keep inventory to a minimum.
- Pilferage.
- rechauffe.

Purchasing of the items - raw material purchased from reliable market or in bulk will help in reducing the cost:

- **Control portion sizes:** portion helps in controlling the amount to be served. It can be done by using portioning equipments like spoon, ladle, bowl, cup etc. It is a standard procedure of serving the food. Like fried fish means two fillet of cod fish weight 150 g with 80 g French fries.
- **Minimize wastages in the kitchen:** Chef must do his best to minimize the wastages of food. It stars from menu only. While planning a menu he should consider the dishes which are using the proper quantity. Like if menu has "stuff chicken leg" then other chicken dish like "chicken a la king" should be kept in menu. In which boneless chicken breast should be used. Others way of minimizing wastages are by using trimmings or using food for staff also included.
- **Yield testing**-yield testing is done to know the value of the food which is used. Yield test will tell the amount of raw material which is actually utilized and unutilised. **Each product** has its own yield value for example average fish yield value is 40 —60 per cent.

Most of the items are not immediately ready to use after purchase they require some sort of pre-preparation like peeling, trimming etc. This adds to the cost of the item. To control the cost one should use the yield testing of each items listed in menu and ensure that proper yield is taking out.

For example a 10 kg sheep can yield

Lamb Chops	500 g
Boneless	02 kg
Keema	1.600 kg
Kidney	150 g
Neck	500 g
Fat	1.4 kg
Bones	1.5 kg
Curry pieces	02.35 kg

- **Organize the storage room and keep inventory to a minimum.** Store organisation is very important task. As all food must be stored at its proper place. Usually FIFO method of storing is used i.e. first in first out. One should avoid the maximum storage as large quantity of storage invites more spoilage. Proper temperature and space should be arranged to stop the contamination.
- **Pilferage** - It means stealing of food items especially which are very expensive. Like caviar, seafood, saffrons etc. should be kept in proper locking system. Staff

should be checked thoroughly after duty off and regular inventory helps in knowing the pilferage.

- **Rechauffing -** It means reheating or reusing. It is done to minimize food wastages and utilization of the raw material. Rechauffing is done in very careful manner so that it does not affect the quality of food. Rechauffing require a great skill and application of mind. For examples vegetable cutlets can be prepare by using the vegetable trimmings. Even leftover food can be used for the staff cafeteria but without compromising the nutritional value of food.

Purchasing. Purchasing require following steps-

1. Procurement-recognizing the product and finding it. Also to decide what, when, where, why and how to purchase.
2. Buying-forming a team and buying as per the standard, quantity and rules. It can be done through open market, contract basis, by inviting quotation and even in case of emergency.
3. Receiving-food receiving as per correct specification and sorting them, include washing, cleaning for vegetable and fruits.
4. Storing as per the nature like meat store perishable, groceries etc.

Points to Consider for Purchasing Procedure

1. type and image of establishment
2. style of operation
3. occasion
4. amount of storage available
5. finance and supply policies.
6. availability, season, price trend and supply.

QUANTITY REQUIREMENT

The quantity of items to be purchased depends upon certain factors like:

1. number of people to be served in a given period
2. sale history
3. portion size - one must know about the yield of every product

POINTS TO BE CONSIDERED IN PURCHASING FOOD ITEM

1. yield test
2. standard purchase specification
3. method of purchasing
4. record keeping

1. **Yield test** is done to check the waste, portion, size and usable part of the product liken vegetables, fruit, meat etc.
2. **A standard purchase specification** is a concise description of the product. It helps in giving uniformity and consistency. Information regarding the product name, intention, grade, unit and other information. Three copy of purchase order is made by the purchase manager and out of this
   - 1st copy goes to the supplier
   - 2nd copy is kept for verify and then goes to accounts
   - 3rd copy is retained by the purchase manager for reference only.
3. **Method of purchasing** depends upon quantity, quality, availability, time, reason.
   - Open market purchasing-in this type of purchasing a team is formed of professionals authorize for purchasing the prelisted priced items. Quantity and quality is decided in advance.
- contract purchasing-a source of supply established for a specific period of time,

Contracts purchasing can be for:

A. Indefinite quantities to be ordered on an "as needed" basis - purchasing are done in case of new and variety.

B. Contracts specifying definite quantities with deliveries extended over the contract period called standing order.

   - Quotation purchasing-various quotations are invited and a selection committee chooses the best as per the quality and rate.
   - Emergency purchasing-for urgent purpose only.

4. **Record keeping** - requisition form, ordering form

Receiving Control

1. To ensure to get the right quality
2. To ensure to get the right quantity.
3. To ensure that materials are received at right time.

Procedure

1. A copy of the purchase specification must be given to the receiving man. This copy then becomes receiving specification. Receiving specification and purchase specification must be identical. Deviation must not be permitted.
2. Receiving clerk should check the invoice or the delivery and count or weigh the items against the invoice copy of purchase order. He also should check the quality against the order.
3. Any item that is unsatisfactory because of weight, count, or quality should be refused.

4. After getting satisfied he should sign the delivery bill and receiving will be recorded in books.

6. Storage

Three types of stores are used:

1. **Perishable**- easily spoils food items like milk, fish, egg and milk items which are high in protein and carrying very low shelf life.
2. Dry groceries, spices etc. which has a long shelf life.
3. Fresh like vegetables, meat, poultry, fruits etc.

Some rules of thumb for storing food.

FRESH VEGETABLES

1. Vegetables should be stored by Removing air from the package at 5-7°C refrigerated temperatures,
2. Maintaining the humidity (95 to 100%) extend shelf-life of fresh vegetables. Most fresh vegetables may be stored up to 5 days in the refrigerator. It is advisable to wrap or cover fresh leafy vegetables in moisture-proof bags to retain product moisture and prevent decaying.
3. Common vegetables like potatoes, garlic, onions, etc. should be stored in a cool well-ventilated place between 12°C and 15°C. Tomatoes continue to ripen after harvesting and should be stored at room temperature.
4. Cleaning and removing the tops of carrots, radishes, and beets prior to refrigerator storage will reduce loss of moisture and extend shelf-life. Palatability of corn reduces during cold storage due to elevated starch content. Corn and peas should be stored in a ventilated container.
5. Leafy vegetables like Lettuce and spinach should be rinsed under cold running water, drained, packaged in plastic bags, and refrigerated. Proper storage of fresh vegetables will maintain quality and nutritive value. Spinach can be blanched and squeezed completely to remove moisture will extend the shelf life.
6. Processed Vegetables or Canned vegetables can be stored in dry area at room temperature below for up to one year. However too hot temperatures reduce the quality or may spoil the vegetables. Discard badly dented, swollen, and/or rusty cans.

Fresh Fruit

1. Store fresh fruit in the refrigerator by using, covered containers to extend shelf-life and to reduce loss of moisture. Never store fruit for long period. Always store fresh fruit in a separate storage area in the refrigerator, since they can absorb odors from other foods. Prior to consumption, wipe fresh fruits and vegetables to remove possible pesticide residues, soil, and/or bacteria.

2. Apples should be stored separately from other foods in the refrigerator for few days only. Apples stored at room temperature will soften rapidly within a few days. Remember to remove apples that are bruised or decayed prior to storage in the refrigerator. Do not wash apples prior to storage.
3. Green pears and apricots should be ripened at room temperature and then stored in the refrigerator for 5-day only.
4. Ripe peaches Grapes and plums should be stored in the refrigerator and eaten fresh within 5 days of purchase. Store unwashed grapes separately from other foods in the refrigerator and wash prior to consumption.
5. Ripe strawberries can be stored in the refrigerator separately from other foods for approximately 3 days. Strawberries should be washed and stemmed prior to consumption.
6. Citrus fruits, such as lemons, sweet limes, Grapefruit and oranges, can be stored in the refrigerator for 10 days.
7. Melons, such as the honeydew melon, cantaloupe, and watermelon, may be in the refrigerator for two weeks.

DAIRY PRODUCTS

1. Milk should be stored in the refrigerator 0-5°C for 8 to 20 days depending upon the storage conditions. Milk is a very nutritious and highly perishable food. Milk should never be left at room temperature and always storage in clean and close container. Keep it away from acid and heat during storage.
2. Dry milk may be stored at cool temperatures (10°C to 15°C) in airtight containers for one year.
3. Canned evaporated milk and sweetened condensed milk may be stored at room temperature as per the manufacturer instructions but opened one should be consumed within 8 to 20 days.
4. Natural and processed cheese should be kept tightly packaged in moisture-resistant wrappers and stored below 40°F.

BREADS, CEREALS, FLOUR AND RICE

1. Bread should be consumed fresh but can be stored in the refrigerator temperature for 5 to 7 days.
2. Cereals and spices may be stored at room temperature in tightly closed containers to keep out moisture and insects. Whole wheat flour may be stored in the refrigerator or freezer to retard rancidity of the natural oils.
3. Store raw white rice in tightly closed containers at room temperature and use within one year. One should avoid the storage of cooked rice.

MEATS, POULTRY, FISH, AND EGGS

1. Meat, poultry, fish, and eggs are highly perishable and potentially hazardous due to their high moisture and high protein content. Whole cuts of meat may be stored in the freezer ranging from 4 to 12 months.
2. Ground meats should be stored on the lower shelf of the refrigerator but one should try to use immediately. Refrigerator storage slows bacterial growth; however, the product will eventually spoil. Optimum storage temperature of refrigerated meats, including ground beef, is 1-3°C. Always thaw meat in thaw room only or in refrigerator.
3. Cured meats, such as ham, sausages, and bacon, should be stored in their original packaging in the refrigerators for one week. They have a tendency to become rancid when exposed to air.
4. Poultry should be stored in the freezer (-10°C) for 12 months. Thaw poultry in the refrigerator only.
5. Fresh fish, shrimp, and crab stored in the refrigerator (slightly below 0°C) should be consumed within 1 to 2 days in packet only separate from the other material. Frozen fresh lean fish and seafood may be stored for 3 to 6 months at -20°C.
6. Eggs should be purchased refrigerated and stored in the refrigerator at cooling temperature in their original carton away from the food imparting strong smell. Use eggs within 3 weeks after purchasing. Never freeze the egg or at room temperature for longer period.

QUESTIONS

1. What are the factors which influence the planning of menu in quantity cooking?
2. What are the principles of quantity cooking?
3. How will you plan the food quantity while making a menu?
4. Plan a 6 course Indian menu for 500 pax and write down the required quantity of ingredients for it.
5. Define recipe. What are the benefits of making recipe?
6. How the recipe is formed? Write a detailed procedure. What are the different types of recipes are there?
7. What do you understand by production management and its function? Mention the various techniques which may be used for improving productivity for efficient production management?
8. How the kitchen is managed by chef in star hotel? Write in detail.
9. Why food trials are essentials for the success of restaurant?
10. What is the use of Orgenoleptic and sensory evaluation test? How this test is done?

11. What should be the standard purchase specification of following in your view:
    a. mutton leg
    b. Fisn and shell fish
    c. broiler chicken
    d. cauliflower e.-milk
12. As a chef how will you control the raised food cost in he kitchen.
13. Explain following terms:
    a) indenting
    b) procurement
    c) instructional recipe
    d) conversion factor
    e) food costing
    f) food cost percentage
    g) standard purchasing
    h) rechauffe
14. What are the principles of storing different food items? Explain in details.

Bibliography

Beranbaum, Rose Levy, *The Cake Bible.*

Cracknell, H. L. and R. J. Kaufman, *Escoffier.*

Culinary Institute of America, *The Professional Chef,* Seventh Edition,

Dubey, S.C., *Basic Bakery.*

Fuller, John, *Chef's Manual of Kitchen Management*; Batsford London.

Hazan, Marcella, *Essentials of Classic Italian Cooking.*

Hemphill, Ian, *The Spice and Herb Bible.*

Hobb, Betty. C, *Hygienic Food Handling's,* John Ambulance, London.

Hume, R., *Dawnes, Cordon Bleu Cook Book,* Lon. Wciandred.

Jaffery, Madhur, *Taste of India.*

Kasper, Lynne R., *The Splendid Table.*

Kinton, S., *Cesroni Theory of Catering,* Adward Arnold Pub Ltd., London.

Kotas, R., *An Approach to Food Costing*; Lon. Berrie & Rockliff.

Koteschevar, *Standard Principle and Technique in Quantity Food Production,* California.

Labensky, Sarah R., *On Cooking: Techniques From Expert Chefs.*

Montagne, Prosper, *Larousse Gastronomique.*

Peterson, James, *Sauces.*

Philip, Thangam, *Modern Cookery,* New Delhi, Oriental Longman.

Prizeman, John, *Kitchen a Design, Layout and Equipment,* Macdonald & Co., London.

Rai, Ranjit, *Tandoor: The Great Indian Barbecue.*

Saraswat, Arvind, *Professional Chef.*

Saulinier, L., *Le repertoire de la cusine,* Lon Leon Jaggi & Sons.

Singh, Balbir, *Indian Cookery,* Mills & Boon Ltd.

Index